METALCASTING

Look for these other Craftmaster books by McGraw-Hill

Geary ▪ *Welding*
Phillips ▪ *Locksmithing*

METALCASTING

C. W. Ammen

McGraw-Hill

New York   San Francisco   Washington, D.C.   Auckland   Bogotá
Caracas   Lisbon   London   Madrid   Mexico City   Milan
Montreal   New Delhi   San Juan   Singapore
Sydney   Tokyo   Toronto

Library of Congress Cataloging-in-Publication Data

Ammen, C. W.
    Metalcasting / C. W. Ammen.
        p.   cm.
    ISBN 0-07-134246-X
    1. Founding. 2. Metal castings. I. Title.
TS230.A635   2000
671.2—dc21   99-33560
                                        CIP

McGraw-Hill

A Division of The McGraw-Hill Companies

1 2 3 4 5 6 7 8 9 0   AGM/AGM   9 0 4 3 2 1 0 9

ISBN 0-07-134246-X

The sponsoring editor for this book was Zoe G. Foundotos, the editing supervisor was Joanne Woy, and the production supervisor was Pamela A. Pelton. This book was revised by Charlie Self and was set in Melior by Wanda Ditch through the services of Barry E. Brown (Broker—Editing, Design and Production).

Printed and bound by Quebecor/Martinsburg.

Previously published as *The Metalcaster's Bible*, copyright © 1980 by The McGraw-Hill Companies, Inc.

McGraw-Hill books are available at special quantity discounts to use as premiums and sales promotions, or for use in corporate training programs. For more information, please write to the Director of Special Sales, McGraw-Hill, 11 West 19 Street, New York, NY 10011. Or contact your local bookstore.

 This book is printed on recycled, acid-free paper containing a minimum of 50% recycled de-inked fiber.

CONTENTS

INTRODUCTION

For the newly fledged novice metal caster, the person working for his or her own amusement, a hobby foundry is easy to start, lots of fun, and easy to advance from to larger or more intricate set-ups should those become desirable.

Any such foundry can be fully or partially self-sufficient, allowing the metal caster to work either for the fun of it, or for a large enough profit to pay expenses (and maybe a bit more). Items cast for sale become products, and the process acquires a further complexity because of that (tax time, folks). But for those around you, you suddenly become the person to see when a small part for a tool, or other device, cannot be found. Quantities too small to interest the average job shop, as well as jobs that are overly complex or involved, or that require lots of labor in relation to return in other ways, can be your meat, while the job shop eats up the big stuff. . .leaving the entire small item field hobby and small job metal caster who operates out of his or her backyard (essentially: that's more of a figure of speech than a reality for some people who are overpowered by zoning laws, if not by neighborly disapproval of noise and odor).

The metal casting industry has followed a familiar pattern in this country, moving from what was basically a cottage craft, with craftsmen working to turn out from one to however many items were needed, on to a larger industry where the small job needs of many are lost in the shuffle. Limits have been added to the alloys with which a particular foundry might work, as well as limits being stuck on weights of castings, types of castings and so on.

As specialization increased, cost-control became a major factor, and *captive shops,* tightly controlled within the parent industry, came into being. As recently as thirty years ago, there were thousands of foundries of small to medium size in the country: today, a fraction of that number remains, and many of the independent middling large foundries are in trouble.

The jobbing foundry is predicted to be almost extinct in the not-so-distant future: that change is an opportunity for those among you who wish to carry on a hobby that pays for itself. . .or maybe more than pays for itself.

The demand for one-shot metalcasting job work will exists, as does lots of other low production work where a few units of varied sizes may be needed, and may always do so, but the work often goes begging for lack of anyone to do it. And, of course, there's always the jewelry casting market, if one wishes to go beyond casting for one's own pleasure and use. If your own business has a need for cast parts, then, of course, you're going to have a running start with a small foundry of your own, functioning something like the captive foundries of big business, but on a smaller, more personal, and lower production scale.

If, for whatever reason, you wish to cast parts for sale, whether as art or practical accessories for living, low volume sand casting is the way to go. Casting metal parts can be one of the most creative and rewarding activities for the home craftsman, or woman, to undertake. Not as many amateurs try the work as might enjoy it. The assumptions made are often wrong: equipment levels need not be high (though like all other equipment intensive hobbies, this one is apt to create a desire for more gear as time goes on); skill and know-how can be picked up in the same manner as many people pick up woodworking skills (though there are few adult education courses in metalcasting, reading books and talking to other metal casters and starting small and working up do wonderfully well). There is seldom a valid reason that the home shop can't become a site for metal casting activity.

Advice is easy: don't expect to learn it all in a week; don't expect to be a successful professional without more than a small amount of work, even on a very reduced scale; don't rush. There's not really a need to have an ultimate, or immediate, goal in mind at the outset. If the work looks as if you'll enjoy it, give it at try.

A word to the wise, though: if you spend lots of time worrying about the condition of your nails, how your hair is combed, and the details of your clothing, you're probably not going to like metalcasting. The work is often physically demanding and dirty, though anyone with average strength and manual dexterity should be able to easily handle foundry work.

Casting Processes

There are a number of basic casting processes that are available to the small-job metalcaster. Some of these processes are among the earliest attempts by mankind to form and manipulate metals.

Sand Casting

Of the total tonnage of castings produced each year, the greatest percentage is produced by sand casting. Crude methods of sand casting were practiced before the beginning of recorded history.

The ancient Chinese produced a large quantity of extremely fine and complicated bronzes, some of which were quite massive. Careful, unbiased studies of these bronzes through X-ray examination and chemical analysis of the core materials has been most enlightening. Some consist of many sand castings assembled with cleverly designed hidden joints (undetectable except by X-ray examination). The surface texture, in the majority of cases, is not an as-cast finish, but a carefully chased and hand-engraved one. The mold material consisted of fine silica and natural cement (a sand loam) and in some cases, a natural bonded green sand very similar to French sand. Not only were the Chinese clever at making joints, they made some highly complicated piece molds.

(When examining a bronze, you are not looking at the item as cast but, rather, the finished chased and patined work: it might have been produced by any number of methods. The T. F. McGann & Sons Co. of Boston produced countless fine statuary bronzes in French molding sand by the green sand molding process.)

New York is the home of over 300 examples of buildings made from iron members cast in sand; some, highly ornamented, were produced before structural steel was widely used. The French Quarter of New Orleans has fine examples of balconies and fences commonly thought to be wrought iron; they are for the most part not wrought iron at all, but gray iron cast in sand. Some were produced in France from finely carved wooden patterns.

Sand casting consists of pouring a molten metal or alloy into a mold of earth or sand and allowing it to solidify. Molding material is cheap and plentiful. It is also readily worked into suitable molds, making sand casting the most economical method. Machining or building up a part by welding, riveting, or brazing is surely more expensive than casting. Sand casting is also an extremely versatile process. Parts can be made in almost any size varying from a fraction of an ounce up to tons in weight.

Green Sand Casting

Green sand refers to molds made and poured with sand simply tempered with water.

Green sand molds are sometimes made in two-part flasks. The pattern is placed on a smooth molding board and covered with an inverted drag flask; green sand is rammed down firmly into drag flask, leveled off with the bottom, and covered with a bottom board. The boards and flask are then overturned and the molding board removed.

This leaves the upper face of the pattern at the flask parting plane. The cope is placed in register on the drag and the sand face of the drag flask is given a light coating of parting powder (a commercial product) to keep the two halves of the mold from sticking together.

A sprue stick is placed in position with the cope and surrounded with sand tamped firmly to the top of the cope flask. After the sand is leveled off, the sprue stick is removed. The cope flask is lifted off and set aside; the pattern is removed from the drag flask and a gate is cut over to the sprue for the entrance of metal to the mold cavity. The entire mold is blown clean of any loose sand and the cope is replaced. The mold is then ready to pour. Weights are placed on the cope to prevent it from lifting when poured (and causing a *run out*).

After pouring, the metal is allowed to solidify, the mold is shaken out, and the casting and gate are removed.

Due to the lack of grain coherence, pure sand is not suitable for making molds. A binder is needed to hold the sand particles together. Clay is perfectly suited for this purpose. However, an abundance of clay is undesirable because the sand then loses its porosity, and porosity is essential for the escape of gases when the molten metal is poured into the mold.

SAND CASTING (CHEMICAL BINDER)

Chemically bonded or *furan molds* are produced by mixing a chemical binder with clean dry silica sand and adding a catalyst to harden the binder.

Chemically bonded molds are a very good medium for large bronzes and can be used with oil-and-clay patterns, as well as for wood. The molds have little strength in the green state and cannot be used like green sand. You must make up the drag half of the mold, allow it to set, and then remove the cope and finish the mold as usual. It has no equal for piece molds and highly complicated molds, once you get the hang of it.

Its high strength when cured allows relatively thin molds for heavy section castings.

QUICK»TIP

A *sprue* is a feeder hole through which molten metal is poured.

Because no moisture is involved, the yield of good castings is extremely high. The basic formula is:

> Binder—2 percent of the weight of sand
> Catalyst—25 percent of the weight of the binder

The binder is furfural alcohol; the catalyst, an 75 percent phosphoric acid solution.

First mix the sand with the acid, then add the binder and mix thoroughly. You have 20 or 30 minutes to work before the sand sets. The catalyst reacts with the binder to produce a hard resin, which cements the grains of sand together to form a hard, yet permeable mold. Any metal can be cast in furan molds.

Unlike green sand molds, where the sand can be retempered and used over again to produce new molds.

SAND CASTING (OIL BINDERS)

Molds and cores can be made by mixing silica sand with linseed oil or any number of commercial drying oils. Because this is the usual method for producing cores, a mold made with a *drying* oil binder, such as linseed oil and silica sand, is called a *core mold*. Due to its low green strength, it requires special pattern equipment and rigging; it has been largely replaced with furan methods. To make such a mold mix 40 parts (by volume) of clean silica sand with one part (by volume) of linseed oil. Dry the mold completely at 350 F. The oil oxidizes during drying, binding the sand grains together. Like furan molds, it is a one-time material. Unlike furan, oil binders require baking to set a bond.

TOOLS *Binders* hold the sand in shape once the pattern is removed and until the pour is finished. There are a number of binders available, some simple (mostly clays) and others more sophisticated (some clays, chemical and oil binders, silicate of soda gassed with CO_2).

SAND CASTING (CARBON DIOXIDE OR SILICATE OF SODA)

The CO_2 system, or *silicate of soda method* is, like the furan system, very widely used.

When CO_2 contacts the water in silicate of soda, carbonic acid is formed. The acid neutralizes the silicate of soda, forming a glass bond for the molding sand.

Cores and molds may require as little as 2½ percent silicate of soda binder, to as much as 4 percent, depending upon the mass involved. Various grades and formulations of silicate of soda are available for a wide range of applications. The advantage over furan binders is the short time it takes to "gas" a mold or core—in some cases, 10 seconds or less.

After the sand and silicate of soda are gassed, the mold is ready to pour. This makes for very rapid production. It is not as versatile as the furan method, in that manifolds, probes, a tank of CO_2, a regulator, hoses, and gassing cups are required.

Sand Casting With Styrofoam Molds

In this method, the object to be cast or reproduced in metal is first made as a Styrofoam pattern. The Styrofoam pattern is surrounded with green sand in a flask. When molten metal enters the mold, the heat vaporizes the Styrofoam.

This system is ideally suited to large and chunky castings due to its simplicity. However, its voluminous output of noxious smoke has caused considerable grumbling from the EPA; and, it is outlawed in some areas. Done on a small scale, and infrequently, it might be tolerated. You need a new pattern for each casting.

Die Casting

Die casting is a very rapid method of producing large quantities of castings. As the name implies, the mold cavity is a *die*—a permanent metal mold into which casting metal is introduced under pressure.

The process is suitable only to relatively high production jobs, where a large quantity of a given casting is desired. The initial cost to make the die and the high cost of die-casting machines make it imperative that sufficient quantities of a given casting are needed to justify the high cost.

Basically, there are two distinct types of die-casting equipment: the *hot chamber* and the *cold chamber*. In the hot chamber (Figure 1.1), the mechanism that shoots the metal into the die to produce each cast is submerged under the molten metal in the machine's melting pot. This makes it automatic in the sense that the "shot" cylinder is auto-

FIGURE 1.1

Hot chamber die casting.

matically filled with metal for each shot, making it unnecessary for the operator to ladle metal into the cylinder for each casting or shot.

The cold chamber machine (Figure 1.2) requires that the shot cylinder be filled manually by the operator for each casting (or shot). The required amount of metal is poured into the shot cylinder and the shot piston is advanced, shooting the metal into the die cavity.

Plaster Mold Casting

Plaster mold casting has a number of applications. The method is a variation of sand casting. Instead of using sand to make the mold a mixture of plaster, talc, and water flow up around the pattern. After the plaster has set, the pattern is withdrawn. The mold is then baked in an oven, driving off moisture. This process is more expensive than sand casting, but it does offer a higher degree of dimensional accuracy.

FIGURE 1.2

Cold chamber die casting.

Shell Mold Casting

Shell molding is sometimes called the *Croning Process* after the inventor. It uses a mixture of sand and thermosetting resin. This mixture is usually phenol-formaldehyde and it forms the mold. This sand-resin mixture is brought into contact with a heated pattern. The mixture closest to the pattern forms a thin shell due to the polymerization of the resin, which binds the sand particles. The thin shell is then used as a mold, backed up by loose sand or shot to give it strength. Excellent finish and dimensional accuracy are thus obtained. Shell molding is a large-scale industrial process because of the required expensive production machinery.

Slush Casting

In slush casting, a metal mold in two or more parts is used. The mold is filled with metal and rocked back and forth until the metal (touching the mold surfaces) solidifies in the desired thickness. When this point is reached, the liquid metal remaining in the mold is poured out, resulting in a hollow casting. This system is used only for low-melting lead and zinc-based metals, and to produce ornamental items that need not be strong.

This system is similar to the process used to slip-cast clay pottery. The slip in this case is metal, and, the mold is made of metal (usually bronze) rather than plaster of paris.

Permanent Molds

Permanent molds are metal molds designed to be opened and closed. The metal is poured into the mold, and when solidified, the mold is opened and the casting is removed; the cycle is then repeated.

> **QUICK»TIP**
>
> Industrial processes are those that are too costly in terms of materials or tools for the small shop. These include *die casting*—the use of permanent metal molds, or dies, and pressurized injection of metal (the need for very large quantities, however, may reduce the cost per unit to a profit-making level for even small shops); and *shell mold casting*—the use of sand and a thermoset resin to bind the sand—which is cost-prohibitive for small foundries.

Two very common types of permanent molds, which have been around for many years, are those used to make bullets and sinkers for fishing. However, permanent molds are not limited to these types of castings. Hundreds of thousands of different kinds of permanent mold castings in many sizes are made each year. Over 90 percent of all automotive aluminum pistons and most cast aluminum cookware are produced in permanent cast-iron molds.

There are other casting methods; but by and large, the methods described account for the largest portion of the castings produced today.

Casting Defects

A knowledge of casting defects is essential. If you cannot pinpoint the cause of a defect there is no way of correcting the problem. Some defects are quite obvious, along with the cause. Some types of defects can often resemble each other in appearance and separating them is difficult. A drawing or photograph of a defect is one thing and looking at the actual defect is another. You learn about defects by analyzing your own and those of others.

Here is a list of defects and their causes, which should include anything you might even encounter:

- **Blacking or Mold Wash Scab.** Occasionally the blacking or wash on the mold or core breaks away during heating, lifts off the surface like a leaf, and is retained in or on the metal. This is a form of scab. The cause is a poor binder in the wash, improperly dried wash, a poor wash formula, or all of the above.

- **Bleeder.** A bleeder is caused by shaking the casting out of the mold too soon, while a part of the casting is still liquid. The section runs out, leaving a defect. In extreme cases, the entire center section may run out—onto the shake-out man's feet.

- **Blister.** A blister is a shallow blow (*see below*) covered with a thin film metal. It has many of the same causes and cures as blows.

- **Blows.** Blows are round to elongated holes caused by the accumulation of trapped gases. The usual cause of blow holes is sand that is rammed too hard, which decreases its permeability. Other causes are sand permeability too low for the job; sand and core too wet; insufficient or closed-off core vent; green core not properly dried; an incompletely dried core or mold wash; insufficient mold venting, insufficient hydrostatic pressure (cope too short); cope bars too close to the mold cavity; wet gagger or solder too close to the mold cavity; or poor grain distribution. Any combination of hot or cold materials that could lead to condensation as the hot core sets in a cold mold, or vice versa, can cause blows, as can a cold chill, or wet or rusty chaplets.

■ **Bobble.** The casting was poured short, usually with a slacked or interrupted pour. When pouring a casting, the metal must be poured at a constant velocity to hold choke. Slacking off or reducing velocity causes bobble. A completely interrupted pour, with a start and stop and another start even for a second or so can create bobble. Many lost castings are caused by improper pours.

■ **Broken Casting.** May be caused by improper casting design. Improper filleting, along with improper handling anywhere along the line may break the casting. Copper base castings—red brass, yellow brass, and so on—are known as *hot short*, which means they break easily when hot. Therefore, a casting shaken out of the mold before it has cooled enough may be very easily broken. A mold or core with too high a hot strength doesn't give or collapse enough to give the casting room to move as it shrinks; this also may be a cause of broken castings.

■ **Cold Shut.** A cold shut occurs when two streams of metal coming together in a mold fail to weld. Cold shuts are usually caused by a too-cold metal poured too slowly, or an improperly designed gating system, where the mold cannot be filled fast enough.

■ **Core Rise.** Core rise creates a variation in wall thickness, or a complete lack of metal at the point where the core touches the cope. The cause is the core rising toward the cope surface. With green sand, the core may shift because the drag cracks at its base (which happens when drawing the pattern) and floats toward the cope. Dry sand cores float if the unsupported span of a thin and insufficiently rodded core is too great. The core is forced into an upward bend because of the buoyancy of the molten metal. Other causes are insufficient core prints, both in number and design, insufficient chaplets, slipped chaplets, chaplets left out by the molder, or poor core design. Core rise is easy to spot and fix.

■ **Crush.** Crush is caused by the actual crushing of the mold, causing indentations in the casting surface. The indentations are caused by flask equipment, such as bottom boards or cores that are too tall or too large for the prints or jackets. Rough handling can also cause crush.

■ **Drops.** Drops occur when a portion of the cope sand drops into the mold cavity before or during pouring. Causes are bumping with weights, rough clamping, weak molding sand (low green strength), rough closing, jackets placed on roughly, and other rough treatment.

■ **Fin.** A fin of metal on the casting is caused by a crack in the cope or drag. The crack is caused by wrenched flasks, bad jackets, bad setting of jackets, uneven and warped bottom boards, uneven strike off, lack of sufficient cope or drag depth, a bottom board not properly rubbed, or a drag mold sitting unevenly so that it rocks.

■ **Fusion.** Fusion is a rough, glassy surface of fused, melted sand on the casting surface, either on the outside or on a cored surface. It is caused by a too low sintering or melting point of the sand or core. The fault is quite common when a small diameter core runs through an exceptionally heavy section (of great heat) which may actually melt the core. Fusion may also be caused by pouring much too hot for the sand or cores. A mold or core wash can prevent fusion in some cases, but if the sintering point of your sand is too low for the class of work, you must find a more refractory sand.

■ **Gas Porosity.** Gas porosity causes widely dispersed, bright, round holes on fractured and machined surfaces. They are caused by gasses being absorbed in the metal during melting. The gas is released during solidification of the casting. The cause is poor melting practice (oxidizing conditions) and poor de-oxidizing practice.

■ **Hot Tears.** A hot tear is actually a tear or separation fracture brought on by the physical restriction of the mold or the core upon the shrinking casting. The most usual cause is a too-high hot strength of the core or molding sands. These defects may be external or internal. A core that is overly reinforced with rods or an arbor will not collapse. If you restrict the movement of the casting during its shrink-down from solidification to room temperature, it will literally tear itself apart.

■ **Inclusions.** Inclusions are dirt, slag, and other debris. They are caused by failure to maintain a choke during pouring, dirty molding, failure to blow out the mold properly prior to closing, and sloppy core setting that causes the edges of the print in the mold to break away and fall into the mold. The drag should be blown out, the cores set and blown out again. Dirt falling down the sprue prior to the mold being poured, or knocked down during jacketing, must be blown out. For the most part, the cause is dirty molding.

■ **Inverse Chill.** Found in gray iron castings, this is hard or chilled iron in the center sandwiched between soft iron. The cause can be incorrect carbon equivalent for the job or the presence of non-ferrous metals in the charge; metals such as lead, antimony, or tellurium are detrimental impurities.

■ **Kish (Cast Iron).** If the carbon equivalent of the iron is too high for the section poured, and the cooling rate is too slow, free graphite forms on the cope surface, creating black, shiny flakes free of the casting. This causes rough, holey defects, usually widespread in the casting. *Carbon equivalent* is the relationship of total carbon to the silicon and phosphorous content of the iron. It is controlled by the make-up charge and by silicon added at the spout. It is called *carbon* equivalent because the addition of silicon or phosphorous is only about a third as effective as carbon; the carbon equivalent of the three additives is equal to the total percentage of pure carbon plus one third the percentage of silicon and phosphorous combined. The carbon equivalent is varied by the foundryman depending on the type of iron being produced.

■ **Lead Sweat.** Lead sweat is a covering of lead teardrops on the outside of a high-leaded bronze or brass casting, with underlying holes or porosity (red metals containing a large percentage of lead, such as leaded bearing bronze, are most affected). Because lead has the lowest melting point of the metals in highly leaded bronze (copper, 70 percent; tin, 5 percent; lead, 25 percent) and is not in solution with the tin and copper, it remains liquid until the casting is below 620 degrees Fahrenheit. If the casting is shaken out before it is below 620 degrees F., the lead sweats out from between the copper and tin crystals.

■ **Metal Penetration.** Metal penetration is a rough, unsightly mixture of sand and metal caused by the metal penetrating the mold wall or the surfaces of a core. It should not be confused with an *expansion scab*, which is attached to the casting by a thin vein of metal. Metal penetration is primarily caused by too soft and uneven ramming of the mold or core, making the sand too open and porous. Another cause is a too-high pouring temperature. Too-sharp corners (insufficient filleting) may make it impossible to ram the sand tight enough. There may also be localized overheating of the sand because of poor gating practice, or molding with a sand too open for the job. Penetration in brass castings is sometimes traced to excessive phosphorous used in de-oxidizing the metal, making it excessively fluid.

■ **Misrun.** A misrun occurs when a part of the casting fails to run due to cold metal, slow pouring, insufficient hydrostatic pressure, or sluggish metal (sluggish metal is nonfluid because it is badly gassed or oxidized).

■ **Omission of a Core.** Leave out the core and the results are obvious.

■ **Pin Holes.** A surface pitted with pin holes may also be an indicator of many subsurface blow holes.

■ **Poured Short.** Incomplete casting because the mold wasn't filled. A stupid trick that sooner or later everyone does. It is caused by insufficient metal in the ladle. Going back and touching up the mold will not correct it.

■ **Ram Off.** Ram off the result of a section of the mold forced away from the pattern by continuing to ram sand after it has conformed to the pattern shape. Careless ramming is the cause, where the mold is first rammed vertically, then on an angle. This causes the rammed sand to slide sideways and leave a gap between the pattern and the sand. The result is a deformed casting. Ram off may also occur when you use sand with a poor or low flowability (too much clay, or sand that's too fine).

■ **Run Out.** Run out is caused by metal in the mold running out of the joint of the flask. Run off can drain any part of the casting above the parting line. The run out may come between the drag and the bottom board in a cracked drag mold. It may also come from between a loose and improperly fitted core and the core print. Other causes include insufficient room between the flask and the cavity, insufficient weight on the copy (so that the cope rises during pouring), or improperly clamped molds. Excessive hydrostatic pressure (too tall a sprue for the job), or no dough roll between cope and drag on large jobs are two other causes. Run out also may be caused by a combination of the above reasons. Attempting to stop or prevent an immanent run out by placing a foot on top of the cope and applying pressure is dangerous and foolhardy. There is also no sense in trying to stop the run out with clay or sand.

■ **Sag.** Sag is a decrease in a metal section when the core or cope sags. It is caused by too few cope bars, too small a flask for the job, or lack of sufficient cope depth. Sag can also create misruns.

■ **Scab.** Rough, thin scabs of metal are attached to the casting by thin veins and are separated from the casting by a thin layer of sand. Scabs are usually found on flat surfaces and are caused by hard ramming, low permeability, and insufficient hot strength in the mold. Sand may not have enough cushion material, such as wood flour, to allow it to expand when heating. When it is unable to expand, the sand buckles and causes scabs along with—although not always—rattails and grooves under the scabs, which are called *pull downs*. Pull downs cause the scabs.

■ **Shifts.** Shifts come in two varieties: *mold shift* and *core shift*. A mold shift occurs when the parting lines are not matched as the mold is closed. The result is a casting offset or mismatch at the parting. The mold shift is caused by excessive rapping of a loose pattern, reversing the cope on the drag, too loose a fit of the pattern pins and dowels, faulty and mismatched flasks, too much play between pins and guides, faulty clamping, improper fitting (racking) of jackets, and improper placing of jackets. A core shift is caused by misalignment of the core halves, so that they are not true and proper when they're assembled.

■ **Shrink Cavity and Shrink Depression.** These defects are caused by a lack of feed metal, which causes a depression or concavity in the surface of the casting. The shrink cavity is a cavity below the surface but connected to the surface with a dendrite crystal structure.

■ **Slag Inclusion.** Slag on the face of the casting and down the sides of the sprue is called included slag. The case is improper ladle skimming, not choking the sprue (keep it brimming full from start to finish of the pour), a sprue that is so large it cannot be kept choked, and a gating system that is improperly choked.

■ **Steam Gas Porosity.** This usually shows up as round holes, like those in Swiss cheese, just under the cope surface of the casting. Often, steam gas porosity doesn't come to light until machining. The cause is a wet ladle, where the ladle lining was not properly and thoroughly dried. In more extreme cases of wet ladle, the metal will kick and boil in the ladle. The concept of pigging the metal in a wet ladle, then refilling the ladle, in the hope that the pigging finished the drying process, is sheer folly.

■ **Sticker.** Sticker is a lump or bump (rat) on the surface of the casting, and is caused by a part of the mold face sticking to the pattern and being removed with the pattern. The sticker is caused by poorly cleaned, shellacked, or polished pattern; rough pattern; cheap or tacky shellac; sticking liquid parting; a cold pattern against hot sand; or insufficient draft.

■ **Swell.** Swell is a deformation of the casting caused by the pressure of the metal moving or displacing the sand. It is usually caused by a soft spot in the mold or an overall too-soft mold.

■ **Washing and Erosion.** Washing and erosion occurs when the sand is eroded and washed around the mold, and some of that sand then finds its way to the cope surface of the casting, where it becomes dirt-sand inclusions. Washing and erosion can come from the gating system or the mold cavity. Causes are a too-low hot strength, too-dry molding sand, poor gating design, a deep drop into the mold, washing at the point of impact, metal washing over a sharp edge at the gate, or metal hitting against a core or vertical wall during the pour.

■ **Zinc Tracks.**   Found on the cope surface of high-zinc alloy castings, these defects are caused by the zinc distilling out of the metal during pouring. Zinc oxide floats up to the cope and forms worm-track lines on the casting when the metal sets against the cope. Zinc tracks are caused by pouring too hot (metal flaring) in the ladle or crucible, pouring the mold too slowly, or insufficient gates. The mold must be filled quickly to prevent damage.

Mold Making

Foundries throughout the world are rapidly turning to new types of sand molding to improve casting quality, productivity, profits, and working conditions.

In the casting process a pattern is encased in an aggregate of materials to form a mold; this material is called the *investment*. The word is derived from a term once used to describe special apparel, such as a cloak or uniform. Thus, the pattern "cloaked" in material is called an investment mold.

Investments

Two basic investments are used for casting. For nonferrous metals cast at no more than 2000 F., the most commonly used investment is calcium sulfate semi-hydrate or plaster of paris. It is mixed with various *refractories*. Refractories, such as calcined silica or talc, are heat-

QUICK»TIP

As with all crafts, preparation carries the day. The time spent planning and working up the basic steps are all-important, starting with the selection of the investment.

resistant materials. Some investment forms of plaster of paris contain fibers for added strength in both the "green" and dry states; they can be fiberglass or ceramic fibers. Also, ingredients are often added to promote permeability.

Ferrous and nonferrous metals intended for casting temperatures up to 3100 F. are used with hydrolyzed ethyl silicate, a binder, combined with various refractory material, such as zircon, calcined mullite, or fused silica, to which is added a small amount of gelling agent (usually a 7.5 percent ammonium carbonate solution). Hydrolyzed alkysilicate is also used as a binder in some formulas.

A phosphate-bonded refractory investment is frequently used as a backup mix for flask-molded patterns which have been precoated with a hydrolyzed ethyl silicate investment. Common investment formulas and their applications are given in Table 2.1.

Investment formulas for nonferrous metals are many, but basically they consist of a binder and a refractory, often combined with various items for increased strength and permeability.

■ Binders include:
  –Plaster of paris
  –Portland cement
  –Linseed oil
  –Clay
  –Ethyl silicate
  –Phosphates
  –Resins
  –Silicate of soda

■ Refractories include:
  –Wollastonite
  –Silica sand
  –Brick dust
  –Fiberfrax
  –Chrysolite
  –Zircon sand
  –Olivine sand
  –Mullite
  –Ceramic grog
  –Asbestos
  –Vermiculite

Table 2.1

Commercially Prepared Investments	Mold Construction	Casting Metals	Max Pouring Temp
Hydro Perm (U.S. Gypsum Co.)	Flask mold Full mold	Brass Bronze Aluminum	2000°F
Investment R Investment R 555 (Ransom & Randolph Co.)	Flask molds Hand-built molds	All (below max pouring temp)	2000°F
Duracast 20 (Derr Mfg. Co.)	Flask molds Hand-built molds	All (below max pouring temp)	2000°F
No. 1 molding plaster (Georgia Pacific Inc.)	All	All (below max pouring temp)	2000°F

Noncommercial Investments	Mold Construction	Casting Metals	Max Pouring Temp
95% talc 4% Hi-Early cement 1% asbestos (by weight)	All	Brass Aluminum Bronze	2000°F
silica sand and fireclay (1:1 by volume)	Full molds	All	2000°F
70% No1 1 molding plaster 29% talc 1% hydrated lime 0.34 portland cement (by weight)	All	Brass Bronze Aluminum	2000°F
54% .100-mesh silica sand 32% No. 1 molding plaster 13% talc 1% Hi-Early cement (by weight)	All	Brass Bronze Aluminum	200°F
200-mesh olivine flour and No. 1 molding plaster (3:2 by volume)	All	Brass Bronze Aluminum	2000°F
Calcined plaster of paris (gypsum)	Flask molds Full molds	Aluminum	(none)
Plaster of paris and silica flour (1:1 by volume)	All	Brass Bronze Aluminum	2000°F
Brick dust and plaster of paris (3:2 by volume)	All	Brass Bronze Aluminum	2000°F
100-mesh silica sand and Hi-Early cement (10:1 by volume)	Flask molds Full molds	All	2000°F

■ For strength, one of the following can be added to the investment:
  –Fiberglass
  –Ceramic fibers
  –Chicken wire
  –Hardware cloth
  –Metal rods (gaggers)

■ Permeability can be increased with:
  –Foaming agents
  –Wood flour
  –Sea coal (crushed coke)
  –Perlite
  –Course grog
  –Luto (reused plastic of paris binder)
  –String
  –Paper
  –Coke breeze

Some investment molds are made by casting the pattern in an investment of one kind, and then making the remainder of the mold with another. These are called *backup* investments. The initial coating is called a *precoat mix*.

The precoat mix provides maximum detail, refractory properties, and texture. The backup mix gives the mold strength and necessary permeability. Because the metal does not come in direct contact with the backup mix, it can be made of coarser and cheaper materials, reducing the overall mold cost. This practice is widespread in the manufacture of nonferrous castings, as well as for full ceramic molds. Commonly, the pattern is coated with a good commercial investment to a thickness of ¼ inch, and the remainder of the mold is made with 1 part 60-mesh silica sand to 1 part plaster of paris, by volume. Some fibers are added for strength, and wood flour for permeability.

Another common backup mix, used the same way, is 60 percent vermiculite, 30 percent plaster of paris, and 10 percent asbestos.

In ceramic investment molds using an ethyl silicate bonded refractory precoat, the backup mix often contains a phosphate binder to conserve costs.

The surface finish of a cast bronze is a matter of relative considerations. A rough finish on a large bronze would be more acceptable than on a smaller piece. The purpose for the piece and its statement as a design will determine its finish also. The final surface treatment has a bearing on the investment method chosen. For example, a bronze that is going to be polished and buffed over its entire surface could be invested in a simple, cheap, and foolproof cement-bonded sand mold: 10 parts sand to 1 part cement.

Whether one should compound an investment or purchase one commercially prepared is a matter of choice and conditions. By and large, a commercial investment will produce more consistent results. The initial cost is often lower than for one you compound yourself because manufacturers of investments purchase the ingredients in large quantities. They also have the advantage of facilities to manufacture the product under careful quality control. On the other hand, if you are a great distance from a source of raw materials, freight cost becomes a factor. Also, if you are a consumer of small quantities of investments, casting will be more costly to you; small lots of commercial investments are expensive. In some cases, certain materials are unavailable in small lots because it is not profitable for a supplier to break a bulk lot. If your location and financial position is such that you cannot get what you want, but you can buy, say, plaster of paris and some bricks locally, this is the route to take.

Before you decide that the investment you're using is not performing correctly, carefully analyze your complete operation—pouring, calcining, etc. Often, after a series of bad or unsatisfactory castings from a given investment, the investment is blamed and a new one tried, only to have the trouble persist, proving the fault to be elsewhere. I have seen beautiful, flawless castings made from cheap homebrew investments, and some very bad castings that came from complicated, expensive investments. The point is clear: each stage, from pattern development through the final patina, must be carried out with care to achieve good results.

The end use, design, size, surface treatment, composition, and pouring temperature of a casting are all factors that have a definite bearing on the choice of investment and method you use.

Direct Casting Investment Mold

The direct investment casting mold is one in which the core, pattern, and mold are all made progressively, in that order, to produce a *one-time* or *unique* casting. The first step is to build an *armature*, or framework, of steel or soft iron wire.

FIGURE 2.1

The core for a mold can be built up directly on a metal framework called an armature.

FIGURE 2.2

The final shape and wall thickness of a hollow mold built around an armature is determined by the wax layer over the investment core.

The core, which resembles the general shape of the casting, is modeled on the armature (Figure 2.1) with investment mixed thickly in small amounts and progressively built up with spatula and hands. The surface is kept damp so that each succeeding application of investment adheres to the last.

The next step is to build up the final shape with *victory wax* in the thickness desired for the casting (Figure 2.2). The wax is applied in small patties or balls, welded with a warm modeling tool. Make the wax as uniformly solid as possible. The surface of the wax is then detailed as desired, and nails are inserted through the wax and into the core. These will support the core after the mold has been dewaxed, and the necessary gating work attached.

Foamed Plaster Investment Molds

These molds are smooth, with air cells just below the surface. During setting and subsequent drying, the air cells become interconnected, permitting gases to escape when the metal is poured. Just about any conventional formula used for regular investment molds can be used for foamed plaster molds by adding a foaming agent.

The pattern and gating are prepared in the conventional manner and filleted down to a shellacked molding board. The pattern is then given a thin coat of unfoamed investment.

A flask or sleeve is placed around the pattern and carefully secured to the molding board.

Foamed, highly permeable molds can be produced with three parts silica flour and two parts No. 1 molding plaster mixed with any dishwashing liquid.

A rubber-disc mixer can be driven with a hand drill or drill press. The usual investment mix is one part water to one part dry investment.

The desired weight of water is placed in a clean mixing bucket, and the correct weight of investment is added, followed by a small squirt of dishwashing liquid. Then the mix is allowed to stand for 30 seconds or so. The mixer disc is started and lowered to within 1 or 2 inches of the bottom of the bucket and the investment is mixed until well wetted.

Then the disc is raised to a point at which a vortex is created that will make a foam of the investment.

The investment, as it foams, increases in volume by as much as 70 percent in 60 seconds. The trick is to lower and raise the disc to control the size of the air cells. A very fine, even cell structure along with approximately a 50 percent increase in volume signals the end of the process. The mixture is poured into the pattern flask. After the flask has been filled with the foamed mixture, it is jiggled slightly to dislodge any big bubbles that were formed during pouring.

Some commercial investment mixes contain a foaming agent, making the agitation described unnecessary. When making molds from these mixes, it is important that enough is mixed each time to completely fill the flask. A fresh batch often will not bond to the previous dry batch.

Foamed investments can be used to produce full molds with expendable patterns, two-part flask molds using flexible rubber patterns, or rigid, properly drafted patterns.

Cored Molds

Any bronze with a section much thicker than ¾ to 1 inch should not, if at all possible, be poured solid. Aside from the weight of the piece, problems with shrinkage, risering, chilling, and a rough surface caused by heating the inner wall of the mold cavity to excess, will be encountered.

A *core* is a body of investment, or refractory aggregate, used to make a casting hollow. Its external shape becomes the internal shape of the casting.

The process for a cored bronze is the same used for a solid bronze, with one exception: the pattern for a cored bronze must be hollow. Small galvanized steel nails or *chaplets* are pushed halfway through the wall of a hollow wax pattern. The cavity of the wax pattern is filled with the same kind of mix used for a backup investment, and provided with a wax or string vent for gas that will escape from the core when the metal is poured in around it. The mold for the casting is produced like any other bronze mold. When the mold is dewaxed and

FIGURE 2.3

Chaplets (support nails) are used to hold the mold core within the final investment once the wax has melted away.

calcined, the nails (embedded in both the core and the mold wall) support the core and maintain its correct position in relation to the mold wall (Figure 2.3). After casting, the chaplets are cut off and chased down to the level of the outer surface of the casting—or they can be punched out and the resulting holes stopped with brass plugs.

Never use copper or bronze boat nails for chaplets because they will oxidize badly during calcining and become thin and weak. Use galvanized-steel nails or, for extremely large cores, stainless-steel nails. Steel rods (gaggers) are used to reinforce some large cores, but always present the hazard of expanding and contracting during calcining and fracturing the ore.

The core investment should have sufficient permeability and be vented to the outside of the mold. The core is, in most cases, nearly completely surrounded by metal. The gases generated during pouring must be free to get out of the core through a vent. Otherwise, the gases will have to exit through the surrounding liquid metal, causing holes to develop.

Because the texture of the internal core surface is of little consequence in most cases and permeability is desirable, the core investment is made of coarse materials and contains some wood flour and sea coal. In some cases, it is made of a foamed, Hydro-Perm investment (described later).

Often, large or extremely tall hollow wax patterns are held upright on the surface of a water-filled container while they are being filled with core investment. As the investment fills the interior of the pattern, it sinks progressively into the water, preventing the pattern from distorting.

Cores can also be poured in the hollow wax while it is supported by the rubber mold in which it was slip-cast (Figure 2.4). With this

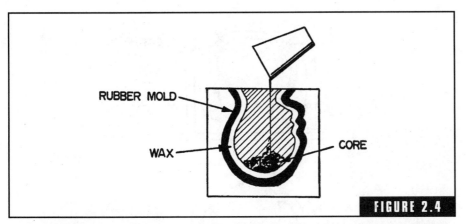

The rubber mold that formed the wax pattern can be used to hold the pattern while the core is poured.

method, the chaplets are located after the wax, with its core, is removed from the rubber mold. The disadvantage here is that if the wax is not removed from the rubber mold prior to pouring the core, there will be no way to determine whether the wax has any thin spots or defects that require fixing from the inside. Once the wax has been removed from a rubber mold for inspection or further work, there is no way to return it properly to the rubber mold for pouring the core.

Hollow castings also are constructed by first placing the pattern on a molding board, running the chaplets into position, and completing the gating system as far as possible down to the board (Figure 2.5A). The pattern is then coated with investment, and the *major mold body* of backing investment is fashioned down to the board (Figure 2.5B).

When the mold has set, it is removed from the board, turned over, and supported within a box (a crate will do).

Nails are driven around the top of the mold projecting from the box, and the gating system is completed (Figure 2.6). A paper sleeve is placed around the mold and extending to the level of the pouring basin. It is sealed with wax where it joins the top face of the mold. The core investment is then poured into the pattern (Figure 2.7) up to the top edge of the pouring basin, completing the mold. Before it sets completely, a welding rod is used to vent the core in several places.

Sometimes a core is in an area that cannot be filled through a large opening. The horse in Figure 2.8A represents such a problem. The

FIGURE 2.5

Some molds can be partially made on the molding board. After the pattern is secured and the chaplets installed (A), a half mold is constructed (B).

FIGURE 2.6

The half mold, built on the molding board, is inverted into a box for support so that its gating can be completed.

way to accomplish the pouring, in this case, is to cut a ½-inch hole in the bottom of the belly. Chaplets, to support the core, are placed in position along with a waxed string vent. The horse is turned over on its back, and the cavity is filled completely with investment using a bulb syringe. When set, the mold is completed normally.

A sleeve or *print* around the bottom of a pattern can be used to form a substantial base on the end of the core, and in cases when the core configuration is simple and its bulk sufficient, chaplets are unnecessary. The print (Figure 2.9) supports the core and keeps it from moving during pouring. When the core is set, the sleeve is removed, and a groove is cut midway around the print to act as a lock to prevent vertical core movement after the mold proper has been made. The pattern is set upright on its print, gated, and the mold is completed in the usual manner.

A paper sleeve is placed around the half mold and the investment is poured in to the level of the pouring basin. This process completes the mold.

QUICK»TIP

Proper planning of the core is essential to success. Avoid thin sections, and don't allow pinching of the core (between two gaps).

Avoid cores that require very thin sections; they will be fragile and cannot be supported properly. Also be careful to prevent stress due to shrinkage when a core is pinched between two cavities. To prevent metal from closing off a vent and causing a hole to be blown through the casting, fit a small ceramic sleeve or steel tube through the vent to hold it open.

Some recommended core mixes are Hydro-Perm, made by U.S. Gypsum Inc.; two parts No. 1 molding plaster to three parts 70-mesh olivine sand to three parts luto; and one part 100-mesh sharp silica to one part No. 1 molding plaster to two parts perlite. (The ingredients for the last two mixes are added by volume.)

FIGURE 2.8

A small, hollow pattern for a horse (A) would not have a large opening through which it can be filled with core investment. A hole must be made, and the investment injected (B).

FIGURE 2.9

The core print will support simple cores within the final mold, making chaplets unnecessary.

Most commercial investments, containing a few parts wood flour or coral for permeability, work well.

Half-inch chopped fiberglass strands can be added to any core mix (other than Hydro-Perm) to increase the dry strength of a core.

Hand-Built Molds, Step by Step

Assuming that the pattern has been fitted with a gating and pouring system, we can construct the investment mold, step by step. Silica flour and plaster makes the investment material for this exercise.

Start to construct the investment mold proper by taking a ¾-inch plywood board big enough to work on, and give the surface two coats of orange shellac. Let it dry to a hard coat.

You are now ready to start the mold. Wash the entire pattern and the gating system with alcohol, then let it dry completely. The alcohol lowers the surface tension so that when wet investment is applied to it, it will not bead up or leave uncoated areas. It will coat evenly and cover completely.

FIGURE 2.10

A gated wax pattern, suitable for a hand-built mold, is first secured to the molding board with a fillet of wax fashioned from the pattern's pouring basin with a warm wax tool.

Next, attach the pattern with its gating system to the center of the board, upside down. Run a hot tool around the top of the pouring basin to melt some wax and weld the whole assembly down (Figure 2.10).

Add enough chopped fiberglass to a dry mix of three parts 200-mesh silica flour (a refractory) to two parts No. 1 molding plaster (a binder) so that it is distributed evenly throughout the mix (¼ ounce of ½-inch chopped fiberglass to a 3-pound batch of silica flour and plaster should be enough). Mix the dry ingredients well and place the mixture in a dry tin can.

In a shallow container, put a small amount of water (¼ cup or less). To this water, slowly add the dry investment mix, stirring with a ½-inch brush until the mix is creamy enough to adhere to your wax pattern without running excessively.

Working from the bottom up, coat the entire assembly, taking pains to avoid bubbles. Work the investment very carefully into all details and pockets so that no air spaces are left. Recesses may have to be stippled with the brush to be filled.

Because investment will begin to set once it is added to water, work with small amounts at a time and apply it quickly.

When the investment in your mixing container gets too hard to handle, throw it out, clean the container, and start a new batch.

Allow each coat to dry firm—but still damp—before applying the next. Paint on coats until you have covered the entire wax pattern and gating assembly to a thickness between 3⁄16 inch and ¼ inch. Now allow the entire assembly to set—but not completely dry.

The backup investment I recommended is, by volume, one part coarse 50- to 60-mesh silica sand—washed and dried—to one part No. 1 molding plaster. It is all mixed very well together with chopped fiberglass.

The backup mix is used to make up the bulk of the mold and requires more permeability. Because it is thicker than the painted-on coat, use a coarse silica sand in place of flour. Mix the backup investment with water until it forms a thick, spreadable consistency.

Apply the backup mix to the pattern with your hands, starting from the board and working up. Avoid overlaps and bubbles.

The thickness of the backup investment depends on the size of the casting you are making. One-inch sides are the minimum for small to medium-sized patterns, and from 6 to 8 inches all around for larger patterns. Play it safe; don't try to be too conservative—you might lose the casting.

Cement Molds

Cement investment molds are made in either two-part, cylindrical metal flasks or in rosin-paper flasks.

The investment cannot be poured; it must be tamped down around the pattern. The investment consists of 10 parts (by volume) of 100-mesh silica sand to one part Hi-Early cement.

The pattern should be made of three parts pine rosin (by weight) to one part victory wax. The cement and sand are mixed dry, and then tempered on the heavy side to about 8 percent moisture.

The pattern is embedded in 4 or 5 inches of cement and sand and tamped down in the bottom of the flask. Then the mold is progressively built up by tamping to the required height and leveled off. The mold is allowed to set overnight, then inverted and dewaxed at 600 F. The cement mold does not require calcining at all, only dewaxing. The mold, when cold, can be filled with any metal or alloy up to 2800 F. in its molten state. Large cast-iron fountains and architectural pieces are often made this way.

For large gray iron and bronze pieces, where surface smoothness is a factor, the wax pattern can be embedded within the drag half of a two-part flask. Then it is parted (generally, at midpoint) and the half-mold is allowed to set overnight. The parting plane is coated with 10-weight motor oil, and the cope half is made and allowed to set. The mold is clamped together and dewaxed. After dewaxing, the mold is separated. The entire cavity, which at this point is exposed, is washed with a core wash, such as Zirc-O-Graph mixed with naptha. The naptha is ignited and burns off, setting the wash. The mold is then reassembled, clamped together, and filled.

If the piece is to be cored, it is lined with clay to the desired metal thickness and provided with the necessary prints for support. The core is made of the same mix used for the mold. The reason for using a rosin-wax pattern is that in dewaxing a cement mold, you do not calcine; heat is only used to melt the wax out. Thus, some wax is absorbed back into the mold face, making it soft during this operation. However, when the mold cools to room temperature, the rosin will reharden the mold face.

Extremely large castings have been successfully cast in bronze and iron this way, some of 20 tons or more in weight. Cement molds are best poured through bottom gating with several whistler vents on top, because wax left in the mold will ignite and burn and the fumes must have free passage out.

Ceramic Shell Molds

Usually, ceramic shell molds are made by dipping the gated wax pattern in a watery mixture or *slurry* of ethyl silicate (insoluable) mixed with a suitable refractory, such as fused quartz sand. Like silica sand, quartz sand is graded into various *meshes*, from 200-mesh (flour-fine) to 30-mesh (very coarse).

With a change in the acid–alkaline balance of the ethyl silicate solution, silica precipitates as a gel. The gelling occurs when the ethyl silicate and alcohol mixture is hydrolyzed by adding water and a catalyst, such as hydrochloric acid (HCL). A common ethyl silicate formula is made up of 2666 cc of ethyl silicate, 660 cc of isopropyl alcohol, 15 cc of HCL (concentrated), and 4000 cc of distilled water. The ingredients are mixed until completely hydrolyzed, then diluted with an equal portion of isopropyl alcohol (by volume). Use only stainless-steel tools and plastic mixing containers for this solution.

To make up the slurry, add 6.65 quarts of ethyl silicate solution to 22.5 pounds of 200-mesh fused silica flour. Dip the clean pattern in the ceramic slurry and drain off the excess; then stucco it lightly by sifting on a mixture of 50- and 100-mesh silica sand through a riddle. After it dries, repeat the procedure until the proper shell thickness is built up. Some operators, after two dips and stuccoing, progressively decrease the fineness of the stucco.

Phosphate-bonded investments are cheaper than ethyl silicate and are used as a backup for full ceramic molds. The thickness depends upon the size of the casting. The average thickness is ¼ inch, but shells up to ½ inch thick are common. The full-ceramic investment mold is produced by two methods. One involves making a shell on the wax pattern, placing the encased pattern in a flask, and surrounding it with a phosphate-bonded investment. The second method uses a two-part flask molding in the same manner.

There are several precoat formulas and backup mixes on the market for specific uses. The molten pouring temperature, metal composition, and the molding method are the determining factors in their selection.

Green Sand Molding

In green sand molding, a mold is produced with an aggregate consisting of refractory material and a binder. The basic ingredients are silica sand, the aggregate, and a refractory clay as the binder. Two types of green sand are commonly used: natural, bonded molding sand and so-called synthetic sand.

Natural, bonded sand is a mixture of sand and clay, ingredients found in Nature, mined and sold to foundries by foundry suppliers. They are graded according to their best application. It is common to find several grades in one mine or digging. A much-used natural bonded molding is called Albany sand—from Albany, New York. It is strip mined in seven grades from No. 00 for very small iron, brass, and aluminum castings, to a No. 3 for heavy castings. See Chapter 2 for more information on molding sands.

French sand, as its name implies, comes from France. It is used for fine bronze and aluminum castings; in particular, bronze tablets and plaques.

French sand consists of 16.6 percent clay and is available in particle sizes from 135 to 170 mesh. Natural bonded molding sands are found in numerous locations throughout the U.S. and are usually named for the location. Greely sand, good for brass and aluminum castings, comes from a pit near Greely, Colorado.

Synthetic sands consist of sharp clay-free silica sand with southern or western bentonite added as a binder.

By selecting the proper base sand, and adding the required amount of binder, any type of molding sand you need can be formulated. For example, 100 pounds of washed and dried silica sand with an average fineness of 140- to 160-mesh, 5 pounds of southern bentonite, 4 pounds of sea coal (ground coke), mixed with 4.5 percent moisture, would yield a good molding compound for light cast iron or heavy bronze. For heavy work, try a mixture of 100 pounds of clean, dry silica sand with an average fineness of 58- to 69-mesh, combined with 1 pound of southern bentonite, 1 pound of western bentonite, 1 pound of pitch, 2 pounds of sea coal, and 5 percent moisture. The basic disadvantage of synthetic sands is that they require a *muller* to mix them and to develop the necessary green strength.

> **TOOLS**
>
> Mullers are expensive, but the cost may be reduced for small applications by using a small cement mixer. You can rent a cement mixer, but these rental units may be too dirty for use as a sand muller.

> **TOOLS**
>
> Green sand, like lost wax, sounds exotic, but it is simply the name of a molding sand that has been tempered with water (plus or minus some other materials). In some types of sand molds, good, old-fashioned molasses serves as a serviceable binder.

Natural bonded sands can be mixed with a riddle and cut by hand with a molder's shovel. They carry more moisture for a given bond strength—a disadvantage. However, most bronze and aluminum is cast in natural bonded sands except in highly mechanized operations.

Skin-Dried Sand Molds

The skin-dried mold is produced like a green sand mold with one exception: prior to closing the mold for pouring, spray every interior surface of it with a mixture of 10 parts water to one part molasses or lignin sulphite. Dry the sprayed areas with a torch using a low, broad flame kept in motion to dry the sand slowly and to avoid excessive heat that might scorch the surface. You want to simply drive out the surface moisture and supply enough heat to set the molasses or lingnin binder.

Dry the mold surface to about ⅛ to ¼ inch in depth, leaving a smooth, hard skin.

Although this system seems quite simple, it takes quite a bit of skill and practice to do properly. This kind of mold is commonly used for tablets, grave markers, and highly ornamented castings. This method prevents small sand protrusions on the mold surface from being washed away when the mold is poured. A skin-dried French sand mold will produce a casting with a surface finish superior to that of an investment casting.

Skin-dried molds are best made in metal flasks—wood flasks might burn. After the mold is carefully dried, allow it to cool and then close it. Pour the mold shortly after closing it; otherwise, the moisture in the sand behind the dried surface will eventually migrate to the surface, defeating the purpose of the whole operation.

Dry Sand Molds

Dry sand molds are made in steel flasks. Green sand is mixed with a binder such as pitch, linseed oil, lignin sulphite, or a commercial binder. Make the mold as in green sand casting and, when finished, spray it with molasses water and dry it overnight at 350 to 400 F. Dry sand molds are usually made when thick metal sections are anticipated, and a tough mold is required. Steel castings are commonly poured in dry sand molds. A typical dry sand formula for heavy work is 100 pounds of sand, 3 pounds of plastic fireclay, 3 pounds of bentonite, and 2 pounds of pitch.

No-Bake Molds

No-bake molding involves the controlled mixing of two or more chemicals with sand to form a filled mold that cures or air hardens within minutes at room temperature. No fuel for baking or curing is needed. One of the chemicals, a catalyst or hardener, causes the resin binder, which coats the sand grains, to undergo a chemical reaction. As time passes, the sand grains are bound together and the mixture sets up or *cures*.

Variables such as temperature, humidity, and the reaction rate between the liquid binder and catalyst affect *work time* and *strip time*. Work time is the period during which the sand mixture can be used to produce satisfactory molds. Strip time is the time after mixing when the pattern can be removed.

Proven Advantages

No-bake molding offers the foundry numerous advantages. These advantages can be most fully realized when the no-bake process is combined with an environmentally designed, energy-efficient system that can process the sand for re-use. In this sense, *sand reclamation* is the logical extension of no-bake molding.

Energy and Time. Significant saving in the cost of thermal energy is achieved because baking or curing is eliminated or greatly reduced. As fuel shortages become more acute and costs rise, this will become even more important. Short, controllable cure times and simpler, more efficient molding procedures also permit high-production schedules to be met. The no-bake process is ideal for producing a wide variety of casting sizes where metal pouring flexibility is required.

Sand and Equipment Costs. Less sand is needed because the sand-to-metal ratio for no-bake molding is lower than that for green sand. The advantages of flaskless molding are important. The cost of flasks, handling, and maintenance is often eliminated. Casting removal and cleaning are also easier. In addition, the overall capital investment for equipment is usually lower.

Casting Quality. More accurate, truer-to-pattern reproduction improves casting quality. With no-bake's rigid wall molds, less scrap loss and higher yields are often recorded. These dimensionally consistent castings require less cleaning, finishing, and machining set-up time.

Economics. Just as in green sand molding, typically 80 to 90 percent of the reclaimed sand from a no-bake mold typically is reusable. Casting producers can stretch supplies of dwindling and ever more costly virgin molding sands. At the same time they significantly reduce the cost of disposal.

Total System Approach

To gain maximum benefit from no-bake molding, a *total system* includes:

- Automated, continuous sand mixing
- Mechanized mold and core handling
- Controlled metal pouring and cooling
- Casting removal, cleaning, and sand reclamation, ideally accomplished by an environmentally designed, single-step system
- Closed-system sand return

Before embarking on no-bake molding in a large operation, foundrymen must consider several factors. These factors include the type of metal; weight and size of casting; production requirements per pattern; type and cost of sand and binder; sand-to-metal ratio; type of mixing equipment; casting cleaning; and the sand reclamation system.

It is common practice with large flask molds to face the pattern with a no-bake mix, then back it up with system sand.

In no-bake molding, internal cores are usually made with the same sand mix. In essence a no-bake mold is a core mold.

No-Bake Binders

Both organic and inorganic binder systems are available for no-bake molding. In order to coat individual sand grains readily, binders are applied as individual liquid resins. Depending upon the binder system, the hardening additive or catalyst can be introduced into the sand mixture in the form of a liquid, a finely divided solid, or a gas.

ORGANIC BINDERS

Furans. The furan series is the oldest of the no-bake systems and sometimes is called *acid no-bake* because an acid acts as a catalyst. The series exhibits high strength and exceptionally well-elevated temperature properties. Cores and molds can be poured four hours after they have been stripped. Furan binders are available with different levels of nitrogen and water. The grade of binder varies with specific use. Steel producers usually want very low or zero nitrogen and a water content less than 1.0 percent. On the other hand, most gray iron producers prefer 4–5 percent nitrogen and 12–20 percent water. The cost of the binder generally is related to the nitrogen and water content. The lower the nitrogen and water, the higher the cost.

Oil-Urethane (Alkyd). This binder can be used as either a two- or three-part system. The binder portion is an alkyd resin. The catalyst consists of two parts: a polymeric isocyanate and a metallic dryer (a lead or cobalt compound in liquid form). The purpose of the metallic dryer is to speed up the reaction.

The oil-urethane system is among the least sensitive to sand temperature and moisture variables. Mold stripping and release properties are excellent. The system contains no water, is low in nitrogen, and does not produce unpleasant fumes.

Before cores and molds can accept molten metal, they need to air cure for 8 to 12 hours after stripping. To allow quicker pour-off, some users apply heat in a post-bake cycle.

Phenolic-Urethane. This three-part system consists of a phenolic resin, a polymeric isocyanate, and a catalyst to regulate curing speed.

INORGANIC BINDERS

Silicate Binders. Two methods are used to harden silicate no-bake binders. In the first method, sand coated with sodium silicate is exposed to carbon dioxide (CO_2) gas. The reaction produces a silica gel that binds the sand particles together. The other method employs an ester setting additive to air-harden the coated sand mixture.

Silicate-type binders have high hot strength and good ecological properties with low gas and low or no odor, stains, or toxicity. However, the curing process is sensitive to sand impurities, moisture, and temperature. Low internal strength, poor handling properties, and poor shakeout are also characteristic.

Phosphate Binders. This zero-nitrogen, zero-silicate no-bake system is composed of a phosphate solution and an inorganic powdered hardener to control hardening speed. Strip time can be varied from 20 minutes to 1 hour. Pouring can begin 1 hour after strip.

Sand mixes are clean. Handling and gas problems are minimal. Tucking and compacting may be necessary in corners and pockets, because flowability is less than that found in organic sand mixes. Also, sand impurities may alter the work-time–strip-time relationship. Shakeout properties compare with those of organic no-bake binders. The nitrogen content is low and there is no water.

Speed, control of work time, strip time and economically favorable low-binder–level requirements make the phenolic-urethane system especially attractive for high-production operations. Intervals of as little as two minutes have been reported from filling to strip. Castings can be poured within one hour after stripping. Sand impurities, however, can affect cure rate and strength. During casting some fuming may also occur.

A typical furan mix has a binder of 2 percent of the weight of the sand and the catalyst 25 percent of the weight of the binder. The mix could be 100 pounds sand, 2 pounds binder, and ½ pound catalyst. The catalyst most often used is 75% phosphoric acid.

Molding Sands

When we speak of sand casting the first thing that comes to the minds of most people is the sand on the beach or the desert, but there are many other places to find sand.

You can prospect for your own molding sands by looking for deposits along creek beds, river banks, and cliffs as well as the beach and desert. The typical molding sand for foundry use resembles ordinary sand, usually screened to a definite size fraction and mixed with 10 to 20 percent clay to act as a binder to hold the sand grains together. Molding sand is ordinarily quite inexpensive. In fact, natural molding sands are found in many areas which contain the correct proportions of sand and clay, and it is only necessary to dig the material out of the ground. Very few natural sands possess the desired properties in all proportions, however, so it is usual to add other ingredients to improve them.

Molding Sand Properties

Molding sand must possess several characteristics. First, it must be cohesive so that the individual grains stick together while the pattern

Table 3.1 Sand Characteristics for Various Metal Castings

Light gray iron	
Fineness	175
Clay	12%
Moisture	7.4%
Permeability	15
Green compression	4.0
Medium gray iron	
Fineness	111
Clay	15%
Moisture	7.5%
Permeability	40
Green compression	4.0
Heavy gray iron	
Fineness	73
Clay	18%
Moisture	7.6%
Permeability	70
Green compression	5.0
Heavy brass	
Fineness	108
Clay	12%
Moisture	7%
Permeability	51
Green compression	4.0
Light to medium brass	
Fineness	218
Clay	13%
Moisture	8%
Permeability	18
Green compression	4.0
Aluminum	
Fineness	232
Clay	19%
Moisture	8%
Green compression	5.0

is being removed, otherwise the mold will break apart. Second, it must be porous enough so that gases and water vapor can escape when molten metal is poured into the mold. To a certain degree, the properties of cohesion and porosity work at cross purposes. The addition of clay or clay-like material improves the cohesiveness of the sand grains, but at the same time tends to reduce porosity. Molding sand must also be refractory to withstand the high temperature of molten metal.

Table 3.1 lists the characteristics of molding sands used for the production of castings in various metals and sizes. Notice that the grain fineness and the permeability required in a sand used to make a mold for a gray iron casting is different compared to the fineness and permeability required in a sand for use in making a mold for aluminum.

Cohesiveness

The size and shape of the sand grains influences the properties of the molding sands. Rounded grains, such as beach sands, do not cohere nearly as well as sharp, irregular grains, which interlock and provide a stronger structure when rammed into the mold. Sharp grained sands, therefore, are to be preferred as less clay is required for bonding and the sands will be more porous.

Your local foundry supplier should be able to furnish clay-bonded moldings sands, of the type described, in 100-pound bags. Molding sands of this type are usually shipped dry, and before use it is necessary to "condition" them by adding water until the sand develops the correct adhesion. The conditioning process is best carried out by sprinkling the sand with water as it is turned over with a trowel or shovel. Enough water is added so that a handful of the sand compressed by clenching the fingers sticks together like a snowball, leaving a distinct pattern of the fingers and lines in the palm. Excessive water should be avoided. Molding sands of this kind can be used over and over, being reconditioned whenever necessary, although they will eventually "wear out" and should then be discarded.

To sand cast make a mold around a pattern, open the mold, remove the pattern, close the mold, and fill the cavity left in the sand with molten metal. When the metal has solidified, shake out the mold and expose an exact duplicate of our pattern in metal.

Anyone who has built sand castles on the beach can attest to how fragile they are. But if you mix enough clay with beach sand to give each grain a coating of clay (which is sticky when damp), you could make great sand castles. Clay and sand castles are not nearly as fragile as beach castles that depend upon water alone as a medium to bond the grains together.

A mold made of beach sand, clay, and water can be used to hold molten metal. When the mold is filled with hot metal, it doesn't crumble or explode because of the moisture content because as the molten metal enters the mold cavity the radiant heat from the metal dries the mold material in advance of the metal flow. The moisture is changed to steam and moves out of the mold through the mold walls because of the porous nature of the molding sand.

Permeability

The ability of the mold material to allow the steam to pass through the walls is called permeability. Permeability can be measured with a meter that measures the volume of air that will pass through a test specimen per minute under a standard pressure. Some instruments are designed to measure a pressure differential, indicated on a water tube gauge expressed in permeability units.

In this book we are for the most part concerned with natural bonded sands, to be used in green sand molding. A natural bonded sand contains enough bonding material that it can be used for molding purposes just as it is found in the ground.

Natural molding sands contain from 8 to 20 percent natural clay; the remaining material consists of a refractory aggregate, usually silica grains.

Any natural sand containing less than 5 percent natural clay is called a *tank sand* and is used for cores or as a base for synthetic molding sand.

Commercial molding sands mined by various companies usually acquire the name of the area where they are mined. The most popular natural bonded molding sand is called Albany, and is mined in several different grades by the Albany Sand & Supply Co., Albany, New York. The origin of this sand is from the Pleistocene ice sheet of approximately 20,000 years ago, which swept down from the north and completely overran what is now known as the Albany District. The result is a seam of fine molding sand approximately 15 inches thick directly under an overburden of 8 inches of top soil.

Fineness

This is a measure of the actual grain size of a sand mixture. It is made by passing a standard sample, usually 100 grams, through a series of graded sieves. About 10 different sieve sizes are used. Because most sands are composed of a mixture of various size grains there is a distribution of sands remaining on the measuring sieves.

The fineness number assigned to a sample is approximately the sieve (screen) which would just pass the sample if its grains were all the same size.

Additives

When you fully understand the relationship between the required permeability for a given metal and its pouring temperature and the relationship of grain fineness to permeability, you will be able to establish what sand you need for a given metal and casting size. As an example, gray iron is poured at a temperature of 2700 F. and is three times the weight of aluminum which is poured at 1400 F.

Although we are primarily interested in natural bonded sands, their use and properties, we will, however, cover some aspects of synthetic molding sands. Both sands have their good and bad features and the choice depends upon the class of work and the equipment available.

The basic components of most molding sands are silica and a clay bond. However molding sands can also be made up of other types of refractory materials such as zircon, olivine, carbon, magnetsite, sillimanite, ceramic dolomite, and others.

Molding sand is defined as a mixture of sand or gravel with a suitable clay bond. Natural sands can be used for producing molds as they are found in nature. Synthetic molding sands are weak or clay free sands to which suitable clay or clays are added to give them the properties needed.

You should be aware, however, that in the recent past there has been a real crop of sand medicine men who sell all types of additives and dopes for molding sands to cure the foundryman's problems.

> **QUICK»TIP**
>
> *Caveat emptor* or "buyer beware" is always a good policy, but it is especially important in areas where knowing the contents of a product is essential to safely producing the work you want. Always learn the contents of molding sand or other foundry products. If the manufacturer, distributor, or salesperson cannot or will not tell you what's in a product, take your business to another company.

Most of these products are simple additives that have been disguised in some manner. Make it a point never to buy any sand additive or product if the manufacturer refuses to divulge exactly what the product is.

We are living in an age of rediscovery and many of these rediscoveries are disguised to look like new products. To know and control your sand you must know exactly what you are adding and using. There must be no unknowns, otherwise you are in the dark.

Avoid complicated sand mixtures; they only lead to confusion and are most difficult to control. A simple sand with the proper grain size and distribution, with sufficient bond and moisture, will give much better results than one which is complex. Complex sands are usually a product of experimentation, with various additives trying to accomplish some particular illusive result. This is usually due to insufficient understanding of molding sands, their formulation, limitations, and uses.

Keep the types, kinds, number, and amounts of sand additives to a minimum for best results.

Avoid the use of products which are sold as cure alls. No product can offset poor practice.

> **QUICK»TIP**
>
> There's an old adage that's not polite, but sometimes helps me remember not ot over-complicate things: KISS (Keep It Simple, Stupid). Molding sands need the KISS approach, so keep the types, kinds, numbers, and amounts of additives to an absolute minimum and you'll see an improvement in results.

Refractoriness

Refractoriness is the ability of sand to withstand high temperatures without fusing or breaking down. From this we can deduce that a sand used for casting steel must be more refractory than one for brass or aluminum because of the greater pouring temperature involved. Also, a sand used to cast large heavy castings must be more refractory than one used for light thin castings of the same metal.

Because we are primarily dealing with natural bonded sands, the refractoriness of the sands can vary over a wide range. When a naturally bonded sand contains appreciable amounts of fluxing agents (various mineral salts, organic material, and oxides) that lower the fusion point of the sand, it may melt or fuse to the casting. There are various costly instruments used to determine the refractoriness of molding sands. In the absence of such testing equipment we must pour samples of various thickness into the sand in question and examine the surface of these test castings for sand fused to the casting. This actual experience will be more useful to you than all the instruments in the world. This is what we call getting your hands in the sand. In order to start our testing we need a wood pattern (Figure 3.1). This is a step pattern, 6 inches long, with three different step thicknesses.

We make a mold of our step pattern in the conventional manner with the sand in question and cast it in brass or bronze at 2200 F. Allow the casting to cool to room temperature in the mold, then shake it out (Figure 3.2).

1" · $\frac{1}{2}$" · ¼"

1° DRAFT ON ALL VERTICAL SURFACES

FIGURE 3.1

Step pattern.

Casting step pattern.

The cold casting is carefully examined for adhered sand that will not peel off easily with a wire hand brush. Any area on which the sand will not peel off is examined carefully with a magnifying glass. This examination will readily show if the sand has indeed melted or vitrified under the heat of casting and has in fact welded or fluxed itself to the casting.

Let's say that the ¼ inch thick section and the ½ inch thick section peeled nicely and is free of any adhered sand and presents a nice smooth metal surface, but the 1 inch section does not peel clean and shows vitrified sand on its surface. This would indicate that the sand has a suitable refractoriness for light brass and bronze up to ½ inch in section thickness but is unsuitable for 1 inch and thicker sections.

Should all surfaces peel cleanly, you must work up a new and thicker pattern. By experimenting you can readily determine the limits of the sand in question.

The reason brass or bronze is used for the test and not aluminum is because aluminum pours at such a low temperature. It would be hard to find any sand that would fuse at these lower temperatures. When performing the refractoriness test, the mold must be carefully made and rammed properly. A soft mold (under-rammed) or a mold which has not been rammed evenly could give you a *penetration defect* which you might falsely identify as poor refractoriness. In this case the surface is rough and contains metal mixed in the sand.

Green Bond Strength

Green bond strength is the strength of a tempered sand expressed by its ability to hold a mold in shape. Sand molds are subjected to compressive, tensile, shearing, and transverse stresses. Which of these stresses is more important to the sand's molding properties is a point of controversy.

To test for green compressive strength test, a rammed specimen of tempered molding sand is produced that is 2 inches in diameter and 2 inches in height. The rammed sample is then subjected to a load, which is gradually increased until the sample breaks. The point where the sample breaks is taken as the green compression strength.

The devices made to crush the specimen are of several types and quite costly. The readings are in pounds per square inch. It sure wouldn't take much thinking or doing to come up with a homemade rammer or a compression device. As you are only interested in whether the sand is weak, strong, or very strong, the figures you give for values are only relative and you can call them whatever you like.

Tensile Strength

Tensile strength is the force that holds the sand up in the cope. And, because molding sands are many times stronger in compression than tensile strength, we must take the tensile strength into account. Mold failure is more apt to occur under tensile forces.

FIGURE 3.3

Squeezed sample of sand.

Where compression strength is measured in pounds per square inch, the tensile strength of molding sands is measured in ounces per square inch.

The tensile strength, which is the force required to pull the sample apart, is determined very easily.

Pick up a handful of riddled tempered sand and squeeze it tightly with your palm up. Open your hand and observe if the sand took a good sharp impression (Figure 3.3).

Now grab the squeezed sample between the thumb and first finger of both hands and pull it apart.

Examine the break. It should be sharp and clean, not crumbly. By observing the break and noting the force required to pull the sample apart you can tell a lot about the tensile strength and general condition of the sand. Make another sample. This time grab it about midway with the right hand thumb and first finger, shaking it until the end that protrudes breaks off. Note how much force was required to make it break (Figure 3.4).

FIGURE 3.4

Sharp clean breaks.

Dry Strength

A mold must not only hold its shape in the green state, it must also hold its shape in the dry state. This is an important property and is measured as *dry compression*. It allows the test specimen to dry out before testing, which is then carried out in the same manner as for green strength. A good average figure is 30 pounds per square inch. Dry strength should be no higher than necessary. Excessive dry strength results in a critical sand. If the molding sand has a too-high dry strength it will not give or break down as the casting shrinks during solidification. This will cause hot tearing of the casting.

Durability

Durability is the measure of the ability of the sand to withstand repeated usage without losing its properties and to recover its bond strength after repeated use. The sand's fineness and the type and amount of clay bond determines the sand's durability. The ability of the bonding clay to retain its moisture is also an important factor.

Moldability

Moldability is also related to the nature of the bonding clay and the fineness of the sand. Because the base sand determines the resulting finish of the casting, it should be selected with care. Keep in mind the type, weight, and class of casting desired. The three or four types of screened sands formerly used for a base have given way to the practice of blending one coarse sand with a fine sand to result in a better grain distribution. This has been found to produce a better finish and texture. Each of the two sands selected should have a good grain distribution within itself. Contrary to popular belief, additives of an organic or carbonaceous nature do not improve the finish but only furnish combustibles resulting in better peel.

Blended Sands

Use the following suggested sand blends as a guide when selecting your own basic blends. Start with a good high grade silica, washed, dried, screened, and graded. Adjustments can be made to the base after sufficient tracking is done.

- For heavy iron use green or dry sand. Fineness 61 and 50. Permeability 80 to 120.
- For medium iron, green sand. Fineness 70 and 45. Permeability 50 to 70.
- For light squeezer iron, green sand. Fineness 110 and 80. Permeability 20 to 30.
- For stove plate iron, green sand. Fineness 200 and 160. Permeability 9 to 17.
- For heavy green steel, green sand. Fineness 60 and 35. Permeability 140 to 290.
- For heavy steel, dry sand. Fineness 55 and 40. Permeability 90 to 250.
- For light squeezer malleable iron. Fineness 130 and 95. Permeability 20 to 40.
- For heavy malleable iron. Fineness 80 and 70. Permeability 40 to 70.
- For copper and monel. Fineness 150 and 120. Permeability 30 to 60.
- For aluminum. Fineness 250 and 150. Permeability 6 to 15.
- For general brass. Fineness 150 and 120. Permeability 12 to 20.

Petro Bond Molding Sands

When Petro Bond first arrived on the scene more than 20 years ago, it seemed to be panacea for the small foundry. With the passage of time, however, this did not pan out for some of the following reasons:

- It cannot be mixed by hand. Requires a muller or some sort of mechanical electric mixer to restore it's homogeneity and to make it reusable. This is a problem for the back yard founder.

- It is extremely smokey during pouring—not advisable for the kitchen table founder.

- It is a dirty sand because it arrives in a state of inconsistency. Batches are not always the same, like material from different dye lots.

- It has a relatively short life due to burning back at the casting skin.

- It is very expensive. Be adventurous and try it, but you won't find a commercial foundry that uses petro bond sand as their system sand.

Parting Dust and Graphite Powder

To facilitate the separation of the two halves of a mold and to prevent the sand from sticking to the patterns, a material called *parting dust* is required. Your foundry supplier will stock this material. There is also a liquid parting compound, but it is not recommended for use with Petro Bond sands. About 10 to 25 pounds of parting dust will last the average home craftsman for years so don't buy too much if it can be avoided. Unfortunately, the minimum package amounts of some foundry products are rather more than the typical amateur needs. A sympathetic supplier will break a package to sell smaller than minimum shipping quantities. At the same time, buy some graphite powder, which is useful for dusting onto patterns to keep sand from sticking to them. Buy only a small quantity as a pound or two will go a long way.

This is a good time to mention that stockmen or warehousemen around foundry suppliers have often been foundry workers at one time. If any one of them takes an interest in what you are doing, he may very well offer some good advice about what material to buy. His advice can be very helpful.

Generally, regular parting dust is so cheap that substitutes are a waste of time, but the other materials can be used when you're out of the official stuff. In a pinch, you can use talcum powder (baby powder), finely powdered charcoal, corn starch, or diatomaceous earth (swimming pool filters use this). Put the dust in a sock and shake it over the surface to be parted to give a fine dusting—all that is really needed. The best material for high quality work is lycopodium, which can be obtained from a druggist.

Synthetic Sands

There is no mystery to synthetic sands whatsoever. But the word synthetic is erroneous and misleading. Synthetic sand is not synthetic in any way. It is basically a combination of natural materials provided by Mother Nature, mixed in proportions desired to give certain properties wanted by the user. Natural bonded sand is mixed by Mother Nature and comes as is.

Let's look this synthetic sand business right in the teeth for what it is. Don't start out under the illusion that it is the answer to all your problems and will produce miracles of some sort. It is in reality a very simple and effective sand mixture, which, when properly prepared and used will give good results. In general it requires no more equipment to test than you should have and use with your naturally bonded sand. It does, however, require a muller or paddle mill to give the correct results. The muller is preferred and is the heart of the system. It is necessary in bonding new and used synthetic sand, which requires a kneading and plowing action to develop its properties fully in the shortest time and to produce uniform sand, batch after batch. Also, the muller develops green strength well.

Remember, sand control is the most effective tool you can use to reduce losses and to produce top quality work. Without it you cannot produce consistent results. The lack of sand control by routine testing explains why sand is allowed to become unsatisfactory and difficult to revive. In extreme cases it must be replaced altogether. Even 10 percent of control added to your sand preparation will produce amazing results.

In selecting the base sand, the best rule-of-thumb is to use the weakest, driest, finest sand you can obtain, which will give you the best castings. This mixture can be found only by actual practice.

Popular Sand Mixtures

The following are four of the most popular synthetic sands in use today with nonferrous work:

■ Aluminum and brass—Penn wash float silica, AFS fineness 160; southern bentonite, 4 percent by weight; hardwood flour, 200 mesh, 1 to 1.5 percent.

■ Semi-synthetic, brass and aluminum—60 percent washed and dried silica, AFS fineness 120, 40 percent naturally bonded sand, Albany O; sufficient southern bentonite to give the desired green strength (7 to 8 psi); hardwood flour, 200 mesh, 1 percent.

■ Brass—washed and dried silica, AFS fineness 120; southern bentonite, 4 percent by weight; hardwood flour, 1 to 1.5 percent.

■ Copper—washed and dried silica, AFS fineness 130; southern bentonite, 4 to 4.5 percent by weight; hardwood flour, 1 to 1.5 percent; silica flour sufficient to drop permeability to between 40 and 50 if needed.

Held to within reasonable limits of the following values, the first, third, and fourth sand mixtures will generally give a higher percentage of good results.

■ Mix No. 1: Permeability, 8 to 16; moisture, 3 to 5 percent, as low as possible; green compression, 7 to 8 psi; AFS fineness, 200–160.

■ Mix No. 2 carries about 6 to 7 percent moisture.

■ Mix No. 3: permeability, 12 to 20; moisture, 3 to 5 percent, as low as possible; green compression, 7 to 8 psi; AFS fineness, 160 to 120.

■ Mix No. 4: permeability, 35 to 50; moisture, 3 to 5 percent, as low as possible; green compression, 7 to 8 psi.

For heavy brass and aluminum, vary your sand accordingly for high permeability. Use a coarser sand and hold your moisture as low as possible. Bentonite has its greatest bonding strength with optimum moisture.

It is difficult or even impossible to set down any hard and fast rules. The acid test is in the end results. You are shooting for a sand that will give you sufficient strength, permeability, and lowest moisture, yet produce a good finish.

Permeability can be controlled with silica flour, which closes up sand, and with coarse sand, which opens it up if the moisture remains constant. Bentonite will control the green strength if the moisture remains constant. Wood flour gives a cushion to prevent over-ramming. It improves the finish, shakeout, and collapsibility as well as providing a reducing atmosphere in the mold cavity. Coarse sand will tend to open the sand up. Fines will tend to close it up. The trend will show readily from daily sand tests and casting inspection. For some unknown reason, mix No. 1 is preferred in the eastern and southern sections and mix No. 3 is in wide use along the west coast. Because of their low moisture and high permeability, they can be rammed very hard and will produce castings with a nice peel that are close to size. Either of these sands can be rammed like bricks. They can be sprayed with a suitable binder such as a lignin sulphite binder and water. The skin can also be dried with excellent results on special work. No mention of sintering point is made since most base sands are above 2300 F. and are suitable for nonferrous work. Core sand or sands should be as close as possible to the same fineness as your selected base sand so as to have a minimum effect on physical properties as it enters the system. Whether it be washed and dried silica sand, crude silica, lightly bonded sand, beach or lake sand, bank or dune, the base sand should have as wide a grain distribution as possible. Such a distribution will give you your best overall working conditions.

You will find that the permeability and other figures given in the recommended limits for the four mixes are to be used as a guide. Permeability will run higher than the value given due to the low moisture used. The highest permeability possible at which you can get a satisfactory finish is the best point. The wood flour can be deleted but it is very beneficial and a most useful tool in control.

Some metalcasters put in a small percentage of cereal bond with or without the wood flour. This is a matter you must decide for yourself. The sand which produces the best results day in and day out is the best mix for you, regardless of what's in it.

Daily checks and tests kept in an accurate and systematic manner can be easily correlated with your practice. The correct amounts of binders, wood flour, or what have you to be added or left out per batch depends entirely upon your operation—thus the reason for control by testing. You can graph the results of your daily tests, checking continuously as to where your sand is headed to prevent it from falling off too sharply. When it starts off in the wrong direction, you can pull it back before any harm is done.

Keeping Molding Sand in Condition

When starting a job with new sand that is either natural or synthetic, you will find that the castings will improve with use as the system builds up some burned sand and clay and becomes evenly tempered. The sand will peak out and start downhill as core sand and burnt clay build up in the system. In general, the addition of new sand to replace the sand lost to drag out on castings and the floor, will keep the system in condition unless you contaminate or throw the entire system off kilter by too heavy additions of sea coal, wood flour, pitch, etc. Then you start over. A lot depends upon the ability of your selected sand to take repeated heating and conditioning as well as its ability to recover time and time again (durability).

If your selection of sand is not suited for the weight range and pouring temperature, you are dead at the start. A fine naturally bonded sand for casting light aluminum could last for years with good results, but if used as a mold material for medium to heavy cast iron, it wouldn't last long at all.

Select the correct sand for the work at hand and avoid too many additives. The percentage of new sand added to maintain the heap also depends upon the daily use. You need approximately 10 pounds of sand per each pound of metal poured per day. Keep your sand free from shot metal and trash. Also, keep it tempered properly.

Dry Sand Molds

The number-one advantage of a dry sand mold is insurance. There is an even greater strength on large molds requiring a large volume of metal. A dry sand mold is free from moisture and you are not troubled with the defects caused by steam and rapid chilling. Make sure that the added cost of going to a dry sand mold is justified by the added assurance of a sound casting.

A skin-dried mold will often suffice in place of a fully dried mold if it is poured soon after the skin has been dried.

Molding Tools and Equipment

The basic equipment and materials needed to perform casting operations will be discussed in this chapter. These items are just about the same as any foundry would use, except the amateur's equipment will probably be on a much smaller scale.

Trowels

Next to the molder's shovel, the most used hand tool is the molder's finishing trowel.

The #1 standard finishing trowel comes in three widths: 1¼ inch, 1½ inches, and 1¾ inches. The blade length is standard for any width—6 inches long. The 1½ inch width is standard. The blade tapers from 1½ inches wide at the handle end to 1 inch wide at the end

TOOLS

Molding tools and gear range from tiny pieces of wire to absolutely immense and massive flasks. The overall goal of all the bits and pieces is to produce a mold that lets you pour exactly what you wish to pour, with the final quality you want. Select tools with care, and learn to use them in practice as much as possible before getting into hot situations. Finishing tools may take more finesse to use, but overall, the level of importance of molding tools and equipment is very high.

FIGURE 4.1

Molder's trowels.

of the rounded blade. The handle tang comes up straight from the blade about 2 inches, then is bent parallel to the blade to receive the round wooden handle. The 2-inch rise gives you knuckle room when troweling on a large flat surface. The only difference between a #1 trowel and a #2 is that the #2 finishing trowel has a more pointed nose (Figure 4.1).

Finishing Trowel

The finishing trowel is used to sleek down a surface, to repair a surface, or cut away the sand around the cope of a snap flask.

Heart Trowel

The heart trowel is a handy little trowel for general molding and, as its name implies, has a heart-shaped blade. They run in size from 2 inches wide to 3 inches wide in ¼-inch steps (Figure 4.2).

FIGURE 4.2

Heart trowel.

Core Maker's Trowel

The core maker's trowel is much like a finishing trowel except that the blade

FIGURE 4.3

Core maker's trowel.

edges are parallel along its entire length and the nose is perfectly square. Core maker's trowels come in widths from 1 to 2 inches, in ¼ inch steps, and blade lengths of 4½ to 7 inches, in ½ inch steps. This trowel is used to strike off core boxes and, because it is parallel and square ended, a core can be easily trimmed or repaired and the sides can be squared up (Figure 4.3).

Brushes and Swabs

The most popular type of brush for general bench work and light floor work is the block brush. It is 1⅛ inches wide and 9 inches long with four rows of bristles. Its main use is to brush off the pattern, the matchplate, the bench, and sometimes the molder himself.

Camel Hair Swab

A round camel hair brush (swab) is used to apply wet mold wash and core wash or blacking to a mold or core prior to drying. Most molders carry two sizes—one ⅝ inches in diameter and one ⅞ inches in diameter (Figure 4.4).

Flax Swab

Also called a *horse tail*, the flax swab is used to swab the sand around the pattern at the junction of the pattern and sand. To dampen this sand to prevent it from breaking away when the pattern is rapped and lifted from the sand, it is dampened by dipping it into a pail of water and shaking

FIGURE 4.4

Camel's hair swab.

FIGURE 4.5

Use of flax swab.

FIGURE 4.6

Molder's blow can.

it out well. It is used on floor work where the pattern presents a fair-sized perimeter (Figure 4.5).

The swab is also used by some molders to apply wet mold wash or blacking to a mold surface; however, this requires great dexterity.

Blow Can

The blow can is a simple mouth spray used to apply liquid mold coats and washes to molds and cores, or with water to dampen a large area. It can also be operated with the air hose like the sucker (Figure 4.6).

Bulb Sponge

The bulb sponge consists of a rubber bulb with a hollow brass stem terminating in a soft brush. The stem is pulled out and the bulb filled about three-fourths full of water. The stem is then replaced. The bulb sponge is used to swab around the pattern prior to drawing it—the same as the flax swab is used for floor molding. The bulb is gently squeezed to keep the brush wet while swabbing (Figure 4.7).

FIGURE 4.7

Bulb sponge.

Sprues and Cutters

You can turn sprues or purchase them in various diameters and use them to form sprue and pouring basins in sand molds. In time you will wind up with a wide selection (Figure 4.8).

FIGURE 4.8

Wood sprues.

Tubular Sprue Cutters

Tubular sprue cutters are tapered steel or brass tubes used to cut sprue holes in the cope half of a sand mold. They are sold in sizes from ⅞ to 1¼ inches in diameter. All are 6 inches long (Figure 4.9).

FIGURE 4.9

Tubular sprue cutter.

Gate Cutter

The best gate cutter is made from a section of a Prince Albert tobacco can or can of similar size (Figure 4.10).

To cut a gate or runner in green sand, the tab is held between the thumb and first finger and the gate or runner is cut just as you would cut a groove or channel in wood with a gouge. The width is controlled by bending the cutter's sides in and out. The depth is controlled by the operator.

FIGURE 4.10

Gate cutter.

Ramming and Rapping Tools

Various tools are used by the metalcaster for the ramming and rapping operations involved during molding.

Bench Rammer

A bench rammer (Figure 4.11) can be made of oiled maple. You can buy one or turn one on a lathe. Use a bandsaw to cut the wedge-shaped peen end.

FIGURE 4.11

Bench rammer.

FIGURE 4.12

Floor rammer.

FIGURE 4.13

Rapping bar and rapper.

The butt end is used to actually ram the sand into the flask around the pattern. The peen end is used to *peen* or ram the sand tightly around the inside perimeter of the flask to prevent the cope or drag mold from falling out when either half is moved, rolled over, or lifted.

Floor Rammer

The floor rammer has the same purpose and design as a bench rammer except the butt and peen ends are made of cast iron and attached to each end of a piece of pipe or hickory handle. The average length is 42 inches (Figure 4.12).

Rapping Bar and Rapper

The rapping bar consists of a piece of brass or steel (cold roll) rod which is machined or ground to a tapered point. The rapper is made of steel or brass and is shaped exactly like the frame of a slingshot (Figure 4.13).

The purpose of these tools is to rap or shake the pattern loose from the sand mold in order to draw it easily from the sand. When you shake the pattern in all directions, it drives the sand slightly away from the pattern. The resulting mold cavity will actually be a bit larger than the pattern. The pattern should only be rapped enough to free it from the sand. You will be able to see when it is loose all around by the movement of the pattern. Over-rapping will distort the mold cavity, which may or may not matter depending on how close you wish the casting to hold a tolerance (Figure 4.14).

The operation is quite simple. The bar point of the rapping bar is pressed down into a dimple in the parting face of the pattern with the left hand. The rapper is used to strike the bar with the inner faces of the yoke.

Hand Riddles

You need two 18-inch diameter riddles— one with #4 mesh and one with #8 mesh galvanized iron screen. The #4 mesh will be used for general bench work and floor molding. It will riddle the first sand over the pattern before filling the mold with the shovel and ramming. The #8 mesh serves the same purpose but also applies fine facing sand to special jobs such as plaques or grave markers (Figure 4.15).

FIGURE 4.14

Rapping.

FIGURE 4.15

Hand riddler.

Bellows

In general there are two types of bellows. One has a short snout and it is called a *bench bellow*. The other one has a long snout and is called a *floor bellow*. The theory is that a molder can wreck a bench mold when blowing it out with a long snout floor bellow by hitting the sand with the snout. This is true due to the different stance and angle when blowing a mold bench high, or on the ground. With care one only needs a 9- or 10-inch floor bellow to blow out cope and drag molds, sprue hole, and gates (Figure 4.16).

Strike Off Bar

Each time a mold is rammed up the sand must be struck off level with the flask cope and drag. The bar simply consists of a metal or hardwood straightedge of sufficient length (Figure 4.17).

Rawhide Mallet

The mallet is a minimum weight of 21 ounces and is used to rap patterns or draw pikes to loosen the pattern from the sand so it can be smoothly withdrawn from the mold without damage to the mold or pattern.

FIGURE 4.16

Molder's bellows.

FIGURE 4.17

Strike-off tool.

Miscellaneous Tools

There are several other tools necessary for the molder to successfully complete his metalcasting operations.

Draw Pins, Screws, and Hooks

These items are used to remove or draw the pattern from the mold. The draw pin is driven into the wooden pattern and used to lift it out as a handle. On a short small pattern one pin in the center will do. If the pattern is long, use one on each end for a two-hand straight lift. The draw hook is used the same way. The draw screw is screwed into the pattern for a better purchase on heavier patterns, and prevents the pattern from accidentally coming loose prematurely and falling, damaging the mold, pattern, or both. In large patterns, plates, which have a tapped hole into which a draw pin with a matching thread is screwed for lifting by hand or with a sling from a crane, are let into the pattern at its parting face. Two or more are usually used (Figure 4.18).

Loose metal patterns are drilled and tapped to receive a draw pin.

Sucker

The sucker is not a purchased tool but one made by the molder. It consists of two pieces of tubing and a tee of copper or iron (Figure 4.19).

The sucker is used to clean out deep pockets in molds where the bellows and lifter fail, or in cases where the pocket or slot is so dirty that using a lifter would take too long. It is also useful where it is impossible to see to use a lifter. The operation is very simple. You simply blow through the elbow with an air hose. This creates a vacuum in the long length, which gives you in effect a vacuum cleaner with a long skinny snout. Now stick the long end down to where the problem is and blow through the elbow. Suckers will lift out small steel shot, a match stick, or material which cannot be wetted such as parting powder or silica sand (Figure 4.20).

Draw pins and draw plate.

Sucker.

Operation of sucker.

FIGURE 4.21

Bench lifter.

FIGURE 4.22

Using the bench lifter.

A word of warning—watch which direction you have the discharge end of your sucker pointed when sucking out a mold. You could accidentally blow sand in someone's eyes.

Bench Lifter

The bench lifter is a simple steel tool with a right-angled square foot on one end of a flat bent blade (Figure 4.21).

This tool's biggest use is to repair sand molds and lift out any tramp or loose sand that might have fallen into a pocket (Figure 4.22).

To remove dirt from a pocket that will not blow out with the bellows, you simply spit on the heel of the lifter and reach down and use the moistened end to pick it up. Then wipe off the heel and go back and slick the spot down a bit.

Lifters come in all sizes from a bench lifter ¼ inch wide by 6 inches long to floor lifters 1 inch wide and 20 inches long. All have the same use. Many molders make their own lifters to suit the class of work they generally do.

Slick and Oval Spoon

The slick and oval spoon is a must for all molders. Again the size needed is determined by the work involved. Most molders have at least four sizes from one ¼ inch wide to one 2 inches wide. This tool is cared a *double ender* in the trade. One end is a slick similar to a heart trowel blade but more oval shaped. The opposite end is spoon shaped. The outside or working surface is convex like the back of a spoon. Its inner face is concave. This face is never used and therefore is usually not finished smooth. When new it is painted black. Both faces of the slick blade are highly polished (Figure 4.23).

The double ender is a general use molding tool used for slicking flat or concave surfaces, for opening-up sprues, etc.

FIGURE 4.23

Slick and oval.

Dust Bags

Two dust bags are needed by the molder—one 5 × 9 inches for parting powder and one 7 × 11 inches for graphite. These bags can be purchased from supply houses, but most give them away. You can, as I do, use an old sock (with no holes) for both parting and

FIGURE 4.24

Vent wire.

blacking. The parting bag is used to shake parting on the pattern and parting line of the mold faces. The blacking bag is used to dust blacking on a mold surface prior to sleeking.

Vent Wire

Vent wire is simply a slender pointed wire with a loop at its top used to punch vent holes in the cope and drag of a sand mold. It provides easy access for steam and gases to the outside during the pouring of the casting. The venting is done prior to the pattern removal. The vent wire is pushed down into the sand to close proximity of the pattern. The first and second finger straddles the wire each time it is withdrawn as a guide (Figure 4.24).

FIGURE 4.25

Basic flask assembly.

FIGURE 4.26

Flask with cheek.

Flasks

Sand molds used in metalcasting are made in wooden frames called *flasks*. They have no resemblance at all to the glass or metal liquid container most people think of when they see or hear the word flask.

They actually are open wooden frames that can be held together with pins and guides. They are separated during the mold preparation process and placed back together for pouring the mold without losing the original register. A flask with good pins and guides will close back together in the exact same place every time. This is essential to avoid shifts in the mold cavity, with a resulting defect.

Basic Flask

The top frame of the flask is called the *cope* and the bottom frame is called the *drag* (Figure 4.25).

In some molding operations you need one or more sections between the cope and the drag. These sections are called *cheeks* (Figure 4.26).

The pins and guides that are used to hold the sections together can be purchased in a wide variety of types and configurations—round and half round, double round, and vee shaped. Single, double, or triple vee shapes are packaged together with matching guides. Both pins and guides have attached mounting plates by which they can be bolted, screwed, or welded to the halves which make up a complete flask set (Figure 4.27).

Homemade Wood Flask

In hobby or small shops you will find wood flasks with simple wood guides and pins. Although they work for a while they soon loosen or burn up from spilled metal. Only resort to this type for a one-time quick job for which you must build a quick flask to fit (Figure 4.28).

ROUND   HALF ROUND   DOUBLE ROUND

V   TRIPLE V (BUCKEYE)

FIGURE 4.27

Alignment pin types.

Floor Flasks

There are some flasks that are too large to be handled on the bench. These can be of wood or metal. The wood flasks are constructed in such a manner that the long sides provide the lifting handles for two-man lifting and handling.

Floor flasks, unlike bench flasks, need support when a certain size is reached: usually, at 18 × 18 inches, support rods are put in the cope. These support members are

FIGURE 4.28

Wood pins and guides.

called *bars*. These bars help support the weight of the sand in the cope to prevent it from dropping out. Bars are required in the drag half of the flask only when it is necessary to roll the job over and lift the drag instead of the cope. In such cases they are called *grids* (Figure 4.29).

The bars do not come all the way to the parting but clear the parting and portion of the pattern that is in the cope by an minimum of ½ inch. These bars, in many cases, have to be contoured to conform to the portion of the pattern that is in the cope (Figure 4.30).

In all cases the bars are brought to a dull point along their lower edge to make it possible to tuck and ram the sand firmly under them (Figure 4.31).

The inside surfaces of both the flask and the bars in the cope section are often covered with large-headed roofing nails with the head

FIGURE 4.29

Wood floor flask.

FIGURE 4.30

Contoured cope bar.

projecting ⅛ to ¼ inch. This gives the entire inner surface an excellent tooth and a good purchase on the sand.

Of course the floor flask, like all others, must be provided with suitable pins and guides on both ends.

Small floor flasks up to 30 × 30 inches with a cope and drag depth of from 5 to 8 inches can be made of 1-inch lumber. From 32 × 32 inches to 48 × 48 inches with 5-inch to 10-inch cope and drag, use 2-inch lumber. From 50 × 50 inches to 62 × 63 inches with 6-inch to 19-inch cope and drag, use 2½-inch lumber. From there up to a flask that measures a maximum of 85 × 85 inches with a cope and drag depth of 7 to 30 inches, use 3-inch lumber. The bars should be made of the same thickness of lumber as the flask. The number of bars required is generally determined so that you have a maximum of 6 inches of sand between them.

If your flask is extremely wide, you might need a cross bar between the bars. This bar is called a *chuck* (Figure 4.32).

When you get to a flask larger than 85 × 85 inches you should move to welded steel.

Where the type of work permits, the floor flask can be fitted with roll-off hinges. These hinges allow the flask to be opened like a book. The pattern is removed and the mold is closed. This operation is completed without lifting the cope (Figure 4.33).

Large Steel Floor Flasks

Large steel floor flasks are more often equipped with female guides on both cope and drag halves with loose pins used for molding and closing. Some have single hole guides, some have double hole guides (Figure 4.34).

Steel flasks can be purchased in all sizes with any size cope and drag depth, or any combination of different cope and drag depths and any type of pin and guide arrangement you desire.

Snap Flask

A snap flask is usually made of cherry wood. After the mold is made, the flask can be removed by opening the flask and lifting it off the mold, leaving the mold as a block of sand on the bottom board (Figure 4.35).

FIGURE 4.31

Contoured bar.

FIGURE 4.32

Cope chucks.

FIGURE 4.33

Roll-off hinge and guide.

In corner A, both the cope and drag have a hinge and in corner B, a cam locking device. In operation the cope and the drag locks are closed tight and the mold is made in the usual manner. When finished, the locks are opened and the flask is opened and removed from the mold. A typical snap flask hinge and lock is shown in Figure 4.36.

The big advantage of the snap flask is that you need only one flask to make as many molds a day as you wish. With rigid flasks you need as many flasks as the number of molds you wish to put up at a time.

FIGURE 4.34

Loose pin and guide.

FIGURE 4.35

Snap flask.

Other Types of Flasks

There are two other types of flasks that are removed from the mold. One is called a *tapered slip flask*. In this type of flask there is a strip of metal on the parting face of the cope that prevents the cope from dropping out while molding, which it would do without the strip, due to the taper on the cope's inner surface. After the mold is made and closed, this strip is retracted by a cam lever. When the strip is retracted the tapered flask is easily removed by simply lifting it from the mold (Figure 4.37).

The other type is called a *pop-off flask*. In this type of flask, both corners that cope and drag diagonally across from one another are clamped by a cam locking device. When the mold is completed the cam is released and the spring-loaded corners pop apart just enough to release the sand mold. These are quite popular and can be had in enormous sizes for floor and crane work as well as small bench sizes.

Jacket

A *jacket* is a wood or metal frame which is placed around a mold made in a snap flask during pouring to support the mold and prevent a run out between the cope and drag.

The common practice is to have as many jackets for each size snap mold as can be poured at one time. When the molds have solidified sufficiently the jackets are removed and placed on the next set of molds to be poured. These are called *jumping jackets*. Jackets must be carefully placed on the molds so as not to shift the cope and drag. The jackets must be kept in good shape and fit the molds like a glove. A tapered snap flask and tapered jackets work best due to the taper (Figure 4.38).

Snap hardware.

Tapered slip flask.

Tapered snap flask.

FIGURE 4.39

Upset.

FIGURE 4.40

Molding board.

Upset

When you need a taller cope section or drag section than the flask on hand, use a frame of the required additional depth. The inside of the frame is provided with four or more metal strips or tabs which fit down into the flask to hold it in place during molding. These strips or bands (they may be sheet iron bands) are called *upsets*. The term *to upset* a cope or drag means to add depth to it (Figure 4.39).

Boards

All boards for molding should be smooth. The pattern and flask rest on such boards when you start to make the mold.

Molding Board

The molding board is a smooth board on which to rest the pattern and flask when starting to make a mold. The board should be as large as the outside of the flask and stiff enough to support the sand and pattern without springing when the sand is rammed. One is needed for each size of flask. Suitable cleats are nailed to the underside of the board. Their purpose is to stiffen the board and to raise it from the bench or floor to allow you to get your fingers under the board to roll over the mold (Figure 4.40).

Bottom Board

The bottom board is used to support the sand mold until the mold is poured. It is constructed like the molding board, but it need not be smooth, only level and stiff. Bottom boards from 10 × 16 inches to 18 × 30 inches should be made of 1-inch thick lumber with two cleats made of 2 × 3-inch stock. Bottom boards 48 × 30 inches use 1½-inch thick lumber with three cleats made of 3 × 3-inch stock. Bottom boards

50 to 80 inches use 2-inch thick lumber with four to five cleats made of 3 × 4-inch stock.

Clamps and Weights

Floor molds are always clamped to pour. Sometimes they are weighted, sometimes not, but they are always clamped.

Floor Mold Clamps

There are two basic types of clamps used (Figure 4.41).

The C-clamp is cast iron or square steel stock. In operation the bottom foot is placed under the bottom board and a wooden or steel wedge is tapped between the top foot and the top of the flask side (Figure 4.42).

A better practice is to place two wedges between the clamp foot and flask by hand, then tighten them with a small pinch bar. Driving them too tightly jolts the mold and could cause internal damage, such as a drop (Figure 4.43).

The jack clamp is the preferred, but most expensive clamp. Its operation is simple. The foot is placed under the bottom board and the clamping foot is slid down against the cope flask. A bar is placed in the cam lever and pushed down until the clamp is snug and tight.

FIGURE 4.41

Floor mold clamps.

FIGURE 4.42

The use of C-clamps.

FIGURE 4.43

Double wedged C-clamps.

FIGURE 4.44

Typical mold weight.

Mold Weights

All snap flask work is weighted before molding. In most cases all that is needed is a standard snap weight. It is usually cast to suit your own snap sizes (Figure 4.44).

The snap flask mold weights are made from 1½ to 2 inches thick cast iron and weigh from 35 to 50 pounds for a 12 × 16-inch mold. The rounded cross-shaped opening through the weight is to accommodate pouring the metal into the mold. The weights are always set so that the pouring basin is free to easily see and pour, not too close to the weight.

In some cases two or more weights are used per mold and are stacked.

FIGURE 4.45

Sad iron weight.

Another type of mold weight which I favor for snap and small rigid flask bench work is the *sad iron* type of weight. They look like the old-time irons heated on the stove for pressing clothes, only heavier (Figure 4.45).

SPRUES

POUR 1,2,THEN 3

FIGURE 4.46

Stacked molds.

Another method used to weight bench molds in rigid full flasks, whether wood or metal, is to stack the molds three high, similar to steps. This method puts weight only on the top mold. This practice was quite common in a great many foundries and is still used today in home casting shops (Figure 4.46).

The lifting or buoyant force on the cope is the product of the horizontal area of the cavity in the cope, the height of the head of metal above this area, and the density of the metal. This lifting force on the cope has to be dealt with by the metalcaster. If the force is greater than the weight of the cope, the cope will be lifted by this force when the mold is poured. It will run out at the joint, resulting in a lost casting. In order to determine how much weight has to be placed on the cope to prevent a lift of the cope, multiply the area of the surface of the metal pressing against the cope by the depth of the cope above the casting and the product by 0.26 for iron, 0.30 for brass, and 0.09 for aluminum. These figures represent the weight in pounds of 1 cubic inch of iron, brass, or aluminum, respectively.

If you are casting a flat plate 12 × 12 inches, the surface area against the cope will be 144 square inches. If this would be molded in a flask which measured 18 × 18 inches with a 5-inch cope and the casting metal would be red brass, we'd have 144 × 5 inches (the height of the cope × 0.30 (the weight of 1 cubic inch of brass). You'd wind up with a lifting force of 216 pounds. One cubic inch of rammed molding sand weighs 0.06 pounds. With that factor, the cope weight would be 18 ×

18 × 5 inches × 0.06 or 97.2 pounds. If you subtract the cope weight from the lifting force—216 pounds minus 97.2 pounds—you are still short by about 119 pounds. This would be the weight you'd have to add to the cope to prevent it from lifting, with no safety factor. With a 20 percent safety factor, add 24 more pounds. You should put 150 pounds on the cope.

Metal Melting Devices

Nonferrous metals are melted in numerous types of furnaces. The crucible furnace is the most common and lowest in initial cost.

Crucible Furnaces

The furnace is essentially a refractory-lined cylinder with a refractory cover, equipped with a burner and blower (Figure 5.1) for the intense combustion of oil or gas. The metal is melted in a crucible (pot) made of clay and graphite, or silica carbide, which is placed in the furnace. When the melting is complete, the furnace is turned off, the furnace cover is opened, and the crucible removed with tongs and placed in a pouring shank. Then the liquid metal is poured into prepared molds.

FIGURE 5.1

Crucible furnace.

A crucible furnace can be made from an old metal drum or metal garbage can, a few pipe fittings, the blower from an old vacuum cleaner, and 30 or 40 dollars worth of castable refractory material. The refractory suppliers can also furnish you with complete advice on what to buy for your particular purpose, along with tips on how to handle the material. Crucibles come in sizes from as small as your thumb to a number 400, which will hold 1200 pounds of molten bronze.

Homemade melting furnaces are simple to construct, and are fun to build and operate. A furnace for a No. 20 crucible, which has a single pour capacity of 60 pounds for bronze, or 20 pounds for aluminum, would be considered average in size.

By weight, crucibles will hold three times as much bronze as aluminum. Always allow some clearance below the top of the crucible for safety—it is dangerous to melt a brimming potful.

Let's assume, for this discussion, that you have chosen a No. 20 crucible: 10⅛ inches high, 7¹³⁄₁₆ inches across the top and bottom, and 8½ inches at its *bilge*, or widest point (its shape resembles that of a barrel). This crucible requires a base in the form of a truncated cone 6 inches across the top, 7 inches across the bottom and 5 inches high. Now we have 15 inches of height and 8 inches in diameter to go into the furnace.

There must be sufficient distance between the crucible and the furnace lining for correct combustion, and for room to fit open tongs around the crucible. Also, enough space between the furnace bottom and the covers is needed for correct combustion and exhaust through the cover opening. A good general rule is to allow 2½ to 3 inches of clearance between the furnace wall and the bilge. Leave 3 inches between the top of the crucible and the cover and above the furnace bottom. In general, the lining should be a minimum of 4 inches thick to insure good insulation.

With this we need a shell for our furnace 22½ inches (inside diameter) by 22⅛ inches high with a cover band (Figure 5.2) 22½ (inside diameter) × 4 inches in height. A safety hole directly in the front of the furnace, flush with the bottom and 3 inches square, is needed. Should the crucible break, the metal will run out of the furnace through the hole.

Without a safety hole, metal could run into the burner pipe, or simply fill up the bottom of the furnace and solidify there, leaving you

COVER BAND

3" DIAMETER HOLE FOR BURN PIPE

3" × 3" OPENING

4" LINING THICKNESS

4"

22⅛"

FOR LOCATION OF THIS HOLE SEE TEXT

22¼" DIAMETER

FIGURE 5.2

Furnace dimensions.

with a hunk of metal next to impossible to remove short of tearing everything apart.

The shell is completed by making a 3-inch hole 6 inches above the bottom of the shell, a third of the shell's circumference away from the safety hole. This is where the burner pipe enters. The burner pipe is brought in 2 inches above the refractory lining of the bottom, and off-center from the diameter of the shell so that the flame will circle the space between the crucible and the lining, spiral around the crucible and out of the vent hole; this gives the highest and most even heat (Figure 5.3).

The cover consists of a metal band formed into a ring 22½ inches in diameter, but tapered slightly (Figure 5.4). Tabs or lifting ears must be riveted on directly across from each other on the cover ring. They should be drilled with holes to clear a ½-inch pipe, which will be used to remove the cover.

The cover ring is placed on a smooth floor covered with newspaper in preparation for making the exhaust hole.

SAFETY TIPS

Clearance between molten metal and the top lip of the crucible is essential: brimful melts are dangerous.

CRUCIBLE

BURNER

FLAME

FIGURE 5.3

Heating method.

FIGURE 5.4

Cover ring.

Within the center of the cover ring, place a 6-inch tin can or jar as a form for the exhaust vent. The castable refractory material is now mixed according to the manufacturer's directions, tamped firmly in place around the vent form, leveled off smoothly with the top of the ring, and left to set overnight.

Now we are ready to line the furnace body. Place a heavy cardboard sleeve 14½ inches in diameter and long enough to extend slightly above the top of the shell in the center of the furnace—22 or 23 inches tall should do.

Once the sleeve is centered, fill the inside of the sleeve with dry sand to give it added strength. Hold it in place while tamping in the lining all the way to the top. Two plugs will be needed for the furnace shell while the lining is being installed: one to fit through the safety hole and against the cardboard sleeve and another to fit the burner port. Dimensions for the plugs are given in Figure 5.5.

Coat each plug with heavy oil or grease, and fit both into their respective places. Use small wooden wedges to get a snug fit.

With both plugs securely in place, start tamping in the lining, making sure the castable refractory is well compressed. Do not place too

FIGURE 5.5

Hole plugs.

much material between the sleeve and the shell at a time; doing so will produce gaps. When the top of the shell is reached, trowel and smooth the refractory. The furnace is now complete.

Burners

Now you must have a suitable burner and a blower that will deliver 300 cubic feet of air per minute.

A blower from an industrial vacuum cleaner will deliver enough air at the right pressure.

The simplest type of gas burner can be made from a pipe 2 feet long. Heat the pipe red-hot at one end and hammer the end partially closed—not much over ¼ inch in all around—so that you are left with an opening 1½ inches wide. Heat the pipe again, 1 foot from the hammered end. Hammer in a neck with an inside diameter 1½ inches that is 1 inch wide (Figure 5.6). In the bottom of the groove left from this *necking down*, burn a hole and fit a ½-inch pipe snugly into it. Weld it in place. You have just made a nipple for the gas line.

Insert the burner pipe into the burner port in the furnace body, attach the blower to the opposite end, connect a stopcock to the nipple, and connect the whole thing to a gas outlet.

The intake of the blower must be provided with a shutter or damper to regulate air going to the burner.

A butterfly valve will fit within the burner pipe. Whether you decide to control the air in the burner pipe or at the blower intake doesn't matter, but it must be constructed in a manner that provides positive action without moving of its own accord.

Small furnaces, or *coffee-can foundries*, are easily made using a large coffee can as the form for the furnace, lining it with refractory material, and using a propane torch to heat and melt small quantities of aluminum, zinc alloys, and similar low-melting point metals. Generally, this furnace should work well with all metals up to some forms of brass.

Make the furnace with two side ports made from plumbing nipples to let the flame in. Supply a vented lid, and use furnace cement as a refractory material (use a can half the size of the original can to form the center, which is surrounded by refractory cement).

This furnace can melt aluminum on a gas range—although your spouse may not appreciate the concept or the action.

FIGURE 5.6

Gas burner.

First Heat

The newly lined furnace should be slowly dried by building a wood fire inside and letting the wood burn down to coals. It takes about two days of this treatment to be safe.

For the first heat, put two thicknesses of cardboard on the crucible support block and place the crucible on the cardboard. With the furnace cover off, place the metal charge loosely in the crucible. Do not wedge the metal in because it must have room to expand without restriction. Wedging metal in a crucible can cause it to split.

Now place a wad of gunnysack material dampened with fuel oil, or charcoal lighting fuel, about 1 foot from the burner port, in line with the firing direction. The lighter wad should be jammed snugly between the support block and the furnace wall. This will prevent it from being blown out of the furnace or away from the burner. The wad has to remain in place, burning until the furnace wall reaches ignition temperature. Prepare to fire the burner by opening the blower's air control valve halfway. Light the wad and allow it to burn briskly. The blower is started up. Check to see if the wad is still burning briskly. Should it blow out, turn off the blower and start over. Once you have determined that the lighter wad will burn with the blower on, open the gas valve until you get ignition.

Adjust the gas to the point that produces maximum ignition—the loudest roar in the furnace. At this point, you have maximum combustion for the blower's output. Allow the furnace to run for 5 minutes at this setting. After 5 minutes have elapsed, the furnace wall should be hot enough to maintain combustion. Place the cover on the furnace, and advance gas intake and blower output to the point where the gas is wide open and the air is adjusted for maximum roar. Now advance the blower output slightly. This will give you a slight oxidation in the furnace, which is the best condition for melting.

During the lighting up and the 5-minute period with the cover off, keep your hand on the gas valve. Should you lose ignition during this period, close the gas valve at once, let the blower run a minute or two to clear the gas-air mixture, then close down the blower and start over.

Never light a furnace without the blower delivering at least half its capacity. A too low setting can result in a backfire into the blower due to back pressure in the furnace. The blower has to be blowing strongly enough to overcome back pressure so that the ignition takes place in

Oil burner designs.

the furnace. Do not light a furnace with the cover on for the same reason. Should the power fail and the blower stop, immediately turn off the gas. Never leave a furnace unattended during the melting process. To shut down the furnace, close off the gas first, then the blower. Oil-fired furnaces (Figure 5.7) are lighted and shut down the same way.

Coke Fired Furnace

Although there are not many in use today, because they are slow and messy in operation, natural-draft coke-fired furnaces are simple in construction and have a low initial cost.

To operate a coke-fired furnace (Figure 5.8), place a fire brick on the grate, cover the grate with wood and paper kindling, and cover the kindling with a 3-inch layer of coke. Light the kindling and when the coke ignites and glows red, add another

Coke burner.

FIGURE 5.9

Pit furnace.

layer. Add layers until you have a deep bed of red-hot coke. Remove some coke from the center and place the crucible in this well; then build up a layer of fresh coke to the top of the crucible. Fill the crucible with metal and put the cover on. Adjust the draft to promote maximum combustion. As the coke burns down and drops into the ash pit, replace it.

When the metal has reached the desired temperature, pick out coke from around the crucible, and pull out the crucible with the tongs, place it in the shank, and pour. The brick in the bottom on the grate is used to support the crucible should it work its way down too far in the furnace.

A crucible furnace can also be easily constructed in the ground (Figure 5.9) in areas where a water table is not too close to the surface.

FIGURE 5.10

Tap type furnace.

Tapped Crucible Furnace

The tap-type crucible furnace is commonly used by people who work alone, casting small- to medium-sized work, or who have a minimum of headroom to pull out the crucible. The furnace (Figure 5.10) is built on four legs with a front opening at the bottom. This opening should be at least 4 × 4 inches. A hole is drilled in the front of the crucible, level with the bottom, to allow the metal to run out.

The furnace is lit and charged in the conventional manner. After 5 minutes the brick is removed, the cover is closed, and combustion is adjusted. A refractory-lined ladle is preheated by placing it on bricks above the exhaust hole in the cover during the melting.

When the metal is ready to pour, the hot ladle is removed with a hand shank (handle) and placed in front of the furnace.

A clay plug in the crucible's tap hole is picked out with a tapping bar made from a ½-inch steel bar sharpened to a point. The metal runs into the hand ladle. The ladle is then used to pour the mold.

To close up the tap hole for the next heating, a cone of *bott* (plus) mix is formed on a bott rod, and firmly pushed into the hole. The bott rod is given a little twist to release the bott. The heat of the furnace and crucible bakes the bott into place.

The crucible is placed in the furnace with the tap hole facing the opening in the front of the furnace. A refractory trough is made from the bottom of the tap hole to the furnace opening to carry the tapped metal out to the ladle. The operation is very simple. The tap hole is stopped with a bolt made of one part sharp silica sand to one part milled fireclay. The mixture is dampened to form stiff mud and pressed firmly into the hole. To light the furnace, the lid is simply propped up at its edge with a chunk of firebrick. If the hole should weep or leak at any time during heating (very rare), put a ball of bott mix on the bott rod and press it over the leak.

Pouring the Casting Mold

The actual pouring of molten metal into molds is a very important phase of the casting operation. More castings are lost due to faulty pouring than to any other single cause. Some basic rules for *gravity casting* a mold poured from a crucible or ladle are:

CASTING SAFETY RULES

- If a mold cracks and the metal starts to run out, don't try to save it.

- If a mold starts to spit metal from the pouring bases or vents, stop the pour. Continuing to fill a wet mold that is spitting back can result in a bomb.

- Don't use weak or otherwise faulty tongs or shanks.

- Don't pour with thin, weak crucibles.

- Wear a face shield and leggings.

- When pouring at night, dust the pouring basin with wheat flour (shake it from a bag) to make a more visible target for pouring.

- When pouring with a two-man shank, make sure the other man knows what he is doing (neither of you should move or jerk back once you start the pour).

- Make sure you have a good, dry pig bed to hold any excess metal after the pour.

- When pouring several molds in a row with a hand shank, start at one end and back up as you go. Going forward to pour brings the knuckles of the hand closest to the ladle right over the mold just poured.

- Don't pour from an awkward position. You must be relaxed to be safe.

- Don't try to lift or pour too much metal by hand. Use a crane or chain fall on a job boom with more than 40 pounds on a hand shank, or 200 pounds on a two-man bull shank. Going heavier invites disaster.

CASTING QUALITY RULES

- Pour with the lip of the ladle or crucible as close to the pouring basin as possible (this is also a safety rule).

- Keep the pouring basin full (choked) during the entire pour.

- Keep the pouring lip clean to avoid dirt or a double stream.

- Use slightly more metal than you think you'll need.

- Pour on the hot side—more castings are ruined by pouring too cold than by pouring too hot.

- Once a choke is started, do not reduce the stream of metal.

- Do not dribble metal into the mold or interrupt the stream of metal.

- When pouring with a hand shank, rest the shank on your knee.

- When pouring several molds from a single ladle or crucible, pour light, thin castings first (the metal is getting colder by the minute).

- Don't try to pour too many molds at a single heating.

- Make sure the flasks are closed and clamped or weighted properly.

- If the metal in the ladle or crucible is not bright, clean, clear, and hot, don't pour it.

Pouring reservoir.

Large molds are often poured by placing a sheet of asbestos over the sprue, on top of which is a large molten metal reservoir made of sand. The amount of metal required for the casting is poured into the reservoir, and a rod is used to puncture the asbestos sheet (Figure 5.11), allowing the metal to fill the mold.

Kilns

The types of kilns used for metal casting are so numerous that a large volume would be needed on this subject alone. The factors influencing their diversity are mold size, mold material, pouring technique, and the availability of fuels.

Small, tin-can molds and stainless-steel flasks for plaster-bonded investments require only a small, box-type oven, fired with a simple gas burner because the maximum temperature won't exceed 1250 F.

An electric kiln would be just as suitable for the same reason. These can be easily built or purchased cheaply.

The *catenary arch*, downdraft oven (Figure 5.12) is recommended for larger flask molds and hand-built molds.

Large molds to be poured in place can be calcined in a stacked kiln built on the spot around the mold from a diagonally

The catenary-arch oven. The shape of the arch can be duplicated by suspending a flexible drain with a uniform cross section between two points.

FIGURE 5.13

A stacked kiln, built around a mold to be filled at the site of its construction.

cut oil drum lined with industrial insulation (Figure 5.13). Regardless of the size chosen or the type of construction, downdraft kilns are best for many molds, especially lost wax molds, because the heat is drawn downward and under the molds, promoting even firing and firing temperatures.

The refractories used for the kiln, regardless of its style or size, are largely a matter of choice. However, with today's modern castable refractories, one-piece construction is by far the easiest method of construction. Brick requires considerably more skill in its use, and is usually heavier in overall weight.

Suppliers of refractory materials carry a wide variety of castable refractories and cast shapes. They can advise you about which is best for your particular needs. Regardless of the kind of kiln you choose, it must be designed to *dry* the molds, not to simply bake or cook them. Dry air must be taken into the oven and take moisture with it when it leaves the stack. If a kiln does not do this, the air will become stagnant and saturated with moisture. When this happens, the mold stops drying and just bakes like a roast in a covered pot. Venting must be good enough to bring in fresh air continuously as moisture-laden air exits.

Cupolas

Although most investment materials are limited to metals poured at 2000 F. or less, ceramic shell molds, and any of the sand systems, are suitable for ferrous castings. Due to a relatively low shrinkage factor and the superior fluidity of cast iron, you need only a minimum amount of gating and risers. The largest percentage of cast iron produced is melted in the *cupola* (Figure 5.14). It is basically a miniature blast furnace. The cupola shown is the basic furnace used to reduce copper ore to *matte* copper. The cupola, besides reducing ore, can melt bronze, brass, or cast iron. Although the cupola is usually thought of as a cast-iron melting furnace, it is excellent for melting bronze, in particular, silicon bronze and bronze low in lead or zinc content. (I have used a small, homemade cupola for many years for all my melting.)

REFRACTORY LINING

STEEL SHELL

COKE

COPPER ORE AND SULPHUR

COKE BED

MELTING ZONE

WIND BELT

HINGED MICA PEEP-HOLE

TUYERE (AIR ENTRANCE)

SAFETY TUYERE

TAP HOLE

DOORS (HINGED)

MOLDING SAND

WEDGES

FIGURE 5.14

The cupola used in the smelting of copper ore.

    Because the cupola melts continuously—as long as it is stoked and fed, it will melt charge after charge. The big advantage of the cupola is that you can pour a large quantity of molds, and collect a sufficient number of charges in a big ladle to pour castings in just about any weight you wish. You can also melt single batches of cast iron or bronze. Commercial cupolas range in size from a No. 0 with an inside diameter of 18 inches that will melt a ton of iron in an hour, to a No. 12, 84 inches in diameter that will melt more than 33 tons an hour.

A cupola is basically a refractory-lined cylinder with openings at the top for the escape of gases and the introduction of a charge. Smaller openings at the bottom are provided for the air blast and the release of molten metal and slag. A bed of fuel is laid on the cupola and ignited, after which alternate layers of metal and fuel are put down and the blast turned on. If a few simple rules are followed, melting will begin quickly and continue for a long time.

The cupola is by far the simplest and most efficient melting furnace. Before getting into its actual operation, let's examine the cupola's construction from the bottom up.

The cupola is supported on four legs and fitted with a pair of perforated, cast-iron doors underneath. The legs are long enough to allow the doors 6 inches of clearance above the floor when they are open (hanging down). When the doors are closed, they are held by a metal pipe wedged in place tightly with a pair of steel or cast-iron wedges (Figure 5.15A). The doors have a mating offset lip (Figure 5.15B) and ledge to insure a good fit. Four or more openings are cut through the

FIGURE 5.15

The bottom of the cupola (A) is high enough off the floor to allow 6 inches of clearance for the open doors (B).

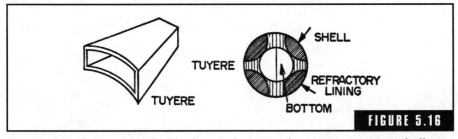

The opening of the tuyeres inside the cupola are so close as to create practically one continuous opening.

lining and shell about 1 foot from the doors for *tuyeres*. They fan out at the inside of the lining and make an almost continuous opening by being close to other adjoining tuyeres (Figure 5.16). The tuyeres are usually formed in cast-iron tuyere boxes installed during the lining of the cupola. To provide a blast of air through the tuyeres, the cupola is constructed with a *wind belt*—a sheetmetal tube encircling the outside of the cupola. There are two basic types. In the most common, air is introduced into the tuyeres through elbow connections extending from the bottom of the wind belt and terminating at the outer tuyere opening (Figure 5.17A). These are called *pendulum* tuyeres. In the second type, the wind belt encircles the tuyeres at their level (Figure 5.17B).

It is customary to place one tuyere lower than the rest; this is a *safety* tuyere. Its purpose is to prevent molten metal from rising above the bottom of the tuyeres and spilling, burning up the wind belt or causing greater havoc. Should the metal rise too high it will spin over

A wind belt can be either above the tuyeres (A) or level with them (B).

FIGURE 5.18

Conditions within the cupola can be observed through a peep hole in the lowest of tuyere pipes.

into the safety tuyere, which is fitted with a lead disc covering a hole in the bottom of the pipe that supplies the blast. The disc would melt quickly, allowing the metal to drop through, thus preventing damage to the cupola.

A ladle is usually placed on the ground below the disc. Each tuyere has a peep hole fitted with a cover and mica window. The cover (Figure 5.18) can be swung aside for access to the tuyeres, or locked in place when the cupola is under blast.

Blast air is supplied to the wind belt by a blast pipe. It enters the wind belt at a point between tuyeres. The blast circulates through the wind belt (Figure 5.19) and enters the cupola through the tuyeres. This type of construction seems to be the best in that the blast is divided more or less evenly, delivering the same volume and pressure to all tuyeres equally. The blast is supplied to the cupola by a blower whose required output is based upon the inside dimensions of the cupola.

Besides tuyeres, the cupola must have a tap hole (Figure 5.20) through which molten metal can be removed. This is located at the bottom front, between two tuyeres. A slag hole is located in the back between two tuyeres, 3 or 4 inches below them. The legs are sections of pipe attached to a plate used to anchor the cupola to the floor.

The blast is divided evenly among the tuyeres by circulation around the wind belt.

Molten metal is drawn from the cupola through a tap hole.

A truly workable cupola, and one that will operate as safely and efficiently as possible, must be constructed according to certain design criteria. The refractory lining, for example, should never be less than 4½ inches thick. The diameter of the lining itself is determined by its thickness. For one thinner than 7 inches, the inside diameter should be no more than 36 inches—a thickness greater than that dictates a diameter from 41 to 56 inches.

Blower output should be 2.5 CFM (cubic feet per minute) per square inch of inside lining area. Always round off the output figure you derive to the next highest blower size available, for safety. The level of the coke bed above the tuyeres is determined by blast pressure. Its height should be equal to the square root of the blast pressure × 10.5 + 6.

A good way to determine the correct bed height is to note the length of time it takes the first drops of iron to fall past the tuyeres after turning on the blast. Iron should be seen at the tuyeres in 4 or 5 minutes; at the tap, in 6 to 8 minutes. If iron can be seen sooner, the bed of coke is too low; if seen later, the bed is too high. This observation can be made at a tuyere window.

The optimum melting rate is based on 10 pounds of iron per square inch of cupola area; that is, a 12-inch cupola should melt 1130 pounds per hour. The amount of iron needed per total charge—fuel plus metal—is based on a *melt ratio*, a value determined by the weight of the coke charges. Enough metal melted by the time 4 inches of the fuel bed have been burned away is optimum. A layer of fuel previously placed above the metal charge will replace the fuel consumed. When another charge of metal is melted away, more fuel will descend. The process is repeated until the end of the *heat*, or until the desired amount of metal is melted.

The constant relating to the weight of metal charges is the weight of 4 inches of coke. Usually, a metal ring 4 inches deep is made that has the same diameter inside as the cupola. It is filled with coke, and then the coke is weighed.

The melt ratio for iron is 9 to 1—9 pounds of iron for each pound of coke. If a cupola took 1 pound of coke to reach a 4-inch level, each iron charge would weigh 45 pounds and each coke charge would be 4 inches high. The melt ratio for copper or bronze is 20 to 1.

Some small cupolas (24 inches tall and 24 inches wide) are used for *batch melting* (one charge of metal).

These extremely short cupolas have a cover similar to those on furnaces used to melt bronze, and have their tuyeres close to the bottom. After each melt, the bed is built up and a new metal charge is added. This is done throughout the day, whenever a melt is needed. The cover has a 6-inch exhaust hole in its center. The cover provides back pressure to drive the blast downward to compensate for the cupola's height.

No two cupolas operate alike, but the guidelines given will put you in the ballpark. The most common type of homemade cupola is two 55-gallon oil drums welded end to end. They will do a remarkable job if built well and properly operated.

Cupola Operations

After raising the bottom doors and propping them up firmly, tamp down a compact layer of tempered molding sand on the bottom of the cupola, making it slope downward from the back and sides toward the tap hole. Cover the bottom with light, dry kindling and light it.

Add enough wood to get a good brisk fire going—approximately half of the bed coke. When this has burned through, add the remaining half. When the entire bed of coke is burning brightly (as seen through the top), add enough coke to bring it to the correct level. At this point, put in the first metal charge, followed by 4 inches of coke. Then add the next metal charge and so forth, until the desired number of charges (Figure 5.21) are in the stack. Allow the cupola to "soak" for about a half-hour. (Whenever the blast is off, open one or more tuyeres to prevent the accumulation of explosive gases in the wind belt.)

The bed should now be properly *burned through* and the cupola charged with alternate layers of metal and coke. Close the tap hole with a bott (clay plug). The bott mix is fire clay and sand in equal amounts, tempered with enough water to make a pliable mixture. Make the bott on the end of a bott rod (Figure 5.22) by first wetting the pad on the bott rod and forming a ball of bott mix there; then form it into a cone. Press the bott firmly into the tap hole, twist the bar to detach the body, and

The operation of a cupola properly charged with fuel and metal.

FIGURE 5.22

A bott bar used to form and install a bott. A clay plug is used for the tap hole.

FIGURE 5.23

Punching out chilled slag.

slide the bar closed. Then turn on the blast and start the metal. The metal will collect in the bottom of the cupola with slag floating on top. When sufficient metal is in the well area, the slag will flow from the slag hole. When iron appears at the slag hole, tap the cupola by picking out the bott with a *tapping bar*—a pointed rod ½ to ¾ inch in diameter with a ring at one end. When enough metal has been tapped, plug the cupola with a fresh bott.

Melting will continue as long as the blast is maintained and metal and coke charges are added. Occasionally, chilled slag will build up around the tuyeres and impede the air blast. They must be cleared by punching them loose with a blunt bar (Figure 5.23). The cupola can be held in a nonmelting state for several hours. Open the tap hole and drain the well area completely; then shut off the blast and open a tuyere cover. Melting will stop when the blast is shut down. To resume melting, close the tap hole, close the tuyere, and start up the air blast.

The blast pipe is provided with a *blast gate* to regulate the blast. A blast gate is helpful to keep track of conditions in the cupola. As you may recall, the fuel bed level above the tuyeres is a function of blast pressure—low blast pressure for a low bed, high pressure for a high bed.

To achieve proper melting, the metal must be melted at maximum heat in the fuel bed melting zone, and the oxygen entering the bed from the tuyeres must be entirely converted into carbon dioxide before coming into contact with the metal. If the bed is too low and the metal melts too close to the tuyeres, it will oxidize badly. If the melt takes place too high, it will be cold.

The two ways of determining if the melting is being accomplished correctly is by noting the time it takes for the first metal charge to melt, and by observing the color of the slag. If an apple green is observed upon fracturing the slag, things are going great and you can be assured that the melting is being accomplished in an area devoid of free oxygen. If the slag is dark brown, it contains some oxides of metal. If black, the metal is melting much too low.

What can be done to correct an oxidizing condition? Examine what's happening. The metal is oxidizing because there is free oxygen in the melting zone. This is caused by incoming oxygen not having time to be converted completely to carbon dioxide before reaching the melting metal. This can be due to too low a fuel bed, a too-high blast pressure, or both. To correct this condition, first lower the blast pressure, put in an extra 8-inch charge of coke, then add a normal metal charge, followed by 4 inches of coke when the 8-inch *split* reaches the bed. This can be determined by comparing the amount of metal tapped to the size of the metal charge. If the bed is too high, reduce the amount of coke between two charges of metal. When this coke reaches the bed, it will be lowered by this amount; or, raise the blast pressure to cause the melting zone to move up. When tapping the metal, watch for excessive sparks (oxidized metal) shooting from the stream issuing from the tap hole, indicating a low bed. The droplets of iron passing by the tuyere peep hole should be bright (hot) without giving off sparks. If they are dull (cold) the bed is too high, the blast too low, or both. If the droplets are bright, but shoot off sparks, the bed is too low, the blast is too high, or both.

After you have done some actual cupola melting and trained your eye to recognize these symptoms, it will all become quite simple. If there is a foundry in your community that runs a cupola, try to get permission to look it over. Watch it operate and talk to the cupola tender. It could be a valuable outing.

When melting bronze, use a low blast pressure (2 ounces average, 3 ounces maximum) and a metal-to-coke ratio of 20 to 1. The tapping temperature should be approximately 2300 F., but no more. If the drops of bronze going past the tuyere peep holes are bright and clear, you are in good shape. If dull, they have become oxidized because of a low fuel bed, excessive blast, or both. If they look cold but don't exhibit signs of oxidation, the bed is too high, the blast is too low, or both.

When you have reached the end of your melting schedule, tap out all the liquid metal, shut down the blast, open a tuyere hole, pull the bottom door prop out, and allow the burning coke and whatever else is left in the cupola to drop out. Quench the residue with a water. When the cupola is cold, you can tell just where the melting occurred by observing the groove burned completely around the refractory lining. The lining must be chipped clean of slag and patched before the

TOOLS Oxygen lances are simple tools, nothing more than a length of ¼-inch black iron pipe, an O_2 bottle, and a regulator. Heat the end of the lance with your welding torch so you've got a slight melt, and crack on the oxygen to support combustion. The lance will burn through any metal that has solidified—turned refractory—in the tap.

next heat. Save the unburned, quenched coke from the *drop*, as well as any unmelted metal, for the next heat. Do not use drop coke in the next bed of coke. Use it between metal charges.

Jammed Taps

Sometimes a cupola is melting and cannot be tapped; if the blast is shut down, it stops melting at once and begins to freeze up. If the blast is continued, it continues to melt and if not tapped, the metal spills over into the safety tuyere or into the wind belt.

You can also lose your blast due to a mechanical or electrical breakdown and find that you cannot get the tap open and drain the stack due to a freeze-up of the breast or a chunk of coke jammed in the way of the tap hole. To open a frozen 'or jammed tap, the simplest method is to burn your way through with an *oxygen lance*, which consists of a length of black iron pipe attached to an oxygen bottle and regulator (Figure 5.24).

A ¼ inch pipe 8 to 10 feet long is needed to operate the lance. The business end is heated with a welding torch until it just starts to melt and the oxygen is turned on. This will support combustion at the end of the tube, which is rapidly oxidizing with intense heat. The lance is used to burn a hole through the breast by melting anything in its way—refractory, metal, etc.

It is common practice in some shops to provide two tap holes in the breast, one above the other. The top one is only opened in case of a freeze of the bottom tap.

FIGURE 5.24

To open a frozen or jammed tap, the simplest method is to burn your way through with an oxygen lance.

Metal Handling and Pouring Devices

There has been a general request by foundrymen, equipment designers, and manufacturers for greater—in fact maximum—safety in metal handling devices such as tongs, pouring shanks, and other equipment. This is certainly all done with good intentions, but not all the equipment that has made it to market is suitable. Metal handling gear that is cumbersome, overly complicated, or poorly balanced defeats any claimed purpose of safety, regardless of the maker's intent.

Crucibles

Crucibles are ceramic pots made of graphite and clay, silicon carbide, or other refractories. They are used for melting and pouring metal, or as a ladle for pouring metal.

Melting and pouring crucibles are standardized by size, and numbered by the various manufacturers, who also make special-purpose crucibles (Table 6.1). The crucibles most used fall into a range of sizes from a No. 10 to a number 400, representing 30 to 1200 pounds capacity for bronze and 10 to 400 pounds for aluminum. Generally a cru-

Table 6.1

Number	HEIGHT OUTSIDE INCHES	TOP DIAMETER OUTSIDE, INCHES	BILGE DIAMETER OUTSIDE, INCHES	BOTTOM DIAMETER OUTSIDE, INCHES	BRIMFUL CAPACITY, CUBIC INCHES	APPROXIMATE WORKING CAPACITY, POUNDS RED BRASS
6	6½	5¼	5¼	3⅞	66.4	19.0
8	7⅛	5⅞	5⅞	4¼	91.3	26.3
10	8¼	6¼	6¾	5	125	35.6
16	9¼	7½	7½	5½	238	68
20	10½	7⅝	8-5/16	6⅛	285	82
30	11⅝	8-9/16	9-5/16	6⅞	437	125
40	12⅝	9⅜	10-3/16	7⅝	581	166
50	13-13/16	10¼	11⅜	8¼	664	190
60	14-9/16	10⅞	12-3/16	8⅞	775	221
70	15¼	11⅜	12-11/16	9¼	858	245
80	15-13/16	11-9/16	12-15/16	9-7/16	997	285
90	16⅜	12⅛	13-5/16	9¾	1052	301
100	16-13/16	12-7/16	13¾	10	1218	348
125	17½	12⅞	14⅛	10⅜	1383	387
150	18½	13¾	15⅛	11	1633	467
175	19⅜	14⅜	15¾	11½	2047	587
200	20¼	15⅝	16¾	12½	2210	634
225	20⅞	15-7/16	16¾	12½	2570	736
250	22½	16	17-3/16	12⅝	2680	769
275	22¼	16¾	18-3/16	13⅜	3040	872
300	22¾	16¾	18-3/16	13⅜	3300	943
400	24½	18½	19⅝	14½	4270	1219
430	25	20½	None	14½	5100	1457
430	25	20½	None	14½	5460	1561
500	22½	22⅜	None	14½	5460	1561
600	27⅜	23⅜	None	14½	6530	1869
700	32	23⅜	None	14½	8170	2338
800	36	23³⁸	None		9420	2693

cible will hold a weight three times its number of bronze or a weight equal to its number of aluminum; that is, a No. 20 crucible has a capacity of 60 pounds of bronze or 20 pounds of aluminum.

Crucible melting was practiced before the Christian era. Historical records mention crucible melting as far back as 5000 B.C.

The conventional pit or crucible furnace is still popular. The majority use a forced draft blower and burner, but a few-natural-draft coke crucibles are still around. The following guidelines are provided to insure the most efficient use of a crucible you might purchase, its longevity, and your safety in handling it:

■ When receiving a new crucible, inspect it carefully for damage in shipment and manufacturing defects. Tap the crucible lightly with a wooden club to check for internal cracks. If the crucible is good, it will produce a clear ring—if not, a dull thud.

■ Store crucibles in a warm, dry place with room for air circulation between them.

■ Roll crucibles by tipping and rolling as you would a barrel, or carry them or use a hand truck.

■ Use a base block made of the same material as the crucible. The base block should be at least as wide as the crucible.

■ Place a piece of cardboard between the crucible and the base block to prevent the crucible from sticking to the block during melting. A stuck crucible has to be rocked to get it loose which is hard on the crucible, often tearing chunks out of its bottom.

■ Do not wedge metal into the crucible. Leave room for metal expansion.

■ Do not let the flame cover the crucible. The flame must be aimed from the side, at the line between the base block and the crucible bottom.

■ Do not use excessive flux, or one that might be injurious to the crucible. Add the flux after the metal has been reduced to a semiliquid.

■ Do not melt very small amounts of metal in a large crucible. This reduces crucible life.

■ Do not allow a ridge of slag and metal oxides to build up in a crucible. It can cause gas bubbles in a casting known as *duck flights*: a trail of progressively smaller indentations caused by bubbles. Oxides will be dislodged from the ridge by molten metal and carried out with the pour. The oxides enter the mold cavity along with deoxidized metal, and start to give up their oxygen as they convert back to liquid metal, leaving a trail of bubbles which may not get out of the metal as it solidifies.

■ Never clean crucibles with a chisel and hammer. Scrape gently while hot with a skimmer bar.

■ Do not wedge blocks all around a crucible in a tilting furnace (in which the crucible is not removed). It must be allowed room to expand.

■ Do not pull a crucible with tongs that do not fit properly, or grab the crucible above the bilge.

FIGURE 6.1

Come-out tongs should fit the bilge of the crucible properly, without being too close to the rest of the crucible.

FIGURE 6.2

Before a pouring shank can be attached to a crucible, the crucible must be resting on a block that is as wide as the crucible's bottom, and taller than the shank ring is wide.

FIGURE 6.3

Double-grab tongs (A) and single-grab tongs (B).

■ Do not use *come-out* tongs (Figure 6.1), even when they fit properly at the bilge, if they do not have sufficient clearance at the top of the crucible.

■ Always use hand shanks and bull shanks that fit the crucible just below the bilge.

■ Do not use, or attempt to make, homemade crucible tongs or pouring shanks. It is impossible to make this equipment properly without the proper jigs, experience, and equipment necessary to do so. All it takes to cause a bad accident is to have an improper weld let go, or an improper fit to cause a dangerous spill. Besides, this equipment will cost you more in time and money to build than to buy.

■ Never place a hot crucible in a draft. Return it to the furnace to cool slowly to avoid thermal shock.

■ When attaching a pouring shank to a crucible, place the crucible on a base block as wide as the bottom of the crucible and extending above the shank ring (Figure 6.2).

■ Do not use wedges to make a shank accommodate a crucible smaller than it was intended for.

■ Never use tongs with single grabs (Figure 6.3).

Two hundred pounds of molten metal is the most weight that should be handled by two men by hand; forty pounds, the most with a one-man hand shank. When you exceed this weight, use a crane or a jib boom.

Ladles

When melting with a tilting-type crucible furnace, a tapped crucible, or any open flame or electric furnace, pour the metal into a ladle used to transport the metal to the molds.

Ladles like these are made in various thicknesses of steel, depending on their size. Bowl-type ladles for a one-man hand shank are made of 14-gauge steel with a bead to catch the shank ring. The two most common sizes are type 14 and type 7. Ladles that fit two-man shanks range from 60 pounds capacity to 250 pounds capacity.

Ladles must be lined with a refractory and properly dried. Small ladles are usually lined with a castable or tamped-in commercial refractory such as A.P. Green, Red X, or Green X ladle lining. A freshly lined ladle should be oven dried completely at a maximum of 300 F. before putting it into service. Large ladles are lined with firebrick and faced with a tamped-in refractory.

A ladle must be brought to a red heat before tapping metal into it. This can be done by placing it on bricks above the furnace exhaust hole during the melting. Larger ladles, which would be cumbersome to heat in this manner, must be heated with a ladle heater.

Care of Crucibles

The prices of crucibles have skyrocketed since 1970, therefore it is a good idea to take good care of them to reduce costs and get the maximum life from them.

Store crucibles in dry places, especially those made of graphite. Do not let them become damp by placing them on concrete floors or on the ground. Graphite crucibles should always be brought up to their operating temperature slowly. Also, never put a cold crucible in a hot furnace or turn the burner flame directly onto a cold crucible. Fire up the furnace for a few minutes. Then shut it off and place the crucible in so that it warms gradually from the residual heat of the furnace, or, the cold crucible can be inverted over the sight hole of the furnace if it is already operating. This procedure will warm and dry the crucible properly and gradually. None of these precautions are necessary with silicon carbide crucibles because they do not absorb moisture and are more resistant to thermal shock.

Cold chunks of metal should never be jammed into a crucible before firing it up. The expansion of the metal could crack the crucible.

Lifting the crucible out of the furnace and pouring the molten metal is the most critical and dangerous operation of metalcasting. The hobbyist must wear heavy leather gloves, leather shoes, and a face shield. He should also wear a heavy leather or canvas leggings, preferably. Foundry suppliers offer a variety of safety equipment of this type, and it is the best investment that can be made by the home shop metalcaster.

Place pieces loosely with plenty of room for expansion. You should never let a molten charge of metal solidify in a crucible. Pour out almost all of the melted charge before it solidifies. The remelting of a solidified charge may cause the crucible to crack from the expansion of the metal.

Never use a crucible which shows any signs of cracking. It could break while lifting or pouring.

A crucible should never be filled excessively. The level of molten metal should never exceed about 4/5 of the maximum capacity of the crucible. Special tongs should be used to lift and pour. No makeshift equipment should ever be used by any metalcaster.

Tongs

Crucible tongs are made in several designs and styles. They can be purchased from foundry suppliers, or you can make your own based on the designs shown in Figure 6.4. The arc-shaped end which grips the sides of the crucible must fit its contour firmly and securely. Therefore, a different size tong will be required for each size of crucible. The L-shaped style shown in Figure 6.4 seems to be safe, although this kind is more difficult to construct.

FIGURE 6.4

Commercial tongs for lifting and handling a small crucible.

Table 6.2

Color	Temperature°F.
Faint red	900
Blood red	1050
Dark cherry red	1150
Medium cherry red	1250
Cherry red	1450
Bright red	1550
Orange	1700
Yellow	1850
Light yellow	2100
White	2300

Temperature Determinations

Many hobbyists are tempted to judge the proper pouring temperatures of their metals by the appearance of the melt alone. This procedure can be used, but it is not recommended.

The *approximate* temperature inside the furnace or crucible can be estimated by looking through the sight hole in the lid and comparing the color with the scale in Table 6.2.

A problem with the use of any color chart is the subjective interpretation we all give to color. The amount and type of illumination also affects color interpretation: what appears bright red in a home shop corner, or on a dull, dark day, may well appear as dull red in a brightly lit environment. Changing the light type to bright fluorescents can also change color interpretation, because standard fluorescent bulbs give off a yellowish-green light that can make metal seem hotter than it is.

Optical Pyrometer

How does one measure the temperature of molten metals far above the range of thermometers? One instrument for such use is the optical pyrometer, but it costs a couple hundred dollars so it is often beyond the reach of typical hobbyists. The optical pyrometer depends on comparing and matching the color of a glowing filament with the color of the object being measured. The electrical current is observed and adjusted through the filament until its image disappears when viewed against the background of the furnace or crucible interior. The filament and object are then at the same temperature. It can be read from a calibrated dial on the instrument. Readings can be taken very rapidly and at some distance from the furnace.

Thermocouple Pyrometer

For measuring high temperatures, a thermocouple pyrometer is used. Its operation works on the principle that when the junction of two dissimilar metals is heated, an electrical voltage is generated. This voltage can be measured in an external circuit by a device such as a meter or potentiometer. The voltages (or currents) generated are quite small but they are measurable with simple equipment.

Connect a thermocouple (the two pieces of dissimilar metal in the form of a pair of wires) to a simple direct current meter. The current and the meter reading depend not only on the temperature of the junction, but also on the resistance of the meter and wires; therefore, a simple instrument of this kind does not measure temperature directly. It is calibrated by comparing the reading at known temperatures.

Buy a 0-50 milliamp direct current meter from an electronic or surplus store. It should have a scale length of at least 2 inches for accuracy and be readable to 1 milliamp or better.

Also obtain a chromel-alumel thermocouple made of 8- to 14-gauge wire. It should be equipped with ceramic insulators and with a minimum length of at least 18 inches. Then connect the two leads of the thermocouple through the intermediate heavy copper or brass wire (Figure 6.5). The connection from the thermocouple wire to the lead

0-50 ma DC PANEL METER

HEAVY COPPER OR BRASS WIRE ABOUT 8 GAUGE LENGTH TO SUIT —PREFERABLY ABOUT 18 INCHES

CHROMEL-ALUMEL THERMOCOUPLE—8 TO 14 GAUGE WIRE FITTED WITH CERAMIC INSULATORS MINIMUM 18 INCHES LONG

FIGURE 6.5

Schematic of a simple thermocouple pyrometer.

wires should be brazed or silver soldered, although good mechanical connectors should work. Tight, secure electrical connections are essential for stable readings of the instrument. The lengths of the intermediate lead wires can be made to suit, but about 18 to 24 inches should suffice for readings in a small furnace.

The thermocouple pyrometer is now ready for calibration. Should the meter needle deflect downscale when the tip of the thermocouple is heated, reverse the leads to the meter. The meter should read zero when the thermocouple is at room temperature. If not, adjust it to zero with the small screw below the face of the meter.

CHAPTER 7

Casting Small Items

The amount of detail required on small surfaces is the primary difference between casting smaller items, such as jewelry, belt buckles, and other decorative or craft items and large, utilitarian items. When casting a large section of iron or steel, or even brass or bronze, less detail allows for smoother, less detailed surfaces, and larger patterns usually do not require the extremely fine details that sometime occurs in smaller, more ornate castings.

Much of the fine detailing can be produced with the refractory material, which allows for good detailing with as smooth as possible finish, but some is better handled in the way the mold is designed.

Lost wax and investment casting are excellent for extreme detail and for fancy shapes. Choosing between sand casting and investment or lost wax casting depends on what you have for a pattern and how clean a final finish you must produce. Lost wax can, with the right investment, reproduce fingerprint detail and reduce machining to a minimum. Sand casting does fairly well too, but is less forgiving to the novice. Ramming that sand and getting the right consistency is an art that takes time to learn. If you make a wax copy of your original, or carve an original out of wax, you can add all kinds of detail, lettering, and undercuts in the wax before you make the rubber mold to produce the wax patterns. On the first pour, you can sprue together as many patterns as you can melt metal. The hard work is in the single original.

RTV silicon mold rubber comes in 5 gallon quantities and is costly. Wax is cheap. Go wax for detail, but remember, there are fewer steps in sand.

Investment Casting Basics

Precision casting, such as that used to make jewelry and small model parts, was first developed to cast precision dental parts. Other industries recognized the usefulness and climbed right on the wagon, so the process is very popular now.

There are five essential steps to precision investment casting:

1. Make the wax pattern—this is expendable before casting, or "lost."
2. Case or *invest* the pattern in a refractory material that can stand high heat and reproduce every detail in the pattern as the mold forms.
3. Burn out the pattern, leaving a negative mold inside the investment material.
4. Cast by filling the mold with metal.
5. Destroy the mold to recover the casting.

It sounds easy, and in most aspects, it is easy, but there are details to be considered that make for a more, or less, perfect job.

Making the Pattern

This step is the most involved and difficult, because the whole idea is to make a complex pattern that reproduces perfectly in reverse (negative) in the investment material. There are a number of kinds of waxes, some for carving and some for molding, each with different features. The only way to decide on a wax for a particular job is to experiment to see which does best in your hands. Blended waxes include waxes like beeswax (usually white), carnuba, ozenite, and synthetic waxes; resins like shellac, rosin, balsam, and other tree saps; and fillers like talc, starch, chalk, pumice, wood flour (fine sawdust), and others.

You need to make or buy a wax that lets you work it as you wish, whether you're carving or molding by hand, or combining the procedures. Carving waxes are readily available in tubes, rods, blocks, and sheets as thick or as thin as you need. Hardness is variable, but most carving wax is not easily bent or finger-shaped. Modeling wax is softer and is easily formed by hand.

Melting wax is a simple process, but needs some care, because liquid and near liquid waxes may reach a flash point and catch fire explosively. Melting wax should be done in a double-boiler arrangement, never in a single pan. This prevents really bad overheating (as long as you keep water in the lower pan). Speaking of water, whenever you're heating wax, keep a pan of cool or cold water nearby. A fast douse with the water can reduce burning considerably, should some hot wax splash on you.

Keep melted wax away from open flames (although an open flame can be used to melt wax enough to weld blocks together). Never set a solid pot of wax on a burner. Wax expands as it heats, and the cap, or top, will heat and melt last, creating a pressure build-up that can be dangerous.

Processes and tools used to work the wax depend on the size and shape of the mold needed: if you're working gold or silver, it's unlikely massive molds will be made, but for fine brass or other castings, larger molds may be needed. It's beyond the province of this book to provide art instruction, but see the appendix for a couple of books that provide lots of model-making information. You will do lots of filing with coarse-toothed files, and eventually will find you need to make many of your own shaping tools, but that process itself becomes a lot of fun, once you decide what you need to do and how best to modify a tool to do a better job.

Carving wax may also be shaped on a lathe, with a soldering iron, or with wood carving tools. Smoothing is done with fine files, or even a nylon stocking or piece of paper towel. Don't use materials like sandpaper or steel wool (no matter how fine) that can leave grit or debris stuck in the wax.

Special wax pens are available for various kinds of shaping uses, which saves the overheating problem common with soldering irons or wood burning tools. If you've already got a soldering iron or wood burning tool on hand, then you can mount a dimmer switch (potentiometer) into a small box, run a cord to a plug, and place the potentiometer in the circuit between the plug and an outlet on your box. Mark the dial around the potentiometer so you can judge heating levels.

Burn-Out Oven

Investment casting demands a burn-out oven of some type. The oven is used to burn out the wax after the investment is poured. You can buy such an oven, or you can make your own. Temperatures above 1250 F. are not needed because that's the absolute vaporization point for the wax. At temperatures above that, the gypsum binder in most investments tends towards instability, creating problems during and after casting of the metal (the released sulfur really messes up silver by darkening it, but there's often also a severe loss of detail, which defeats the entire point of this kind of metalcasting). Firebrick and refractory cement are essential ingredients of any kiln or oven. After meeting that requirement, you can decide how fancy to get. You may choose to work with a gas fuel set-up (propane or MAPP, or MAPP and acetylene) with nichrome heating elements and a pyrometer and control switch. You may also buy an oven directly from a supplier. After the burn-out (oven) kilns, add the following:

The most important considerations with a burn-out kiln are not only temperature but also oxygen once the sprue or pouring basin is white and free from carbon deposit left by the wax. This is no guarantee that the mold is clean and free from carbon deposits inside the mold cavity. If it is not completely free of carbon, the surface of the casting will look like fine orange peel—rough, not smooth. Therefore, sufficient secondary oxygen must come into the combustion chamber in order to reduce the carbon to CO and CO_2.

Electric kilns are, for the most part, not designed for other than a neutral atmosphere, giving you little control. With the gas-fired kiln (i.e., catenary arch kiln fired against bag walls with positive downdraft circulation), you can control the combusion chamber to either oxidation or reducing conditions. The only way to be sure that the carbon left by the wax has been completely eliminated from the cavity (i.e., $C + 0 = CO \; CO_2$) is by inserting a copper tube (¼" tubing) with a short dog-leg on one end into the pouring basin of the funnel down mold in the kiln. You then draw some air out of the mold into your mouth. The heat dissipates through the four feet of tubing, what you draw in is cold or barely warm when it reaches your mouth. If you taste wax in your mouth the mold is not completely free of wax/carbon. The mold should be left in the kiln until the copper-tube test has absolutely no taste whatsoever when you draw on the tube with your mouth. At this point, you have a completely clean cavity, free of wax/carbon and it can be poured without risk or orange-peel surface. This procedure is the only positive test for a clean mold burn-out. Relying on the time and temperature methods is risky if you need a clean mold burn-out.

After a mold is ready to be placed into kiln to be dewaxed and calcined, it must first be placed underwater in a suitable container and weighted down. Weight the mold to keep it submerged. Leave it underwater until it stops bubbling and is completely saturated. This puts everything into a state of equalibrium. The mold is now placed in the kiln—basin down on kiln furniture. The kiln is then fired slowly. The mold should not have random wet ad dry areas that can cause uneven expansion. Always remember to soak the mold to equalibrium when is being dewaxed so that the burn-out starts on a level playing field.

Super Simple Set Up

The simplest burn-out oven is one made of firebrick and heated with a torch. Simply place two firebricks on a flat surface, stand two bricks at each side, and two on top, with a notch cut in the back side of one side brick, and a hole cut in the top. The 2-inch square notch in the side brick lets heat be applied, while the 2-inch square upper notch provides a vent that lets gasses flow out. Use an oxy-MAPP or oxy-acetylene torch to provide heat. Aim for a simple gauge to tell when the burn-out temperature is right. Make a small ball of clay and stick an 8- or 10-penny aluminum nail in the ball. Set it in the oven. When the nail bends, the temperature is about 1200 F., right about where you need to be.

Electrical Burn-Out Ovens

A nichrome-heated burn-out oven (Figure 7.1), with a pyrometer and a control switch, is more complex but relatively easy for any person handy enough to melt metal to make. With a 1000-watt nichrome coil, you'll have an oven capable of producing well over 1500 F. You can use a 660-watt element if you can accept slower burn-out times. Nichrome heated elements are readily available at electrical supply stores.

As the burn-out progresses, you'll want to avoid the room as much as possible. Vaporizing wax doesn't smell good, and in heavy concentrations, it's dangerous. Good ventilation is imperative. Always turn off the oven before you check the mold.

A nichrome-heated oven can be built in your own shop with little more than a chisel, a hacksaw, a couple of metal clamps, and other readily available tools. You may want to get right angle bends in the metal—26 gauge mild steel sheet—done commercially, but you can

FIGURE 7.1

Front side view.

bend it yourself using a couple of pair of metal bending clamps. These
clamps have plates about 2½ to 3 inches wide that make getting clean
corners a lot easier. Most parts can be found with little trouble.

You need six firebricks, type classified at 2400 F. Refractory cement
is needed, too, and a pint is probably enough. The heating element
must have a 110-volt classification; a power control, Type CRS, rated
for 1000 watts; and a pyrometer with a temperature scale that reads
over 1500 F. (to 1800 F. is preferable).

The oven door is pivoted on a rod and closes with a drop bar. See
Figure 7.2 for details and dimensions. The sheetmetal is cut to size, using aviation cutting shears. Fold, or have the parts folded. Make sure
the bricks are sized to fit the three walls, floor, and top. Cut two bricks
to 5½ inch lengths, and cut one brick exactly in half. The remaining

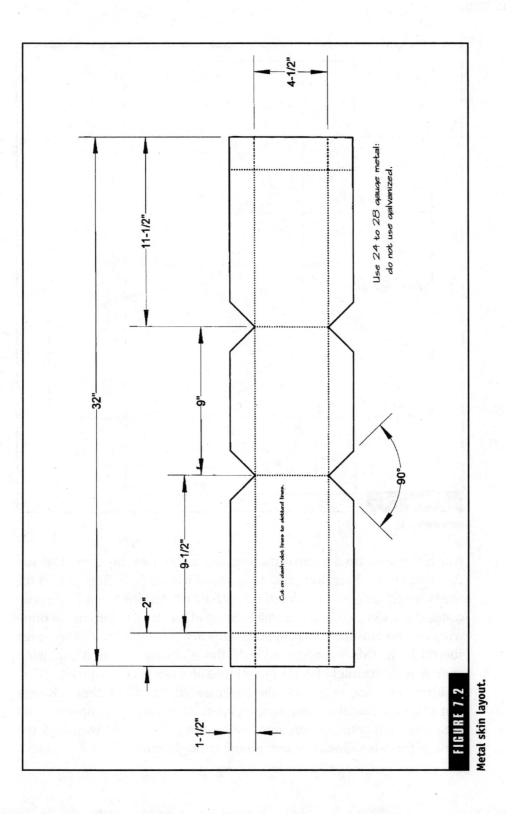

Use 24 to 28 gauge metal; do not use galvanized.

Cut on dash-dot lines to dotted lines.

FIGURE 7.2

Metal skin layout.

119

90°

7-1/2"

4-1/2"

5-1/2"

8-1/2"

1-1/2"

FIGURE 7.3

Door covering.

two full-length bricks make the top and bottom of the oven. Cut the firebrick with a hacksaw (a 12 tooth per inch blade is fine, but 18 tpi works well, too). Now, place the two half bricks down, and carefully gouge them out for the nichrome heating element. The job can be done with a wood chisel of the proper width—about ¼-inch wide. The gouge should be just deep enough to hold the nichrome element and wide enough to fit it snugly (check actual measurements before gouging).

Firebricks are very soft, so use care in handling them. Rough handling guarantees scratches, gouges, and probably breaks. The nichrome coil must be stretched to fit the gouged pathway, and the ends of the wire should be completely straightened.

11"

7"

0-1/2"

3-1/2"

15"

8"

0-1/2"

3-1/2"

Double fold

Fold on dotted lines.

Cut on dot-dash lines.

∅ 0-3/4"

FIGURE 7.4

Back sheetmetal layout.

121

FIGURE 7.5

Main chamber brick layout.

To hold the nichrome in place until it takes its initial set, use staples wide enough to span the gouge and hold the nichrome in place: the nichrome is cut in half (as exactly as possible), and placed. If you have more electrical experience, you can temporarily wire power to the nichrome so that it heats and takes its permanent set while lying outside the oven. This is the easiest, but is dangerous for those who aren't used to working with electricity.

Take several 16-penny nails and cut the heads off. Drill slightly undersized holes in the assembled oven bricks. Set the floor brick down, place the side half bricks on that (making sure the open end of the nichrome loops point in the same direction), and then place the top brick over that. Drill ⅛-inch holes through the top brick down into the side bricks, making sure they're positioned to miss the heating elements. Push fit the headless nails: you may have to drive them, but do so with great care because the brick is fragile. Now, turn the assembly over and repeat the process with the bottom.

Take the 5½ inch bricks and fit them into the ends of the oven, forming a rabbet all the way around so that the bricks fit snugly into place. One brick is part of the door, and one is part of the back of the unit. Size the rabbet to suit your exact dimensions once the top, bot-

FIGURE 7.6

Side brick grooves.

tom, and sides are assembled and pinned in place. The rabbets should be about ¼-inch deep and ¼-inch wide; this may require adjustment.

Form up the metal case using sheetmetal screws. Top, bottom, all four sides.

Slide the firebrick assembly into the case. Attach hinges. The simplest hinge is nothing more than a steel rod through plates on door and oven, two on each, at the base of the unit, so that the door pivots

FIGURE 7.7

Back interior.

upward to close. Holes in the plates allow the door to rotate down
and out of its opening. Years ago, a friend of mine built some wood
stoves that use a wood-handled knob that also works exceptionally
well for this oven. The base of the door is bolted to a couple of steel
flats, through which the hinge rod runs. That rod is bent upwards and
out from the furnace a bit; it has a 1½-inch diameter, 2½-inch long
wood knob placed on the end. Pulling it to the operator opens the
door, pushing it up closes the door, and the knob falls far enough
ahead of the door so that its modest weight, and the weight of the rod,
serve to hold the door closed. If that isn't sufficient, add a counter-
weight at the head of the rod, under the wooden handle and drill the
handle to fit over it.

With the drawer ready, and the sliced brick for the wiring ready,
use furnace cement to form fillets at all corner joints inside the kiln.

FIGURE 7.8

Front door interior.

See Figures 7 for further details.

Clean Burn-Outs

The cleanest burn-out results when you start the work with the sprue hole down. The molten wax then flows out of the sprue hole onto the oven floor. At the point when the wax stops flowing, carefully turn the flask over so the sprue hole is on the top. Gasses escape more efficiently this way. When the edges of the sprue show white, then burn-out is done.

At this point, it is time to pour metal; the best results are had when the investment is still warm from burn-out.

FIGURE 7.9

Front view.

FIGURE 7.10

Oven side view.

Investments

Investments for fine detail are made of gypsum (hydrated calcium sulfate, a white mineral). It makes up as much as 40 percent of the mix. Silica is also used; it is white or colorless and sometimes known as quartz. It cushions the mold and allows for expansion and contraction as the mold heats and cools during burn-out and cool-down. *Cristobalite* is a form of very pure silica formed by heating silica to temperatures up around 3000 F. Other chemicals may be used, including wetting agents, to let the investment flow more readily over the model. Some ingredients may change the setting time of the investment or reduce air bubbles in the mix. Generally, gold, silver, bronze, and most other metals need a standard investment, while platinum needs a high-temperature investment.

The silica used in investments is of such a fine, powdery texture that it is recommended that proper dust masks be worn while using the dry material.

The gypsum used is hygroscopic: it is so thoroughly dried that it actively seeks to draw water from the air. The material must be kept in sealed plastic bags. Buy in quantities that will be used in a few months to prevent contamination.

Investment can be bought through most jewelry suppliers, and may be found through some commercial metalcasters.

Investing

Start by checking the model for debris, dust, or other dirt. Check the fit between the flask and the base to be sure it is watertight. Seal with wax if it isn't. Paint the model with a wetting agent to reduce the possibility of air bubble.

Part of the fun, for many of us, in casting is the mess: investing is a messy process, and some clean-up time must be figured into the job, no matter how careful you are.

As a side note, if you have investment left over, discard it properly. Pouring it down the drain is going to result in a call to the plumber, because the material hardens in the pipes. When working with wax, equipment made of rubber—bowls, spatulas, and similar items—work best and clean easiest.

Investments not otherwise marked have a working time of 9½ minutes. Watch the clock, because taking too short a time to mix the investment means water may settle out when the investment is in place, leaving bubble trails around the mold pattern. Mixing for too long means the investment will have partially set up and won't be liquid enough to flow properly everywhere it's needed.

Water at 72 F. is used at about 38 to 40 parts to 100 parts of powder, by weight. Add powder to the water and make sure the mixing is complete.

A vacuum machine is used to remove bubbles from the mix after it is poured into the flask. Leave about a 2-inch space at the top of the flask for the expansion that happens under vacuum. Without a vacuum machine, use vibration to settle the mix and remove air bubbles.

Make an eccentric cam to fit into an electric drill, and have that turn against a stand that holds the flask.

The *shell method* is probably easiest, because no special gear is needed. Mix investment in small amounts, no more than a quarter cup at a time for jewelry models, and paint the investment onto the model with a soft brush. Make sure to get into the hard-to-reach spots. Sprinkle the painted model with dry investment powder, and repeat the process. The first layer gives the surface quality of your casting, so it is exceptionally important. Once the two layers are dry, surround the entire package with investment. On this step, you can forget about bubbles, because any present have no effect on the final casting.

Once the investment is complete, the mold goes to the burn-out oven.

We're only covering gravity casting, but lots of people use centrifugal force to make sure material is in every cavity in the mold. Extra machinery to spin the mold is needed. If you avoid thin, lacy areas, then gravity casting works fine. If you want thin lacy areas, then get a centrifugal casting machine with a coiled-spring drive unit.

The flask can be quenched in a bucket of water as soon as it is no longer red hot. Most authorities say use a cheap plastic bucket, and hold the flask above the bottom for the first few uses. After the third or so quenching, a layer of silted investment will have built up on the bottom of the bucket, and you have to worry less about setting the flask down and having it melt through. The investment is caustic enough to rot out any metal bucket quickly, so plastic is preferred. The bucket will fill with investment over time and must then be discarded and replaced, because it's just about impossible to clean the semi-hard investment out of the bucket. Discarded drywall buckets from construction sites make excellent recycled quenching buckets.

Metallurgical Properties of Cast Metals

Pure metals are rarely used for making castings. The properties of pure metals can be improved with respect to fluidity, melting point, strength, and hardness by the addition of alloying elements. Metallurgy has resulted in the development of certain standard casting alloys which have ideal properties for given applications, and the hobby metalcaster will find that the use of these materials yields favorable results.

A particular metal or alloy is chosen for a given casting dictated by a number of factors such as required strength, surface finish desired, cost, ductility, and ease of machining and casting. Cast iron does have certain deficiencies, but its low cost offsets the disadvantages.

Popular Alloys

Many aluminum alloys are used for metalcasting. The most versatile are the aluminum-silicon alloys, which combine good castability with excellent corrosion resistance and high strength.

Aluminum

Aluminum alloys cast very easily, and the beginner is encouraged to experiment with aluminum casting first before graduating to the more difficult-to-handle brasses and bronzes. Basically the techniques are the same in all cases, but aluminum alloys are easier to handle and melt.

Scrap aluminum works well if you carefully pick out only scrap castings such as gear cases, cylinder heads, machine parts, etc. Avoid pistons and connecting rods because they are alloyed with other elements which may make the material less suitable. Avoid wrought or structural aluminum scrap completely because it is not alloyed for casting purposes and will give poor results.

Segregating aluminum and magnesium alloys is not always done well by scrap dealers. Do not mix magnesium with aluminum scrap because the accidental melting of magnesium may lead to a fire. Once ignited, magnesium cannot be extinguished. If it should ignite, cover it with sand to slow the burning and let it go. Never apply water to burning magnesium—only dry sand. Sometimes magnesium alloys can be identified by sight. It is grayer and less dense than aluminum. If there is any doubt, apply a drop of 1 percent silver nitrate solution to the filed surface of the metal. A black stain is produced immediately if the metal is magnesium. Aluminum and its alloys remain unchanged.

QUICK»TIP Many aluminum auto and light truck wheels get junked annually, and most of those are about 356 T6 alloy. This is a nicely castable alloy, strong, and with other good features—ductility, resistance to cracking—that make it decent for wheel use. It is particularly important when using aluminum alloy wheels to check each wheel for the possibility of its being magnesium, as tons of that flammable metal are also used for wheels.

Silicon Bronze

Silicon bronze casting alloys have grown in popularity. They have excellent casting properties with strength approaching that of low-carbon steel and good corrosion resistance. Silicon bronze alloys contain about 95 percent copper and 4 to 5 percent silicon. They also contain minor amounts of manganese and zinc.

Silicon bronze has the best combination of properties that appeal to the amateur metalcaster of all readily available copper-based alloys. It is inexpensive and can be repeatedly remelted without changing composition. Silicon bronze is available under the trade names Herculoy and Everdur.

Red Brass

Red brass can be considered as either a brass or a bronze. The composition varies, but the typical red brass contains about 85 percent copper and 5 percent each of tin, lead, and zinc. Red brasses are among the most widely used of all copper-based casting alloys. They have numerous uses in the production of pipe, valves, fittings, pump housings, and plumbing fixtures. They also offer an excellent combination of resistance to corrosion, high strength, and casting properties.

Bronze

Bronze is not an alloy of definite composition. It is an alloy of copper and tin. It may also contain small amounts of other elements. Other bronzes contain relatively little tin, such as manganese bronze, and other alloys contain no tin at all, such as aluminum bronze (copper-aluminum) and silicon bronze (copper-silicon). Some alloys are called bronzes but in reality are brasses, such as architectural bronze (copper-zinc-lead) and commercial bronze (90 percent copper, 10 percent zinc).

The term *bronze* used without qualification usually means tin-bronze. When tin is added to copper it increases its hardness and strength. Zinc is sometimes added in small amounts to improve the casting properties. Lead improves the machining qualities. Tin bronzes contain about 87 to 90 percent copper, 6 to 10 percent tin, and 2 to 4 percent zinc. If lead is added to improve machining, it will usually be present in about 1 percent. The alloy will then be referred to as a *leaded tin bronze*. Tin bronzes have excellent casting properties as well as good mechanical strength and ductility. Tin bronzes do tend to be a little more expensive than yellow brasses which contains no tin.

Bronwite

Bronwite is a patented alloy manufactured by ASARCO. Originally it was developed to replace nickel silver alloys and to avoid the high cost and availability problems involved with nickel. Bronwite contains 59 percent copper, 20 percent zinc, 20 percent manganese, and 1 percent aluminum. With respect to color, corrosion resistance, strength, ductility, and hardness it is the equivalent of nickel silver, but it's easier to cast because of the low melting temperature of 1550 F. Bronwite can be polished to a very high luster. Parts originally made of nickel need not be plated if they are made of Bronwite. Also, its resistance to tarnishing is just as good as nickel.

Zinc

The most common alloys of zinc are the Zamak alloys which contain about 95 percent zinc, with 4 to 5 percent aluminum, and occasionally slight additions of copper and magnesium. Zinc die casting alloys have good strength and casting properties, but they lack corrosion resistance and ductility. The only advantage is the low melting temperature, which reduces the high temperature capabilities required for the melting furnace.

Undesirable Alloys

Many alloys used during metalcasting should be avoided by the beginning metalcaster in the home hobby shop.

Manganese Bronze

A favorite casting alloy for parts requiring high strength and resistance to corrosion is manganese bronze. Manganese bronze compositions vary quite a bit, depending upon the strength characteristics desired, but typical compositions are around 60 percent copper and 25 to 36 percent zinc, together with small amounts of iron, aluminum, and manganese.

Because manganese bronze is not an easy material to cast, the beginning metalcaster should avoid it.

Aluminum Bronze

Aluminum bronze has enormous strength, far exceeding that of mild steel. In addition, it can be heat treated to improve its strength. It has a narrow solidification range and high shrinkage upon solidification, making it an extremely difficult material to cast.

Brass

Brass is readily available in scrap form, which would appear to make it an attractive choice for the amateur. However, brass is not easy material to cast and the hobbyist is likely to experience some difficulties with it, especially at first.

Brass does not denote a specific composition of material. It is a class of alloy. Brass is an alloy of copper and zinc containing more than 50 percent copper. It may also contain minor amounts of other alloying materials. Yellow brass ordinarily contains 65 percent copper and 35 percent zinc. It has a pleasing yellow color. It also polishes well.

The term *brass* used without qualification usually means yellow brass. It contains copper and zinc. Other compositions are also used for specific applications in industry. Scrap brass contains a variety of different compositions mixed indiscriminately. The metalcaster using scrap brass will find that casting properties vary from melt to melt.

When brass is brought to its melting temperature, zinc distills out. It also burns above the molten alloy. This problem can be alleviated by providing a protective cover of flux over the melt.

Scrap Versus Virgin Alloys

Scrap brass and bronze are readily available at scrap metal dealers. They are often at prices about half that of commercial alloy prices. A beginner may be tempted to buy scrap metals for his first castings, but this practice is not to be encouraged. Copper alloys are difficult to identify from appearance alone, so many alloys will end up in the same bin at the scrap dealers. You could end up with a mixture of yellow brass, aluminum bronze, and manganese bronze. Needless to say, you would find uncertain results in the quality of the finished product. Select your

QUICK»TIP

Those interested in precious metal or art casting may start with aluminum and red brass, but eventually move on to costlier substances. Essentially, that means a change in casting alloys to silver and gold.

Yellow gold comes in 10 carat (Kt) form with a melting point of 1450 F., and a flow point of 1635 F. As the alloy gets closer to pure gold, the melting and flow points rise; 18 carat gold melts at 1620 F. and flows at 1715 F.

White gold melts at 1625 F. due to the nickel content. 18 carat gold melts at a lower temperature because it is formed by an isotherm with 75% pure gold content.

Sterling silver melts at 1575 F., and flows at 1660 F.

Casting temperature is from 50 to 100 degrees above the flow temperature. With these precious metals, cast when the metal turns to a clear liquid with a mirror surface. Because the metals will "soak," or pick up impurities if kept heated too long, immediate casting is recommended.

There are different melt and flow points for these alloys because they are alloys, and each metal included has a slightly (or greatly) different melting point. For example, 13½ carat gold contains 56.25 percent gold, 8.8 percent silver, 30.7 percent copper, and 4.25 percent zinc.

Platinum cannot be gravity cast because of its high melting temperature—it is ether liquid or solid regardless of how high you raise its temperature. It freezes at once when you remove te heat used to melt it.

QUICK»TIP You can, however, cast platinum in small castings (i.e., jewelry, or dental casting by using a special vertical casting machine called TROIT). Tubing sheet and so on is produced by hot forging. Cast iron is so-called because it has a wide solidification range, unlike platinum, whereby you can carry a ladle of cast iron around the block and then pour darning needle; it is still liquid like water.

material from a reputable dealer and reject any scrap with an uncertain color.

Casting alloys should really be purchased in ingot form. More uniform results and fewer rejects will make up for the higher raw materials costs. Brass and bronze are usually sold in 25-pound ingots, but they can be cut up into more convenient 4- or 5-pound chunks with a power hacksaw.

Cores and Their Application

A core is a preformed baked sand or green sand aggregate inserted in a mold to shape the interior part of a casting which cannot be shaped by the pattern.

A core box is a wood or metal structure, the cavity of which has the shape of the desired core to be made therein.

A core box, like a pattern, is made by the pattern maker. Cores run from extremely simple to extremely complicated. A core might be a simple round cylinder form needed to core a hole through a hub of a wheel or bushing or it could be a very complicated core used to core out the water cooling channels in a cast iron engine block along with the inside of the cylinders.

Dry sand cores are, for the most part, made of sharp, clay-free, dry silica sand mixed with a binder and baked until cured. The binder cements the sand together. When the mold is poured the core

QUICK»TIP

No matter how small a casting will be, too shallow a core box prevents good casting, because the shallow box tends to collapse around the core. If you have trouble with cores collapsing, before going to a lot of other trouble, try a deeper core box.

holds together long enough for the metal to solidify; the binder is cooked from the heat of the casting until its bonding power is lost or burned out. If the core mix is correct for the job, it can be readily removed from the casting's interior by simply pouring it out as burnt core sand.

This characteristic of a core mix is called its *collapsibility*. The size and pouring temperature of a casting determines how well and how long the core will stay together. A core for a light aluminum casting must collapse much more readily than a core used in steel because of the different time, weight, and heats involved. Core sand, like molding sand, must have the proper permeability for the job intended. The gases generated within the core during pouring must be vented to the outside of the mold to prevent gas porosity and a defect known as a *core blow*. Also, a core must have sufficient hot strength to be handled and used properly. The hot strength refers to its strength while being heated by the casting operation. Because of the shape and size of some cores they must be further strengthened with rods and wires.

A core for a cast bronze water faucet must have a wire in the section which passes through the seat of the valve. Because of the small diameter at this point, core sand alone would not have sufficient dry strength to even get the core set in the mold much less pour the castings (Figure 9.1).

A long span core for a length of cast iron pipe would require rodding to prevent the core from sagging or bending upward when the mold is poured because of the liquid metal exerting a strong pressure during pouring (Figure 9.2).

FIGURE 9.1

Dry sand core with support wire.

VENT   SUPPORT RODS

SAND CORE

FIGURE 9.2

Rodded core.

Binders

There are many types of binders to mix with core sand. A binder should be selected on the basis of the characteristics that are most suitable for your particular use.

Some binders require no baking and become firm at room temperature. Examples are rubber cement, Portland cement, and sodium silicate or water glass. In large foundry operations and in some school foundries, sodium silicate is a popular binder because it can be hardened almost instantly by blowing carbon dioxide gas through the mixture.

Oil binders require heating or baking before they develop sufficient strength to withstand the molten metal. Linseed oil is considered one of the strongest binding oils. Vegetable, mineral, and fish oils are also used.

Sulfite binders also require heating. The most popular of the sulfite binders is a product of the wood pulp industry. It is sold in liquid form under the trade name of Glutrin and in the dry form under the trade name of Goulac.

Furan is the trade name of a chemical binder which is hardened by the use of a catalyst. There are many liquid binders made from starches, cereals, and sugars. They are available under a countless number of trade names.

A good binder will have the following properties:

■ Strength

■ Collapses rapidly when metal starts to shrink

> **QUICK»TIP**
>
> Core sand binders come in two basic types: those that **set at room temperature**; those that **must be heated to set**. Rubber cement and Portland cement need no heat. **Oil binders**, including linseed, **vegetable**, and other oils need to be set by **baking**. Furan uses a chemical catalyst **as a** hardener.

QUICK»TIP Binders increase the properties of strength; collapsibility; non-distortioning; storability; and low water absorption. They disperse properly through the sand mix and produce an easily formed mixture.

- Will not distort core during baking
- Maintains strength during storage time
- Absorbs a minimum of moisture when in the mold or in storage
- Withstands normal handling
- Disperses properly and evenly throughout the sand mix
- Produces a mixture that can be easily formed

Core Mixes

Table 9.1 is a list of core mixes that I have used for a number of years with good success.

If you are confused about core mixes, don't let it worry you. Foundry A produces the same type and weight of castings as Foundry B. Foundry A has 100 or more different core mixes. They use almost a different core mix for each job. Foundry B, doing the same kind of work, uses three different mixes, one for light work, one for medium work, and one for heavy work.

Both produce good work. However, I am sure Foundry B's cost and problems are much less than A. This condition exists throughout the industry. For general all round core work in the small or hobby shop, a simple linseed oil bonded mix will suffice for 90 percent of the work.

The simplest mix is by volume, 40 parts fine sharp washed and dried silica sand and 1 part of linseed oil.

It is common practice to add a small percentage of water and kerosene. This makes it mix better and strip easier from the core box.

If the moisture is too low in the mix, the core will bake out too soft and if the moisture is too high, the core will bake out too hard and stick in the box when making the core. Most mixes work best when just enough water is added to make the mix feel damp but not wet. To blend your core mix start out with dry sand, nearly pure silica sand free from clay. Mix the dry ingredients, add the oil and water, and finish mixing.

Core sand mixes can be combined in a muller or paddle type mixer in small amounts on the bench by hand.

The core is made by ramming the sand into the core box and placing the core on a core plate to bake (Figure 9.3).

The box cavity is dusted with parting powder, usually made of powdered walnut shells, purchased as a core box dry parting. The box is rammed full of sand using the handle of a rawhide mallet to ram. The excess is struck off level with the side of a core maker's trowel. The core is then vented with a vent wire, a core plate placed on top, and the plate and box rolled over on the bench. The box is rapped on one side and then on the front and back to loosen the core.

The box is then lifted (drawn) off leaving the core on the plate. The plate is placed in the oven to be baked or dried. When finished, it is removed from the oven and allowed to cool. It is then ready to use (Figure 9.4).

Stand-Up Cores

Stand-up cores (cores that can be stood on end to dry) are made in a split core box. The box is pinned together with pattern bushings. The box is held together with a C-clamp and it is rammed up using a dowel of suitable diameter. When rammed, it is then vented with a vent wire. The clamp is removed and the box placed on a core plate. The half of the box away from the core maker is removed and the core is slid to the far side of the plate. The

TABLE 9.1

For brass and aluminum	
Fine river sand	10 parts
Wheat flour	¼ parts
Air float sea coal	3 parts
Rosin	1 part
For small castings	
New molding sand	15 parts
Sharp sand	5 parts
Linseed oil	1 part
For aluminum, heavy castings	
Sharp sand	30 parts
New molding sand	10 parts
Wheat flour	2 parts
Temper with molasses water	
For aluminum, medium castings	
Sharp sand	10 parts
New molding sand	5 parts
Wheat flour	1 part
Temper with molasses water	
Good mix for long skinny cores	
Sharp sand	8 quarts
Wheat flour	1 quart
Core oil	⅛ pint
Quick collapse cores for aluminum	
Sharp sand	45 parts
Molding sand	45 parts
Powdered rosin	2 parts
Wheat flour	1 part
Mix for small cores	
Sharp sand	25 quarts
Molding sand	15 quarts
Linseed oil	1 quart
Brass pump core mix	
Silica	32 parts
Fire clay	1 part
Silica flour	4 parts
Add rosin to desired dry strength	
Small diameter bushing cores	
Sharp sand	80 parts
Corn flour	2 parts
Oil	1 part

FIGURE 9.3

Simple dump core boxes.

FIGURE 9.4

Use of dump core box.

remaining half of the box is removed, leaving the core standing free. This is continued until the core plate is full, or until you have sufficient cores. The plate is then ready for the core oven (Figure 9.5).

Stand-up cores are often made in gang core boxes (Figure 9.6). Stock or round cores, when too tall to stand on end, are made in a split box and rolled on to a core plate for drying (Figure 9.7).

Pasted Cores

Cores can be made in halves and after they are dried, glued together to make the complete core. If the core is symmetrical, a half box is all that is needed (Figure 9.8).

After the two halves of the core are dried, a vent is scratched along the center line of one half and the sections are glued together with core paste. The seam is then mudded with a material known as *core daubing*. Both core paste and daubing can be purchased or made. For homemade core paste use enough wheat flour dissolved in cold water to produce a creamy consistency.

For a good core daubing mix, fine graphite is mixed with molasses water (one part molasses to 10 parts water). Enough graphite is added to the molasses water to make a stiff mud.

Another good daubing mix is graphite and linseed oil mixed to a stiff mud.

After a core has been pasted and daubed, it is a good idea to return the core to the core oven for a short period to dry the paste and daubing.

FIGURE 9.5

Stand-up core box.

FIGURE 9.6

Gang core box.

FIGURE 9.7

Use of core plate.

FIGURE 9.8

Pasted cores.

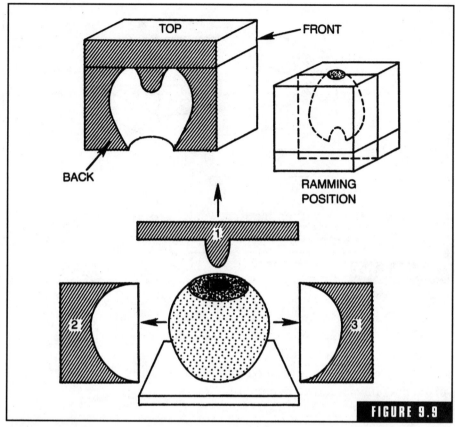

FIGURE 9.9

Three part core box.

Three Part Core Box

This box consists of a top, front, and back section. The box is assembled and placed top down and clamped. You ram it up, put on a core plate, roll it over, and rap it. Remove the top (which forms the negative section on top of the core), then remove the main box from the core as you would any simple split box (Figure 9.9).

Loose Piece Box

A loose piece box is a box which contains a loose piece (or drawback) to form a particular shape to the core. The loose piece is placed in position in the box, the core rammed, rolled over on a plate, rapped, and

FIGURE 9.10

Loose piece core box.

lifted off. The loose piece remains with the core on the plate and is drawn back to remove it (Figure 9.10).

The core box may have one loose piece or many. Sometimes a loose piece may have a loose piece of its own.

Swept Core

A core can be produced by a suitably shaped sweep (or stickel) and guide rails. The guide rails are clamped to a core plate. Core sand is heaped in between the rails and swept to shape by the sweep form. When finished the guide frame is removed and the core dried. The swept core might have several different diameters and may be curved. The shape dictates the frame construction and the number and shape of the strikes. Flat cover or slab cores are more often than not swept up on a core plate with a simple frame and flat strike off bar (Figure 9.11).

Core Driers

A core drier is a support used to keep cores in shape during the baking or drying. Most core driers are made of cast aluminum. The core drier

Swept core.

is similar to a half core box but fits the core more loosely than the box and only sufficiently to prevent the core from collapsing or sagging before and during drying. The core is rammed in the usual manner. The side of the core box that presents the face of the core that will rest in the drier is removed. The drier replaces this half box. The box and drier are rolled over and the box removed, leaving the core resting in the drier ready to be dried (Figure 9.12).

Core driers.

FIGURE 9.13

Green sand drier.

In the case of a green sand drier, you simply make a bed of riddled molding sand to support the core during drying. The core box is rammed, one half of the box removed and replaced by a tapered wooden frame. Dry parting is shaken over the exposed half of the green sand, the unbaked core is filled to the top with lightly riddled, tempered fine molding sand and struck off level with the top of the frame. A core plate is then placed on the frame and the whole assembly rolled over. The remaining half of the core box is removed, then the wooden frame. This leaves the core supported in a bed of molding sand for drying. When dry, the green sand is simply brushed off of the baked core with a molder's brush (Figure 9.13).

Balance Core

FIGURE 9.14

Balance core.

A balance core is a core supported on one end only; the other unsupported end extends a good way into the mold cavity. To prevent the core from being lifted up by the metal coming into the mold, we must extend both the length and diameter of the core section held by the single print (Figure 9.14).

To prevent having to make a balanced core which not only takes up room in the flask, but increases core cost, a better solution is to use one core to produce two castings. A *dumbbell core* produces two castings having a common print (Figure 9.15).

Chaplets

Chaplets consist of metallic supports or spacers used in a mold to maintain cores, which are not self-supporting, in their correct position during the casting process. They are not required when a pattern has a core print or prints which will serve the same purpose. Chaplets are purchased in a wide variety of sizes and shapes to fit just about any need or condition. The three most common types are the stem chaplet, motor chaplet, and radiator chaplet.

Motor chaplets and stem chaplets are placed or set in the mold after the mold is made. Radiator chaplets are rammed up in the mold during the molding operation.

On many gas stove burners, hot water heater burners, and many types of gas furnace burners, you will note that there are a series of projections or little bumps on the casting face both on the cope and drag. They are more noticeable on the bottom face. These bumps or knots are made by radiator chaplets used to hold the core centrally located when these burners are cast. The pattern is drilled wherever a chaplet is needed. These drilled holes are slightly larger in diameter than the stem diameter. The chaplet has a knot behind the business end of its stem that allows the chaplet to only stick into the hole in the pattern as far as this knot. The distance from the knot to the end of the stem represents the metal thickness of the casting. The end of the chaplet that is held in the molding sand has a plate-shaped head to give it a good purchase in the rammed molding sand. This prevents it from moving or being pushed back by the force of the core as it tries to float when the mold is being poured.

QUICK>>>TIP

Chaplets are spacers to maintain cores. Three types are common: stem, motor, and radiator. Stem and motor chaplets are placed after mold is made; radiator chaplets are rammed up in the mold during mold-making.

DUMBBELL CORE

1 COMMON CORE FOR 2 CASTINGS

FIGURE 9.15

Dumbbell core.

The molder sets the stem chaplets into the holes in the drag half of the pattern. He rams the drag, rolls the flask over, and sets the cope chaplets. He then rams and finishes the cope. When the pattern is removed, the stems of the chaplets stick through the molding sand the exact distance required. The core is set on the drag chaplets and the chaplets in the cope come down and clamp the core between the cope and drag chaplets when the mold is closed.

When the casting is poured, the projecting chaplets hold the core in place until the metal starts to solidify, then these projections fuse or weld themselves into the metal that surrounds them.

A leaking hollow casting sometimes results when using radiator chaplets. This problem arises when the casting is not poured hot enough to properly fuse the chaplet, or a rusty or dirty chaplet is used by the molder. After the casting is shaken out, the stem and head that was in the sand is broken off. The chaplet is provided with a break off notch (Figure 9.16).

Chaplets are seldom, if ever, used in nonferrous casting because the pouring temperature is not high enough to melt and fuse the chaplet.

A core which is set in place during the ramming of a mold to cover and complete a cavity partly formed by the withdrawal of a loose piece on the pattern is called a *cover core*.

Ram-Up Core

A ram-up core is a core that is set against the pattern or in a locator (slot, etc.) in the pattern. The mold is rammed and when the pattern is drawn, the core remains in the mold (Figure 9.17).

As you can see, there is an endless variety of types, kinds, and uses of cores. New uses and kinds are continuously coming up as new problems present themselves.

FIGURE 9.16

Chaplets.

Core Washes

Cores are sometimes coated with a refractory wash to increase the core's refractiveness and to produce a smoother metal surface in the cored cavity of the casting. These materials are called *washes*. They can be purchased in a variety of types and refractive strengths. A common homemade wash is graphite and molasses water mixed to a nice paint consistency.

Ram-up core.

Core Plates

Core plates, as you have no doubt guessed by now, are flat plates on which cores are baked in a core oven. They can be made of cast aluminum which has been normalized and machined to a true flat surface. Composition plates of Transite, a composition asbestos mill board manufactured by Johns Manville Co., can be purchased in a range of sizes and thicknesses from any foundry supply house.

Vent Wax

Vent waxes are tapers of various diameters made of a wax and rosin combination. The vent wax is rammed up in the proper position in a core and, when the core is baked, the wax melts, leaving a vent channel. This wax is sold in spools by supply houses.

Core Ovens

Cores are baked to set the binder. The usual temperature range for oil bonded cores is from 300 to 450 F. The time required varies with the bulk of the core. A large core might take several days to bake; a small core might bake out in an hour or less. When an oil core is completely baked the outside is a rich dark brown, not black or burned. The core must be cured completely through with no soft centers. Only experience and trial and error will teach you how to bake cores.

It is common practice to hollow out large cores to decrease the baking time and ensure an even bake throughout.

Another factor which relates to the time and temperature required to properly dry a core is the type and amount of binder used. Oil binders require hotter and quicker baking than rosin, flour, and goulac binders.

The core oven, which is usually a gas fired oven with temperature controls, is equipped with shelves on which to set the core plates and cores for baking. Some have drawers like a file cabinet which pull out to load and unload. When the drawer is pulled completely out, its back closes off the opening in the oven and prevents heat loss. This type of oven is also made with semicircular shelves which swing out.

The core oven can consist of a square or rectangular brick oven with doors. The bottom of the oven is floor level. The cores are placed on racks which, when full, are rolled into the oven. The oven is closed and the cores are baked. It is common practice to load the ovens one day with the cores required for the next day and to dry them over night. The lead time required for cores to the molder will vary from hobby shop to shop.

You can bake cores in your kitchen oven or there are many different kinds of mechanized machinery which can be purchased to make cores, completely automated to semi-automated, blowers, extruders, shell machines, etc.

Shell Coremaking

Shell cores, are coming like shell molding, are becoming more and more popular for certain types of work. Shell cores came to the front very rapidly. One of the most important things to consider in designing with a shell core is to use it when it offers a definite advantage over an existing dry or green sand core.

Carefully consider the casting, its design, etc., to determine whether a decided advantage can be realized by use of a shell core. Look for an overall reduction in cost, less machining, elimination of an operation, etc. Don't use a shell core to core out something like the hole in a frying pan handle or some such foolishness as that.

Sometimes a combination of shell and dry sand cores in the same job is the best practice. Use the methods and types of materials you have to the best advantage. Avoid foolish or ridiculous applications. I have seen some errors, but I also have seen some very ingenious applications of shell cores that resulted in concrete advantages and dollar savings.

So far as I know, there is no difference in the sand, binder, or method employed to make a shell core for use in nodular or any other type of metal, whether ferrous or nonferrous. I have seen shell cores used to make a gray iron casting, then used to produce the same job in brass with no change in equipment or cores. It is my understanding, however, that the most difficult metals to cast in conjunction with shell cores are certain classes of steel and the copper-base alloys with more than 6 percent lead.

A shell core sometimes has a tendency to be thin at the vertical surfaces that are at right angles to the body; that is, the sides of the core that forms the sides of your rings. However, with a ½-inch wall in the casting, the ring projections on the core undoubtedly will fill up completely with sand and be solid (Figure 9.18). Using a thin, hollow shell core over a long unsupported span completely surrounded by metal is

FIGURE 9.18

Ring projections on the core fill up with sand and become solid.

FIGURE 9.19

Cut a groove around the core prints when using shell cores.

like trying to duck a balloon under water. If you have no core rods or other stiffening or supporting members, the lifting force on the core is somewhat greater because of its lightness and its hollowness. I have seen shell cores reinforced internally with molding sand or just plain dry, sharp sand.

The print on the open dump end of some cores should be long enough to ensure a good seal to prevent metal from bleeding or running into the core. Most hobby shops using shell cores cut a groove around the core prints, a little way back from the casting (Figure 9.19). This procedure will give you a little green sand crush to form a tight seal around the core print. Dough roll, core paste, or one of the prepared seals with a little corn flour sprinkled on makes a good seal.

The percentage of resin needed in the mix seems to vary from sand to sand, increasing with sand fineness. The usual amount is about 5 percent by weight, but there is a critical amount which must be worked out. As the amount of resin is increased, the resulting shell or core becomes smoother and harder. It is with this condition that you might run into penetration, cracks, etc. A high percentage of resin makes a hard and brittle core. It seems that above 8 percent resin, cores are too hard and brittle. Below 4 percent, they usually are too weak. I believe that the proper ratio of sand to binder will produce the desired results.

The sand and resin may be mixed dry in a suitable muller or a Y-type blender and used in that condition, or the sand may be resin coated.

Sand may be coated with resin by either the hot or the cold process. Because the latter can be carried out easily in the small shop, I will touch on it briefly.

Sand and the proper amount of resin—about 2.5 pounds per 100 with round grain and 4 pounds with subangular sand—are mixed dry in a muller for 1 to 2 minutes. Then an alcohol–water solvent is added slowly. The solvent is 3 parts denatured ethyl or isopropyl alcohol to 1 part water by weight. The amount varies with resin. Use 0.72-pound solvent for 2.5-pound resin mix, and 1 pound solvent for 4-pound resin mix.

Mulling is continued for 10 to 20 minutes until the solvent has evaporated and the sand is dry. That condition is indicated by appearance and can be checked by picking up a handful of the sand. It should show no strength. Mulling is stopped as soon as the sand mix is dry. If you try this, don't forget that the muller should be hooded and hitched to an exhaust system.

This mixture is designed to coat every grain with a coating or shell of resin, preventing the possibility of segregation, which sometimes occurs in sand resin mixes. Any resin which is capable of heat polymerization can be used, such as urea formaldehyde or phenol formaldehyde. Use a top-quality, clay-free, washed and graded subangular silica. It should be below 2 percent clay AFS.

False Coring of Bas-Reliefs

The field of art casting is for the most part a specialty and is full of tricks requiring lots of experience.

The system most commonly used for making a casting with undercuts, such as bas-reliefs, is called *false coring* (Figure 9.20). Each recess or undercut is filled with sand in such a manner that it leaves a print on the main face of the mold where it can be attached. These portions have to be made so that the main face of the mold can be lifted from the face of the pattern without breaking or tearing up. At the same time, each false core must be made so that it can be removed from the pattern without damage to it and then be placed in its proper print on the mold face.

French sand is used extensively for this type of work because it can be rammed hard and dried hard without the fear of blowing, etc.

FALSE CORES

COMPOUND FALSE CORES

2

1

DRAG

PATTERN

COPE

FIGURE 9.20

Bas relief with a backdraft requires the use of false cores.

French sand comes from a little town near Paris. *Yankee sand* is what often is called synthetic French. It is used widely for fine work. In fact, I have seen Yankee sand do just as well as French sand. With either sand, if the whole mold is put up, it should be rammed carefully and hard, washed with plumbago and oven-dried. If Yankee or French is used as a facing, skin drying alone will suffice.

> **TOOLS**
>
> French and Yankee sands are for fine mold-making. Both can be rammed hard and then dried hard without problems.

French sand has a grain fineness of 140 to 175 with the clay removed, carries about 16 percent clay substance, has a permeability of 18 at 7 percent moisture, and averages a green compression strength of about 10. With Yankee sand, grain fineness is about 184, clay content about 19.5 percent, and permeability approximately 17. Green compression strength runs to an average of 16.

Should the bas-reliefs be flatbacked, as most of them are, the cope is made up flat on a smooth, level board. It is struck off and rolled over on a bed. The pattern is then placed on the cope in the correct position for ramming the drag with the roccoco face up. The next move is to study the arrangement carefully and decide about the type of false cores necessary.

Each is made by carefully ramming into the undercuts, bearing in mind that they later must be removed and reassembled on the drag face of the mold in their correct position. Use wires and metal lifters where necessary. Often because one undercut is above another, one false core requires one or more false cores itself.

Make sure that each false core has a sufficient print to locate it correctly with respect to the finished drag. Each false core must have correct draft to allow the drag to be rammed up and removed in good shape. It should be remembered that if your piece has roccoco and backdrafts on each side, the procedure is the same with the exception that you have to use an odd-size double roll, treating each side singly.

After all the false cores have been made, they are marked in such a manner that they will leave an identifying mark on the drag for relocation. The face is dusted with parting and the drag flask is placed, carefully rammed up, and struck off. A bottom board is rubbed in place. Drag and bottom boards are lifted off and rolled over on rails. The false cores then are finished from the undercuts and glued or nailed into their correct positions on the drag face. The rest is as usual—skin dry, oven dry, or use whatever other system you prefer.

Some operators make up their false cores and bake them with infrared lamps just where they are, on the face of the pattern, before they ram the drag. This procedure can be used with French, Yankee, or oil-sand cores provided that the pattern is made of a material which will take the heat. A wooden soldier here and there, cut to give both a print and a handle by which to handle the false core, sometimes can be used to an advantage.

I have seen some old French patterns carved in mahogany which were loaded with roccoco and gingerbread. They are also loaded with undercuts and backdrafts, which were only optical illusions. To create the illusion of folds and undercuts without actually having any is my idea of being really clever.

I also have seen the old cup, saucer, and spoon made with false cores in a two-part flask. Try that some time.

Patterns and Related Equipment

A pattern is a shaped form of wood or metal around which sand is packed in the mold. When the pattern is removed the resulting cavity is the exact shape of the object to be cast.

The pattern must be designed to be easily removed without damage to the mold. It must be accurately dimensioned and durable enough for the use intended.

Each different item we wish to cast presents unique problems and requirements. Especially in large foundries, there is a close relationship between the pattern maker and the molder. Each is aware of the capabilities and limitations of his own field.

Throughout the industry, pattern making is a field and an art of its own. The pattern maker is not a molder nor the molder a pattern maker. This is not to imply that the pattern maker cannot make a simple mold or the molder make a simple pattern but each may soon reach a point in the other's field beyond his own skill and experience.

In the hobby or one-man shop, however, pattern and mold making are so closely interrelated that they become almost one continuous operation. This chapter will acquaint you with some of the various types of patterns and their requirements.

PARTING
LINE

DRAFT

FIGURE 10.1

Disc pattern.

Draft

To illustrate some of the important pattern characteristics, we will use as an example a simple disc pattern. The object we want to cast is 12 inches in diameter and 1 inch thick. The edge of the disc is tapered from the top face to the bottom face (Figure 10.1). This taper is known as the *pattern draft*. This draft is necessary in order that the pattern can be removed easily from the mold causing no damage to the sand. Pattern draft is defined as the taper on vertical elements in a pattern which allows easy withdrawal of the pattern from the mold. The amount of draft required will vary with the depth of the pattern. The general rule is ⅛-inch taper to the foot which comes out to about 1 degree. On shallow patterns such as a disc, ¹⁄₁₆-inch taper, 0.5 degree, is sufficient.

Shrinkage

Now back to the simple disc pattern. If we wish the casting to come out as cast to the dimensions of 12 inches in diameter and 1 inch thick, we must make the pattern larger and thicker than 12 × 1 inch to compensate for the amount that the metal will shrink when going from a liquid to a solid. This procedure is called *pattern shrinkage*. It varies with each type of metal and the shape of the casting.

The added dimensions are incorporated into the pattern by the pattern maker using what is called *shrink rulers*. These rulers are made of steel and the shrinkage is compensated for by having been worked proportionately over its length. Thus a ³⁄₁₆ inch-shrink rule 12 inches long will be actually 12³⁄₁₆ inches long, but will look like a standard rule. But, when laid out against a standard ruler it will project ³⁄₁₆ inch past the standard ruler. These rulers come in a large variety of shrinks. Generally the shrinkage allowance for brass is ³⁄₁₆ inch per foot, ⅛-inch per foot for cast iron, ¼-inch per foot for aluminum, and ¼ inch for steel. This would hold true for most small to medium work. For larger work, the shrinkage allowance is less, in some cases 50 percent less. Where a small casting in steel would require ¼ inch per foot shrinkage allowance, a very large steel casting might require only ⅛ inch per foot shrinkage allowance. So, from this we see that if we wish to cast a bar in brass 1 foot long we must make the pattern 1 foot, ³⁄₁₆ inches long.

Machining Allowance

Now the plot thickens. Say the disc we want in brass requires that the outer diameter of the casting is to be machined (the 12-inch dimension is a machined dimension). We must then allow for machining to our 12-inch dimension. This allowance must be in addition to the shrinkage and draft allowance taken at the short side of the pattern or smallest diameter (Figure 10.2).

We must have a pattern dimension of 12³⁄₁₆ inches. The ³⁄₁₆ inch allows for shrinkage plus ¹⁄₁₆ inch for metal to come off. So we need an actual diameter on the small end of our pattern of 12⅜ inches.

If we dimension our layout as 12¹⁄₁₆ inches (the ¹⁄₁₆ inch for machining) and we use a ³⁄₁₆-inch shrink ruler to measure this dimension, then

FINISH ALLOWANCE

SHRINKAGE ALLOWANCE

12⅜"

FIGURE 10.2

Finish and shrinkage allowance.

TOOLS   To determine shrinkage allowances, the use of shrink rulers is helpful. Shrink rulers come in different sizes, including ³⁄₁₆-, ³⁄₈-inch, and other sizes.

when you build the pattern it will come out fine. Or, make your pattern layout read 12 inches in diameter taking the 12-inch dimension off of a ³⁄₈-inch shrink ruler.

Approximate finish allowances, including the draft are, brass ¹⁄₁₆ inch; aluminum, ⅛ inch; cast iron, ⅛ inch; cast steel, ¼ inch.

On a blueprint given to the pattern maker for large projects, all finishes should be noted (turned, ground, etc.). He will then know from experience how much to allow and how much shrinkage to add to the pattern.

Production Pattern

In the case of the disc, if you are only going to make a casting from the pattern now and again, one at a time, dimension as just described. This pattern is called a *production pattern*, one from which the actual castings are produced.

Master Pattern

Now suppose we want to make one or more production patterns out of cast aluminum from which we intend to make production aluminum castings. In this case we need a wood pattern from which to cast our production pattern. If we wanted as our finished or end product a cast aluminum disc, we would have to make our wood pattern with a double aluminum shrink rule or ½ inch per foot shrinkage. Because we are going to take ¼-shrinkage in going from our wood pattern to our cast pattern and another ¼ inch to our end product, these rules are called *double shrink rulers*. If we were going from a wood pattern to an aluminum production pattern to a brass casting as an end product the shrinkage allowance on the wood pattern would have to be ¼ × ³⁄₁₆ or ¹²⁄₁₆ inch plus finish, etc., if any. This type of pattern (the wood) is called a *master pattern*—a pattern from which the production pattern or patterns are made.

Parting Line

On the simple disc pattern of Figure 10.1, note that the upper face of the pattern is designated as the *parting line* or *parting face*. By this we

FIGURE 10.3

Parting line.

mean a line or the plane of a pattern corresponding to the point of separation between the cope and drag portions of a sand mold. The parting may be irregular or a plane, because the mold must be opened, the pattern removed, and then closed for pouring without damage to the sand. The

QUICK»TIP

Parting lines must be flat or *drafted* so that the mold can be opened. Drafting is the sloping of vertical areas to allow parting.

parting line must be located where this can be accomplished. The portion of the pattern in the cope must be drafted so the cope can be removed and the same for the drag (Figure 10.3).

Any vertical portion of the pattern in either the cope or drag portion must be drafted or tapered as shown in Figure 10.4. The junction or change of draft angle indicates the proper position of the parting line.

Back Draft

If the pattern were shaped as in Figure 10.5 and the mold parted at its upper face, the back draft would prevent its removal without damage to the mold.

A back draft is a reverse taper which prevents removal of a pattern from the mold.

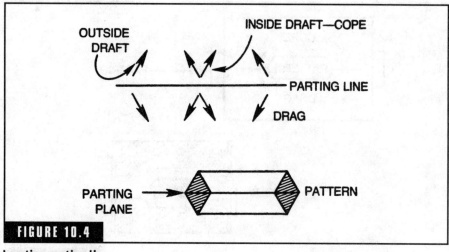

FIGURE 10.4

Locating parting line.

FIGURE 10.5

Back draft.

Gated Pattern

The gate is the channel or channels in a sand mold through which the molten metal enters the cavity left by the pattern. This channel can be made in two ways. One is by cutting the channel or channels with a gate cutter, or by the pattern having a projection attached which will form this gate or gates during the process of ramming up the mold (Figure 10.6).

Gated pattern.

If a pattern is made for a gate, but not attached to a pattern and only placed against it while making the mold, this pattern is called a *set gate pattern*.

Split Pattern

A split pattern is a pattern that is made in two halves split along the parting line. The two halves are held in register by pins called *pattern dowels*. The pattern is split to facilitate molding (Figure 10.7).

The dowels hold the two halves of the pattern together in close, accurate register, but at the same time are free enough that the two

Split pattern.

FIGURE 10.8

Offset pins.

halves can be separated easily for molding like the pins and guides of the flask.

The dowels are usually installed off center in such a manner that the pattern can only be put together correctly (Figure 10.8).

Medium Pattern

A pattern that is used only occasionally or for casting a one time piece is usually constructed as cheaply as possible. If it is a split pattern, wood dowels are used for pins and fit into holes drilled into the matching half. This type of pattern is called a *medium pattern*.

A core of preformed baked sand or green sand aggregate is inserted in a mold to shape the interior part of a casting which cannot be shaped by the pattern.

When a pattern requires a core, a projection must be made on the pattern. This projection forms an impression in the sand of the mold in which to locate the core and hold it during the casting. These projections are called *core prints* and are part of the pattern (Figure 10.9).

Sometimes it is possible to make a pattern in such a way that a core will remain in the sand when the pattern is removed. The pattern for a simple shoring washer, illustrated in Figure 10.10 is made in this way.

Mounted Pattern

When a pattern is mounted to a board to facilitate molding, it is called a mounted pattern. In this case, the mount has guides on each end which match up with the flask used to make the mold. The plate is placed between the cope and drag flask, the drag rammed and rolled over. The cope is then rammed and lifted off. The plate with the pattern attached is lifted off of the drag half. The mold is then finished and closed (Figure 10.11).

Core prints.

Self-coring pattern.

FIGURE 10.11

Mounted pattern.

Matchplate

The matchplate is the same as the mounted pattern with the exception that when you have part of the casting in the cope and part in the drag (split pattern), these parts are attached to the board or plate opposite each other and in the correct location. When the plate is removed and the mold is closed, the cavities in the cope and drag match up correctly. The molding procedure is the same as for one sided mounted plate (Figure 10.12).

In most cases all the necessary gating runners, etc., are built right on the plate. The matchplate might have only one pattern or a large quantity of small patterns.

T OOLS Cope and drag pattern mounts use female guides on the drag (lower part) and male guides on the cope (upper part). These must match the flask used.

Cope and Drag Mounts

In this case you have two separate pattern mounts. One is fitted with female guides for the drag and one is fitted with pins for the cope. These must match up with the flask used.

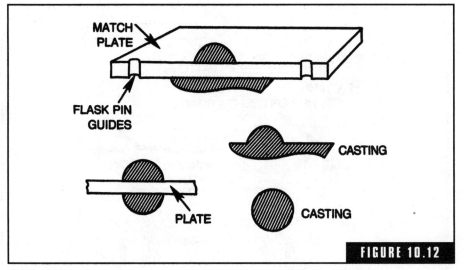

Match plate pattern.

The cope half of the pattern is attached to the cope mount and the drag pattern is attached to the drag mount. The cope and drag molds are produced separately and put together for pouring. The usual practice is for one molder to make copes and another to make the drags. Cope and drag mounts are quite common when making large and very large castings where a matchplate would be out of the question due to its bulk and weight. Cope and drag mounts are sometimes called *tubs* (Figure 10.13).

Cope and drag mounts.

FIGURE 10.14

Follow board.

Follow Board

A board with a cavity or socket in it which conforms to the form of the pattern and defines the parting surface of the drag is called a follow board. It can be made of wood, plaster, or metal. When made of sand it is called a *dry sand match*.

The pattern rests in the follow board while making up the drag half of the mold and in doing so establishes the correct sand parting. The follow board is removed, leaving the pattern rammed in the drag up to the parting. The cope then takes the place of the follow board and is rammed in the usual manner (Figure 10.14).

A simple follow board might consist of a molding board with a hole in it to allow the pattern to rest firmly on the board while the drag is rammed (Figure 10.15).

Miscellaneous Patterns

When several different loosely gated patterns are assembled as a unit to be molded in the same flask, this arrangement is called a *card of patterns*.

Simple follow board.

A *sweep pattern* consists of a board having a profile of the desired mold which, when revolved around a suitable spindle or guide, produces that mold. Two are usually required. One sweeps the cope profile and the other the drag profile (Figure 10.16).

Sweep pattern.

The *skeleton pattern* is a framework of wooden bars which represent the interior and exterior form and the metal thickness of the required casting. This type of pattern is only used for huge castings (Figure 10.17).

An *expendable pattern* is when the pattern is lost. Expendable patterns for sand casting are styrofoam. They are shaped to the desired form with attached styrofoam gates, runners, and risers. The styrofoam pattern is molded with dry clay-free sharp silica sand in a box or steel frame. The pattern is vaporized by the metal poured into the mold, leaving the casting.

Skeleton pattern.

Wood Patterns

Wood patterns used for casting are given several coats of orange shellac to which a pinch of oxalic acid has been added. This gives them a waterproof, smooth, hard surface.

QUICK»TIP

A white pine pattern that weighs 1 pound, will produce an aluminum casting of 8 pounds and a brass casting of 19 pounds.

The majority of wood patterns are made of white pine (sugar pine) as it is easily worked and, when shellacked properly, will not warp under ordinary use.

The approximate weight of a casting can be determined by weighing the wood pattern and multiplying by the appropriate factor indicated. Aluminum 8, cast iron 16.7, copper 19.8, brass 19.0, steel 17.0.

Mounting Patterns

The brass plate method of transfer is an old one and, if done with enough care, usually will do a good job. It is my opinion, however, that the use of a suitable transfer frame or flask and plaster is by far the easiest method of getting a close match.

This system is simple, cheap, and pretty close to foolproof (Figures 10.18 through 10.20). Take a 12 × 18-inch flask, for example, and mount patterns on a plate for use in it. Remove the bushings from both ends of the cope and rebush the flask with tight, round bushings. Allow only about 0.003-inch clearance between the pin and bushing.

To mount a pattern, drag the patterns, plug mounting holes, and pour the plaster.

The second step in mounting a pattern includes removing the plate, fitting the cope patterns to drag patterns and pouring the cope plaster.

FIGURE 10.20

The third pattern mounting step involves removing halves of flask containing plaster, patterns, and plate plugs. Then drill the mounting holes.

Alternatively, you can design, cast, and machine a special aluminum flask with a close fit between the pins and the bushings.

Finish the patterns in the usual manner, pinning them together as if you were going to use them for loose molding, with one exception. In the drag-half patterns, drill suitable holes through the prints, etc., to mount the patterns to the plate in the final steps. Next, fit a suitable 12 × 18 inch aluminum plate to the doctored-up flask with suitable pin lugs. Hold these pin lugs also to a close tolerance—0.003 inch or so clearance between the lugs and the pins.

Place the cope and drag flask together, with the plate between them. Turn the entire rig so that the drag side is up. Locate the drag patterns on the plate where you want them with respect to gating. Glue them in place with shellac or wax. Place suitable dowels in the holes you drilled for use later during mounting. These dowels should stick up out of the pattern not less than an inch or so.

With the drag patterns properly located and stuck down to the plate, and with plugs or dowels in the mounting holes, place a weight on each corner of the flask. To the surface of the plate and patterns, apply a good commercial plaster release. Pour enough plaster into the drag flask to fill it to a depth which will give a good coverage around the patterns, yet leave the dowels sticking through the plaster.

After the plaster has set, remove the plate and the drag half of the flask from the cope half. Apply a little heat to the bottom of the plate to loosen the wax or shellac and remove the plate. Should the patterns come out of the plaster in the drag, simply remove them from the plate and reset them in their respective cavities. The drag is then turned over on its back, parting face up. Clean off patterns and top carefully. Place the cope halves of the patterns over their mating halves. They are embedded to the parting line in plaster in the drag of the special flask. Place the cope on the drag, weighing all four corners with a suitable weight.

Apply a plaster parting or plaster release over the entire surface of the plaster and the cope halves of the patterns. Then pour sufficient plaster into the cope to give good coverage around the cope patterns. Because you have no dowels to worry about, you can cover the patterns up. Part the two flasks. The cope half will contain the cope halves of the patterns and the drag half will contain the drag halves.

Next, return to the aluminum match plate fitted with suitable lugs and replace the cope half. Roll the whole works over to bring the drag up and clamp all four corners. The clamp should extend from the cope or top of the flask to the bottom of the drag half. With the flask in the upside-down position, remove the plugs or dowels in the holes for mounting. Leaving these holes open, take the whole business over to the drill press and drill through the drag patterns, the plate, and the cope. Chip the plaster away until you get down to the pattern. Then drive pins through or screw them down. There are many variations of this method, but this is the basic principle. Remove the special flask and the plaster, leaving the patterns with a very close register. Also remove the special lugs from the plate and mount whatever type of lugs you are using.

This rigging, done in the same manner, is suitable for making cope and drag mounts. It also will work in the mounting of a symmetrical match when the flasks are fitted up with a pin on one end and a bushing on the opposite one. This is the type of equipment used on a pin-lift or stripper. The first half off, the drag, is turned end-for-end, and the second half becomes the cope. It is used in some plumbing shops as well as in hobby shops which engage in the production of small and medium castings. The plaster transfer system for mounting these symmetrical matches is used widely in this type of work.

Although a new 12 x 18-inch steel flask that has been rebushed can be used, I would recommend that you construct a special pattern-mounting frame. This frame, or pair of frames, should be machined up very accurately in a tool and die shop. Special pins and bushings can be made, and you will find this equipment to be more suitable.

In most cases you require only about 2 or 2½ inches of depth per section since it is not necessary for the plaster to cover the entire pattern. Only enough plaster is necessary to grip the pattern and hold it in position until it is mounted firmly to the plate. When mounting patterns on cope and drag plates, be sure that the cope frame and drag fit accurately, that the drag frame fits the drag plate, and that the cope frame fits the cope plate. In the case of cope and drag mounts with an elongated or slotted bushing on one end, the bushing must be removed and replaced with a round bushing during the pattern mounting procedure only. It later is replaced with the original bushing.

There are many variations of the plaster transfer method and with a little fiddling around you might come up with something more suitable to your particular operation than the foregoing method. However, this is the basic procedure. Whether the patterns are pinned or screwed to the plate is a matter of individual preference.

In my opinion, it is poor practice to drill patterns prior to mounting on plates, tap out the drag half or cope half of the pattern, mount the patterns by drilling oversized holes through the matchplate, and rely only upon the screw which passes through the cope half of the pattern and the plate and into the drag half of the pattern.

I have had experience with clamping patterns together and with the screw method. I also have drilled through the two halves of the patterns and mounted the patterns across from each other on a matchplate by driving a pin through the hole and an oversized hole in the plate and into the remaining half of the pattern. If by chance the drill does run off, however, the farther the patterns are separated, the greater the mismatch will be.

With the plaster transfer method, however, it doesn't make much difference which way the drill goes as long as the patterns are secured tightly to the plate prior to the removal of the plaster. The plaster will hold patterns accurately across from each other during the drilling, tapping, or pinning operations. Any type of method for mounting can be used in conjunction with plaster.

The accuracy of this system depends entirely upon how accurately and closely your transfer frames fit up.

Recessed Pattern

When molding a pattern with a deep recess in the cope side of the pattern, even if you don't come up quite straight with your draw and a section of the green sand stays down, you can often still retrieve and save the cope.

In many cases this problem is caused by improperly tempered molding sand and you will find that the sand is dry where the drop broke loose from the cope. A sticky pattern may also be caused by low green strength and soft ramming, or the pocket is too deep or heavy to come up with the cope.

Regardless of the cause, there are two ways of saving the cope. Put the cope back on and roll the mold over. Draw the drag off, leaving the drop resting on its mating surface. Now push a large headed nail carefully into the sand to pin the broken piece to its mate. Turn the cope over and see if you have done a good job. If the piece that stayed down is not too large, the next best bet is to dampen both surfaces with a bulb sponge and sprinkle the surface of the sand piece in the pattern with wheat flour. Put the cope back in place and strike directly over the problem with the butt end of the rammer. Allow a second or two for your flour glue to stick, then draw the cope, roll it over, and nail it. In either case, be sure to patch or slick the junction of the repair.

Glossary

abrasives   Any material for grinding, polishing, blasting, etc. The field of abrasives runs from a very mild abrasive such as *rottenstone* or tin oxide to highly abrasive diamond dust, or grit. Natural abrasives include talc, sand, pumice, emery, corundum, garnet, diamond, etc. The manufactured abrasives are silicon carbide, aluminum oxide, metallic shot, and grit. The forms are as many as the types of abrasives—sandpaper, grinding wheels, rouges, etc.

acetylene   A colorless gas HC:CH. It is used as a fuel in high temperature torches such as the oxygen/acetylene welding and cutting torches. Pure acetylene has a sweet odor but when contaminated with hydrogen sulphide it smells quite bad. It is easily generated by the action of water on calcium carbide. It is sold in pressure tanks, called *bottles*, dissolved in acetone to render it nonexplosive. One volume of acetone will absorb or dissolve 25 volumes of acetylene. It is used to produce other chemicals. Large users often produce their own with a device called an *acetylene generator*. It consists of two chambers, one above the other. The top chamber contains dry calcium carbide. The bottom chamber contains water. The carbide is dispensed into the water by a pressure-regulated valve, or gate, when a predetermined acetylene gas pressure is reached by the reaction in the bottom chamber. The valve closes, preventing any more carbide from entering the water. When the pressure drops due to the use of the acetylene from the bottom chamber, the valve opens and the process is repeated.

   In Sweden during World War I, some automobiles were operated on acetylene gas. Presto-O-Lite™ Union Carbide Co. is the trade name for acetylene dissolved in acetone.

acid   Ceramic refractory materials of a high melting point consisting largely of silica. Thus steel melted in a furnace with an acid refractory bottom under an acid siliceous slag is called *acid steel*.

adjustable jackets A loosely cornered slip jacket which will adjust to the taper of the mold and afford a good close fit (Fig. A-1). A popular brand adjustable jacket sold under the name Wopper Jaw jacket is manufactured by Products Engineering, Cape Girardeau, MO.

FIGURE A.1

An adjustable jacket.

aerators Any device which fluffs up and introduces air into a molding sand to increase the flowability and rammability of the sand (Fig. A-2). It also helps to evenly cool and distribute the moisture. Simple riddling of the sand accomplishes this evenness to some extent. Some machines condition and aerate the sand in the same action. A device widely used in the foundry is the Royer Sand & Blender machine. This machine separates, aerates, and blends all in one action. Royer also produces many types of aerators and conditioners.

FIGURE A.2

An aerator. The refuse falls at the retaining gate.

Most mullers have an aerator at the discharge snoot which consists of a series of knives on a high speed shaft. The sand being discharged must make a trip through these whirling knives, which aerate the sand. Some machines consist of steel brushes rotating at high speed through which the sand must pass. The process is called *aerating*.

Originally patented in 1910, the cleated-belt aerator was introduced to the foundry industry by Royer and was quickly accepted for conditioning sand. Over the years, the design, construction, and materials of the unique machine have been continually improved. The basic aerator has been adapted to meet the industry's ever-increasing requirements for proper sand preparation. The development of new aerators for foundry applications continues to be an on-going process. Royer manufactures a variety of standard aerators: basic stationary and portable units, with or without magnetic cleaning; aerators mounted in bucket elevators; belt-mounted aerators; aerators for feeding automatic molding machines; and aerators on molder's hoppers.

As sand is charged into a Royer Aerator, it falls on an inclined, endless belt which has rows of closely-spaced alloy-steel cleats. With the belt moving at more than 100 fpm, the cleats tear apart lumps and propel the sand up the belt to a *sweep*—a row of flat spring-loaded fingers mounted above the belt at the head pulley. As the sand churns against the sweep, trapped gasses are released and foreign materials, such as wedges and cores, fall to the lower end of the belt. The tumbling-churning-mixing action on the belt aerates and cools the sand. Granular sand, between the rows of cleats, passes under the sweep and is thrown forward. The stream of free-flowing sand continues to cool as it is discharged into the air. This is called the basic cleat-belted principle.

The pattern of cleats, speed, and inclination of the belt and spring tension are basic design parameters. The clearance between the sweep assembly and the belt, however, can be adjusted to achieve the desired degree of aeration. Capacity is determined by the width and length of the belt and the condition of the sand.

A.F.S. clay American Founderman's Association defines clay as the earthy portion of a foundry sand which, when suspended in water, fails to settle at a rate of an inch per minute and consists of particles less than 20 microns (.008 inch) in diameter—a combination of true clay and silt.

A.F.S. grain distribution The distribution in percent of various sizes of grains in a given sand established by running a sample through a standard set of screens and weighing the sand retained on each screen. The distribution is then expressed on a graph (Fig. A-3). Sand with 70 to 80 percent retained on three adjacent screens is considered ideal.

age hardening The property of some ferrous and nonferrous alloys to increase hardness and strength by time alone at room temperature. Tenzaloy™ Federated metals is a popular aluminum casting ingot which has very good properties of age hardening. The normal composition is copper 0.6 percent, zinc 7.5 percent, magnesium 0.4 percent, and the remainder aluminum. Cast aged one day at room temperature has a tensile strength of KSI 29. After 10 to 14 days the tensile jumps to KSI 35. The Brinell hardness (500 Kg) jumps from 60 on the first day to 74 about two weeks later. Permanent mold cast Tenzaloy tensile goes from 30

A.F.S. grain distribution.

to 40. Some soft metals (lead base) go the other way, losing strength with age.

air belt   The belt surrounding the cupola or blast furnace which receives the air from the blower and evenly distributes it to the *tuyeres*. Also called *bustle pipe*.

air dried   A green mold or core which is allowed to dry naturally. Some bonding clays used in green sand molding gain strength after the mold has air dried. This increase in strength is called *air set strength*. Holloysite clay from Utah has this property due to its lath-shaped structure. Also known as *white clay*.

air floaters   Any dry compound that is air floated or capable of floating in the air—fine dust, etc. Compounds of pitch, dry parting, blacking, clays, and flours that are advertised as floaters or air floaters indicate that they are free from any heavy particles. They are lightweight, usually of a fine uniform size, and free from tramp material.

air furnace   A reverberatory type of furnace. The metal is melted on a shallow hearth by the flame from the fuel burning on one end of the hearth passing over the bath on its way to the stack at the other end. The heat is reflected from the roof and sidewalls. Air furnaces are fired with natural gas, oil, and pulverized coal or coke. The passive air furnace is fired by a natural draft pulling the products of combustion across the hearth. A shallow bath is necessary in order to bring the bath temperature up high enough.

A deep bath will not melt properly due to heat convection through the hearth bottom.

The air furnace is widely used in the production of malleable iron. It is hard to control a cupola to produce malleable by itself, but is a fast and efficient method of melting. Very often the metal is melted in a cupola and then tapped into the air furnace for refining to the correct analysis. This process is referred to as *duplexing*. The air furnace is a close cousin to the *open hearth* furnace.

With the older, more passive air furnaces that used coal burning on a grate, it was quite common to use a blower for forced draft along with the *stack draft* (suction). A pulverized coal burner has taken the place of these old jobs. A small air furnace burning coal the old way with some air assistance is a great melter for the backwoods or hobby foundry for ferrous or nonferrous melting. The air furnace is usually provided with a breast and tap hole on each side and is tapped like the cupola. Because you have a rather large metal surface exposed to the products of combustion (unlike a crucible), great care must be exercised as to the conditions of combustion or you can wind up with a highly oxidized melt. This is true of any open hearth air furnace of the small ferrous type and of the nonferrous reverberatory furnaces which have come into popularity.

air hardening   When certain alloys of steel are cooled in air from a temperature above or higher than the transformation range to room temperature and remain hard, they are known as *air-hardening alloys* or *self-hardening steels*. Metal lathe tool bits are self-hardening steel. They are extremely difficult or impossible to anneal.

air hole   Gas holes. Air or gas trapped in the casting during solidification. The major cause of *gas porosity* is gas absorption by the metal from the products of combustion: sulphur dioxide, hydrogen, and oxygen. The least likely cause is a too-hot pouring temperature.

airless blasting   The cleaning of castings by throwing shot or steel grit against the objects to be cleaned. Similar to sand blasting (Fig. A-4). The basic difference is that air is not used to propel the abrasive. The abrasive is thrown by a high-speed impeller wheel. The shot or abrasive is fed through the hub of the impeller wheel where it is picked up by the throwing blades. It is accelerated as it passes to the periphery of the wheel and is thrown at high velocity. There are variations of the machines but the principle is

SHOT WHEEL

SHOT

CASTINGS

ENDLESS
PERFORATED
APRON

CLEAN SHOT RETURNS TO WHEEL

FIGURE A.4

Airless blasting.

the same. Some are continuous and the castings are carried
through the blast chamber in one side and out the other. Some of
the castings are placed on rotary tables in the chamber and others
are rolled back and forth on an endless apron conveyor (metal or
rubber) which tumbles the castings under the blast of abrasive.
The abrasive falls through the perforations in the apron and is
conveyed back to the wheel via a screw and bucket. Along the
way back to the wheel, the shot or grit is cleaned of any sand,
dust, etc.

air pocket (permanent mold)   A defect known as an air pocket caused by
trapped air or gas in the mold cavity. Found with permanent
molds as well as with die casting. First it has to be determined if
the pocket is caused by a low pouring temperature; by pouring
incorrectly (too slow, bubbling, etc.); by the gating system not being properly designed; or by the mold not running hot enough.
When you have eliminated all of these possibilities, then the
mold must be vented.

air rammers   A rammer operated by air introduced into a cylinder
which drives a reciprocating piston and rod (Fig. A-5). A rubber
butt or peen is attached to produce a fast rapid blow. Widely used

OPERATING LEVER

AIR→

ACTION

FIGURE A.5

Air rammer.

for bench, floor molds, and in the ramming of cores. They range from small bench rammers to heavy floor rammers.

air strength   When a green sand specimen is allowed to stand for any length of time and air dry before it is tested for its compressive strength, the air strength will have increased. The difference between a sample tested before and after air drying gives the foundryman an idea of what happens when a mold sits for a length of time and air dries prior to pouring. The increase in strength varies widely depending on the type and kind of clay used as a bond. Most foundrymen pay little attention to the air strength of their molding sand and are puzzled about dirt inclusions in the casting, which they attribute to dirty molding. The problem could be simply that the sand is too low in air strength. During air drying, sharp edges lose strength and crumble off or wash off into the mold cavity. A simple change in clay bond can prevent the problem. The moisture content also plays a part in the loss or gain in air strength of the sand.

air vibrator   Any pneumatic type of vibrator (Fig. A-6). There are two basic operating principles. One is the free piston type where air is introduced into the cylinder and the piston shuttles back and

MATCH PLATE VIBRATOR

AIR FITTING

MOUNTING LOG

FIGURE A.6

Air vibrator.

forth at high speed (a floating piston air engine). The other is the ball type, where a steel ball traveling in a case produces the vibration. The most common type used in the foundry is the *match plate air* (piston) vibrator. It vibrates the pattern to ensure a clean lift of the cope and the pattern.

Albany sand A naturally bonded sand from the district around Albany, New York. This sand was strip mined for years and years in various grades suitable for light aluminum casting to coarse grades for heavy gray iron. The field is pretty well worked out of good quality grades. Synthetic molding sands have just about replaced the use of naturally bonded sands. *Naturally bonded sands*, however, can be found practically anywhere in the United States. As mined, they contain sufficient clay bond and the correct properties needed to make molds.

alkali metals 1A of the periodic table including lithium, sodium, potassium, rubidium, cesium, and francium.

alkaline metals Calcium, strontium, barium, radium, and the group 11A of the periodic table.

allotropy The occurrence of an element in two or more forms such as carbon which occurs in nature as diamonds, soft graphite, and amorphous coal.

alloy A combination of metals melted together. If you take 85 pounds of copper, 5 pounds of tin, 5 pounds of lead, and 5 pounds of zinc and melt them together, you'll have an alloy known as *red brass*. Also called *ounce metal*, it is an old and often used casting alloy. With 50 percent lead and 50 percent tin melted together you have the common soft solder known as 50/50. The percentages of the alloying elements vary to give you an alloy of a different name and characteristic castability, melting point, etc. If you took the amount of lead and tin just described (solder) and raised the percent of tin to 80 percent and lowered the lead to 20 percent, you would have an alloy called *babbit*, a bearing metal. Raise the tin even higher to 90 to 95 percent and lower the lead to 10 or 4 percent and you'll have *pewter*. Some metals or constituents are not compatible in any amounts other than a trace. The trace is called an *impurity*. From extensive metallurgical and physical testing, the amounts of various metals in percents that will successfully alloy with each other have been fairly well established. The development of new, useful, and sometimes sophisticated alloys are being researched and developed daily. For example, silicon bronze, which is an alloy of 3 to 4 percent silicon and the remainder copper is not compatible with lead other than as a very minor trace which is classified as a harmful impurity. Lead in even small amounts in silicon bronze combines with the silicon to form lead silicate (glass). When some element is added to an alloy in a minor amount to change the characteristics of the alloy being produced, it is referred to as a *hardener*. Most babbit metal contains a small percent of antimony, which increases the hardness of the alloy considerably.

alloy cast iron Cast iron is composed of iron, carbon silicon, phosphorous, manganese, and sulphur. The elements which compose the alloy called cast iron or *gray iron* are used in different and varying proportions depending on the grade of casting desired. Typical common gray iron would be approximately 93 percent iron, 3.25 percent carbon, 2.5 percent silicon, .50 percent manganese, .65 percent phosphorous, and .10 percent sulphur. Sulphur is usually considered an impurity.

Alloy cast irons are essentially an alloy or iron and carbon to which an element or elements in various percentages and combinations are added. Sufficient amounts produce a measurable modification of the physical properties of the iron in the section (thickness and weight) under consideration. *Ferro alloys* such as ferrosilicon, and the nonferrous group phos copper, copper nickel, etc., are called *alloying elements*.

Some of these additives include chromium, silicon, molbydenium, vanadium, nickel, titanium, and phosphorous copper. These additions are usually added in the form of ferro alloys purchased by the percent produced by smelting companies. More often than not the elements by themselves are difficult if not impossible to add as is from the physical element as well as the cost due to loss by oxidation. These additives are sold combined with iron in the form of shot wafer briquettes with a percentage of the element combined with the iron. Thus if you purchased 100 pounds of 50 percent ferrosilicon you would have 50 pounds of silicon and 50 pounds of iron for each 100 pounds. When melting with the cupola, these additives are usually added to the stream of metal coming from the spout to the receiving ladle or to the pouring ladle; otherwise most of it would be lost if added to the charge in the cupola. In reverberatory, crucible, or induction melting they can be added directly to the bath. The term *innoculance* is used quite often for these additions.

alpha iron The form of iron characterized by a body-centered cubic crystal structure that is stable below 1670 F. Carbon is practically insoluble in alpha iron when heated to a temperature above 1670 F. The *ferrite* changes from alpha to gamma state, a face-centered cubic form. *Gamma iron* readily dissolves carbon. The solid solution is known as *austenite*.

alumel A nickel-based alloy used chiefly as a component in thermocouples.

aluminite An alumina refractory material.

aluminum A light metal produced from boxite which is not sufficiently strong enough to be used to any extent commercially. It is usually alloyed with silicon, copper, magnesium, nickel, and zinc in various amounts and combinations to produce various physical characteristics like castability, strength, soundness, etc., depending upon the method chosen to cast, the castings, and use. There are a great number of alloys available (Table A-1).

aluminum bronze A copper-base alloy containing 5 to 15 percent aluminum and up to 10 percent iron, with or without manganese or nickel (Fig. A-7).

- Normal composition—88 percent copper, 3 percent iron, 9 percent aluminum.
- .276 pounds per cubic inch.
- Patternmakers shrinkage ¼ inch per foot.
- Pouring temperature: Light castings 2050–2250 F., heavy castings 200–2100 F.
- Tensile strength, KSI 80.

Aluminum bronze is a difficult metal to cast due to its high shrinkage, short freezing range, and the tendency to form *dross* that must be trapped and prevented from getting into the casting. The same precaution on gating applies to both small and large castings. The best method of *gating* is to introduce the metal into the bottom of the mold through an inverted *horn gate* (large end attached to casting), using a *skimmer sprue* between the pouring sprue and the small end of the horn.

TABLE A.1 Common AL Alloys.

Sand Casting Alloys

Copper 1.8%	Silicon 5%	Copper 4%
Manganese 1%	Aluminum 95%	Silicon 1%
Aluminum Remainder		Aluminum 95%
Copper 4%	Copper 4.5%	Copper 3.5%
Silicon 3%	Silicon 5.5%	Silicon 6.5%
Aluminum 93%	Aluminum 90%	Aluminum 90%
Copper 4%	Copper 7%	Copper 6.5%
Silicon 5%	Silicon 3.5%	Silicon 5.5%
		Manganese .3%
Aluminum 88%	Aluminum 89.5%	Aluminum 87.7%
Copper 10%	Copper 10%	
Mangesium .3%	Silicon 4%	
Aluminum 89.7%	Magnesium .3%	
	Aluminum 89.7%	

Permanent Mold AL Alloys

Silicon 5%	Copper 3%	Copper 4%
Aluminum 95%	Silicon 6%	Silicon 3%
	Aluminum 91%	Aluminum 93%
Copper 7%	Copper 10%	
Silicon 5%	Magnesium .3%	
Magnesium .4%	Aluminum 89.7%	
Aluminum 87.64%		

Die Casting AL Alloys

Copper 4%	Silicon 5%	Silicon 9.5%
Silicon 8%	Aluminum 95%	Magnesium .5%
Aluminum 87%		Aluminum 90%

Risers should be one and a half times larger than the section they are to feed. Use large fillets and avoid sharp edges and a gating system that produces turbulence or a *nozzling effect*.

Keep the value of the moisture in the sand as low as possible. The top value should be 6 percent. Large castings should be cast in dry sand molds or no-bake molds. Any cores should be open and free from gas-producing ingredients. Keep flour to a minimum. Use a simple oil sand core. Suitable green molding sand should be somewhere within these limits: permeability, 15 to 20; claybond, 10 to 20; green strength, 5 to 10; moisture, 3 to 6 percent; and sand fineness, 100 to 150.

More often than not the weight of the risers will be equal to or exceed the weight of the casting. Heavy sections which cannot be readily fed should be chilled with adequate *chills*.

Aluminum bronze.

aluminum flux Any material, such as dry nitrogen or other inert gas, bubbled through the molten aluminum to rid it of absorbed gasses or stable metallic salts such as *zinc chloride* or *aluminum chloride*. In some cases a mixture of one or more *chloride, fluoride,* or *cryolite* with aluminum magnesium alloys. One or more alkaline earth salts are used as a flux. With clean metal and good melting practices you can produce satisfactory castings without the use of a flux. Consult your supplier for the recommended flux for the alloy you are melting and the type of melting equipment you are using. The simplest and safest way, which produces no obnoxious poison gas, is to simply bubble dry nitrogen gas through the molten bath.

aluminum nickel bronze When nickel is added to aluminum bronze in the order of from 2 to 5 percent, you gain in strength, reliability, and corrosion resistance. Excellent stability in structure during cooling from the casting temperature prevents the *self annealing* that some bronzes suffer from if allowed to cool too slowly. It can cause deterioration in mechanical properties.

Typical aluminum nickel bronze is composed of copper, 83.0 percent; nickel, 2.5 percent maximum; aluminum, 10.0 to 11.5 percent; manganese, .5 percent maximum; and iron, 3.0 to 5.0 percent.

Aluminum Ni bronze is handled the same way you handle straight aluminum bronze as far as foundry practice is concerned with the exception that the higher the percent of nickel, the hotter you must melt and pour. For example, with 12 percent nickel your pouring range jumps from 2350 to 2550 F. which is

TABLE A.2 Aluminum Solder Components

Soluminium (German) AL Solder	Mourays
55% Tin	80 to 90% Zinc
33% Zinc	3 to 8 Copper
11% Aluminum	6 to 12% Aluminum
Bureau of Standards Aluminum Solder	**Alcoa**
87% tin	95% Zinc
8% zinc	5% Aluminum
5% Aluminum	

Aluminum to Aluminum
91% Tin
9% Zinc

FIGURE A.8

Anchor core.

from 50 to 250 degrees above the freezing point with this much nickel. A common error with all nickel alloys is pouring too cold.

aluminum pattern plate An aluminum plate for mounting wood or metal patterns (*match plate*) for molding. Plates are produced in a wide variety of sizes, thicknesses, and types. The common type is a flat parallel ground plate with ears to handle the plate and attach the lugs (guides) and match plate vibrator (rapper).

aluminum solder For the various components and percentages of aluminum solder, see Table A-2.

ammonium chloride NH_4CL called *sal ammoniac*. Used as a soldering flux for soft solders, a lead flux, and in brick form to clean soldering coppers and irons.

anchor (core) Any device used to hold or anchor a core in place (Fig. A-8). It could be a nail running through a print into the sand to anchor the core or a wire tie used when pouring an open-faced bushing mold. The anchor holds the bushing core down and centered when pouring without a cope.

FIGURE A.9

Angle sleeker.

angle sleeker A molder's hand tool for smoothing or sleeking inside and outside corners of a mold (Fig. A-9). These sleeker tools have a half-round tab on their back surface which is held between the thumb and first finger and used as you would a pressing iron to smooth the area you desire, especially when repairing a mold surface. Avoid excess sleeking using too much pressure. This could compact the sand at the point of sleeking too tightly and result in a kick or blow at that point.

angle stem chaplet A sheet metal chaplet with an open design to permit an adequate flow of molten metal through the chaplet (Fig. A-10). Insures proper burning in.

FIGURE A.10

Angle stem chaplet.

annealing   The process of heating ferrous metals above the *critical temperature*—temperature at which changes take place. critical temperatures are determined by liberation of heat when the metal is heated, thus resulting in halts and arrests on heating or cooling curves. The metal is held at the critical temperature until the transformation is complete. The metal is cooled slowly in a furnace or packed in bone ash or cinders to cool slowly. The metal is then relieved of design and casting stresses and is more ductile and easier to machine.

With copper base and precious metals (gold, silver, etc.), the process is reversed. In this case the metal is heated to its critical temperature—usually a dull red in the dark—and quenched in cold water.

anneal, malleable   This heat treatment involves heating and then slow cooling. With regard to malleable iron, it is the method used to convert the hard brittle iron castings into tough, ductile, malleable iron. This treatment causes the carbon in the white iron to precipitate in the free state in the form of tiny particles instead of flakes as in gray iron.

annealing pots   Iron pots in which castings that are to be annealed or malleabilized are packed to protect them from the furnace atmosphere during the annealing process.

antimony oxide   An oxide of antimony. Its principal foundry use is as a hardener in lead-base alloys.

anti-piping compounds   Carbonous (slow oxidizing) compounds which are sprinkled on the top of the riser to slow down the heat loss, keeping the riser liquid longer so that it can do its job (Fig. A-11). Some are mildly exothermic or quite volatile like the old hot patch. *Insulating sleeves* of plaster of paris, or other insulating materials are sold by foundry suppliers in a wide variety of sizes and materials. Some are simply insulators, others are exothermic. Exothermic anti-piping compound materials are composed chiefly of what is known as *thermit*, but modified to react less violently. Thermit is basically a mixture of powdered aluminum and iron oxide.

The idea is to keep the riser liquid as long as possible. It ensures the proper feeding of liquid metal to the shrinking casting to promote directional feeding.

ANTI-PIPING
COMPOUND

INSULATING
SLEEVE

M
E
T
A
L

COPE
MOLD

CASTING

FIGURE A.11

Anti-piping compounds.

Anti-piping compounds should not be added until the riser will take no more metal. They prevent the compounds from being fed into the casting. Anti-piping compounds and sleeves are widely used in steel and iron founding and to a small extent in large nonferrous work.

arbor A metal (cast or fabricated) form used to support a dry sand or green sand core or mold body for strength (Fig. A-12). Also used extensively in heavy loam molding. Sometimes called a *crab*.

Arbors are usually made to fit a particular job. A common use is in the casting of gray iron soil pipe fittings using green sand cores.

In practice the core is made in a full core box by *booking*. The drag half of the core box is partially filled with green sand and the arbor set in place, then the half core completed. The cope half is then made up and the box booked. The cope box is removed and the core lifted out by the arbor, which supports it. The cope half of the green sand rests on top of the arbor and the drag half, supported on the arbor by the half-round sections, extends into its body. The tip-tail fits into a print made in the drag mold by a print on the pattern. The tip tail does two things: It prevents the core from tipping over and touching in the drag and it locates the core properly in the mold when the mold is closed.

FIGURE A.12

Arbor.

Cores for large cylindrical castings molded horizontally are often swept up (or rammed) on a perforated steel or cast iron core arbor. The arbor is first wrapped with burlap to prevent the sand from going through the vent holes (perforations).

The pattern usually has prints on it to accommodate the arbor as well as the core. Small hollow tin tubes are also sold to strengthen a core section by ramming them up where needed when making the core.

In comparison to the sculptured armature, a core or mold arbor represents extra support and strength. In casting, it often serves several purposes all at the same time, such as creating a path for the core gases to escape through plus the conservation of material. In investment casting (full mold), steel tubing perforated and wrapped with paper is used as a *core support* and *core vent*. More often than not it spells the difference between losing a casting from a broken core and a core blowing. The unperforated section, extending through a section of the mold which will fill with metal when poured, prevents the vent from stopping off and causing a blow. Steel automobile gas line tubing is excellent for this purpose.

arc furnaces There are two basic types in use—the *direct* and *indirect arc* (Fig. A-13). In the direct arc furnace three electrodes in a triangular pattern come through the roof of the furnace through suitable openings. They are provided with a suitable mechanism for raising and lowering them. The metal is melted by direct contact with the electrodes. The electrodes are raised and the charge placed on the hearth. The electrodes are then lowered and the

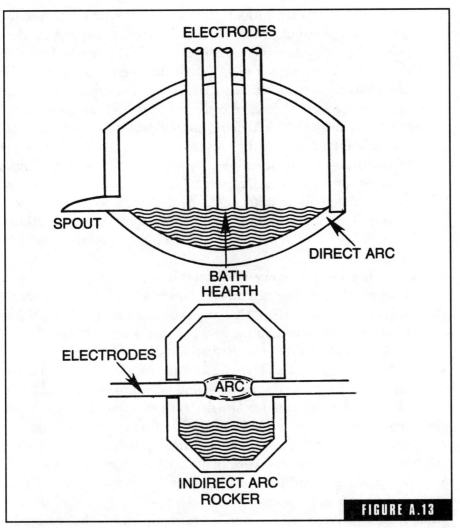

Arc furnaces.

current is turned on. The electrodes melt their way through the charge nearly to the bottom. As the molten metal (bath) rises, the electrodes are raised to the correct height in respect to the bath. As soon as the correct refining period is reached, the current is reduced. The bath is refined and chemically adjusted in the furnace by various slag treatments (boils), oxygen lancings, ferro alloy additions (depending on what is called for as the final analysis), and the starting charge. There are direct-arc furnaces as small as 2 tons to 150 tons and larger. The furnace is tilted to remove the *heat* (molten metal).

In the indirect arc furnace the metal is melted by heat radiation of an arc struck and maintained between two carbon electrodes. The arc is maintained by an automatic screw feed that advances the electrodes to maintain the correct arc gap as the electrodes are consumed. The shell is barrel shaped and rides on a set of rollers and is rocked back and forward through an arc of about 180 degrees. This rocking motion performs the same function as a rotary furnace by carrying the molten metal over the heated lining in all directions, which does the melting. These furnaces are called indirect arc rotating furnaces and *Detroit rockers*. The arc does not come in contact with the charge.

The major manufacturer of this type of furnace is Kuhlman Electric, Detroit. The Detroit rocker is a popular nonferrous melting unit.

arch brick Tapered refractory bricks used to construct a furnace or kiln-arched roof. The two most common sizes are the Number 1 and Number 2 arch (Fig. A-14). By selecting the correct combination of straight brick, splits, and Number 1 and Number 2 arch brick, you can build the desired arch radius.

arsenic trioxide AS_2O_3, also known as *white arsenic*. Used as an alloying ingredient in producing steel and added to antimonial leads, alloys, and white metal bearings. Used as a hardener and to increase fluidity. When added to copper, it increases the annealing temperature for use as radiators. When added to lead it changes the surface tension and permits formation of perfectly spherical shot when dropped from a shot tower. It is usually colored pink to identify it as a poison.

artificial sand Silica sand made by grinding up silical rock and grading it.

atmospheric feeder The theory behind the atmospheric feeder is that upon solidifying and shrinking, the casting forms a partial vacuum in the mold cavity (Fig. A-15). If a connection can be made with the liquid metal in the riser (during this time and action) to the atmosphere, the *atmospheric pressure* will assist in feeding the casting and prevent *shrinkage cavities* due to lack of feed metal. It is a function of differential pressures. By placing a dry sand core extending into a feed riser or gate, you prevent the solidifying skin from closing the liquid metal off from the atmosphere, allowing the atmosphere to exert its pressure to assist in feeding the casting. This system is widely used in steel castings,

BOTH 3½"

NUMBER 1

NUMBER 2

Arc bricks Number 1 and Number 2.

and the author has had great success with large manganese bronze castings using this method.

This method is the principle behind *churning* a riser with an iron bar to affect feed. The object is to keep the riser open to the atmospheric pressure as long as possible. This system has been the subject of several patents by the late George Batty, Henry Phillips, and John Williams.

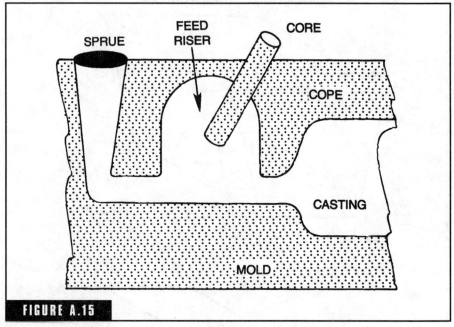

FIGURE A.15

Atmospheric feeder.

auto oxidation   The principle behind the oil oxygen process of core making. It is a form of oxidation by which drying oils absorb oxygen and polymerize the oil to a solid. The process is accelerated by heat and oxygen bearing materials—*perborates, percarbonates,* and *peroxides.*

autogenous heat treating   Shaking out the casting as soon as it has solidified, scraping off the sand, and letting it cool on the foundry floor in a draft. The cooling can be speeded up with a water spray.

autogenous welding   Pouring hot metal into a defect in a casting in hopes it will weld and become part of the parent metal. This is also called *burning in.* It is a hit-or-miss deal at any rate. The hotter the casting being repaired the better chance you have of establishing a good homogenous weld.

babbitt   The original Babbitt, named after its inventor, was 88.9 percent tin, 7.4 percent antimony, and 3.7 percent copper with a melting temperature of 462 F. Used for machinery bearings. However, today there is a large family of tin base alloys called babbitt. Any white alloy used for bearings is currently called babbitt.

babbitt anchors   A tin form filled with baked core sand used to cast an undercut cavity in a casting where a babbitt bearing is going to be poured (cast) (Fig. B-1). The cavity made in the casting provides a lock to hold the babbit in position. The anchors have metal springs to hold them in place in the green sand mold during casting. They can be purchased in diameters from ⅜ inches to 1¼ inches and rectangular from ½ × 1¼ × ³⁄₁₆ inch deep to ⅞ × 3½ × ⅜ inch deep.

back draft   A reverse taper on the vertical surface of a pattern which prevents the removal of the pattern from the mold.

backing board   A second bottom board used to lay the cope over on its back for removing a loose pattern, repair, etc.

backing sand   Foundry floor or system sand used to back or complete a mold after the pattern is covered with a facing sand—new or finer sand, or a facing mix such as #10 facing. (One part sea coal, 10 parts new molding sand with or without an added binder such as *goulac*, wheat flour, etc.) In order to conserve sand and materials on large molds when molding with no-bake or CO_2 sand, the pattern is faced with the no-bake or CO_2 and set, then backed or finished off with floor sand.

baffle plate furnace   A refractory wall in a fire box or furnace to deflect or change the direction of the flame (Fig. B-2). It is also called a *bag wall* or arch baffle. In a reverberatory furnace it is installed at the far end just before the stack, causing the flame to swing back toward the burner or reverberate. In down-draft kilns it directs the flame and

FIGURE B.1

Babbitt anchors.

FIGURE B.2

Baffle plate.

heat upward into the arch to prevent it from heading straight out of the stack.

baffle plate pouring basin Baffle plates are sometimes used in a special type of skimmer type pouring basin (Fig. B-3). This type of runner basin is made up of a cast iron runner box divided into four compartments. The theory is that each compartment allows the slag, dirt, and scum to float to the top of the metal and gives the metal four chances to rid itself of foreign inclusions. When it reaches the sprue, you have only clean metal. The author has constructed various versions of this basin based on a skimmer with a continuous tapped cupola spout. I have had great success,

FIGURE B.3

Baffle plate pouring basin.

especially in pouring large gray iron and bronze castings. The cast iron runner box is lined with loam or monolithic refractory material, blacked, and thoroughly dried. The time it takes to make this type of rig is well worth it.

bag house   A large chamber for holding bags used in the filtration of gasses from a furnace to recover metal oxides, fly ash, and other solids suspended in the gasses. In reality it is a large vacuum cleaner. The bags are made of various materials from cloth to high-temperature ceramic fibers. Aside from the recovery of metal oxides which might have a value, the EPA requires a bag house on many operations as air pollution devices. Bag houses are used alone or in conjunction with electrical precipitators and various washing devices. The exhaust gasses usually have to be cooled down quite a bit prior to entering the bag house to prevent the bags from melting or burning up.

bail   The hoop connection between a ladle and crane hook (Fig. B-4).

baked core   A dry sand core that has been baked to set the binder. A simple oil sand core must be baked at 350 to 400 F. to oxidize the oil and cement the grains of sand together. The core stays together during the casting operation long enough for the metal to take a set. The heat from the cooling casting breaks down the binder (burns it up), destroying its bond and allowing the core to collapse.

A bail.

baked permeability   The property of a baked core cooled to room temperature to pass through those gasses formed while pouring the molten metal into the mold. These gasses must be vented away from the casting through the core vents.

baked strength   The compressive, sheer, tensile strength of a baked core or mold. A measure of its tenacity to a breaking force. The baked strength is far greater than its green unbaked strength.

baking cycle   The time required to bake an oil sand core. Minimum baking cycle in a conventional oven ranges from a minimum of two hours to four to six hours. This will vary with the mix, size, and type of core being baked. The cooling time should also be taken into consideration when planning a schedule in order to have cores to the molders on time. Everything must be considered—inspection, gluing, mudding, sizing, etc.

balance core   A core with only one point of suspension or print (Fig. B-5). The core print is made long enough to have sufficient purchase in the mold to prevent it from moving during casting.

ball mill   A cylindrical device that is revolved. It is partly filled with iron or ceramic (porcelain) balls for grinding or mixing sand or other materials. Widely used in hard-rock mining to reduce the ore-carrying materials to a fine mesh to facilitate the removal of the ore. Ball-mill interiors are often lined with various abrasive-resistant materials.

FIGURE B.5

A balance core.

FIGURE B.6

The base block.

bank sand   Sedimentary sand deposits containing less than 5 percent clay.

base block   Also known as a *pedestal block*, the base block is used to support the crucible in the furnace (Fig. B-6). The base block should be made of the same material as the crucible and be the same diameter as the bottom of the crucible it supports—9 inches in height or of such height that the centerline of the burner is at the junction of the crucible and block.

base exchange of clay   Clay type binders have the ability to exchange some of their ions with other chemicals, such as methylene blue. When the base exchange of a given clay is decreased so is its bonding power. Baroid Chemicals Inc. sells a kit used to determine the amount of effective sand binder in molding sands by methylene blue.

basic   A chemical term referring to any material which gives an alkaline reaction. In a melting furnace with the innerlining and bot-

Basic flask.

tom composed of a basic material such as crushed and burned
dolomite, magnesite or *magnesite bricks*, and using a basic slag,
the reaction is called *basic melting*.

basic flask The top frame of the flask is called the *cope* and the bottom frame is called the *drag* (Fig. B-7). In some molding operations you need one or more sections between the cope and the
drag. These sections are called *cheeks*.

   The pins and guides that are used to hold the sections together can be purchased in a wide variety of types and configurations, round and half round, double round, and vee shaped.
Single, double, or triple vee shapes can be combined together
with matching guides. Both pins and guides have attached
mounting plates by which they can be bolted, screwed, or
welded to the halves, making up a complete flask set.

basic pig iron A special high phosphorous, low sulphur, low silicon
pig iron made for open hearth steel making.

bath Refers to the molten metal on the hearth of a furnace during the
melting process.

battens Wooden bars or strips attached to patterns for rigidity and to
prevent distortion during ramming of the mold (Fig. B-8). Thin
flat patterns are often stiffened with battens for strength after the

FIGURE B.8

Battens.

mold is made. The recess left in the mold by the battens is stopped off with a core or molding sand and sleeked smooth. *Stiffeners*, runner tears on bottom boards, follow boards, etc., are often called *battens*.

bauxite An ore of aluminum, moderately pure hydrated alumina $A1_2O_3 \cdot 2H_2O$. Theoretically 74 percent alumina. Bauxite has a very high melting point (1820 C.) and can be used directly as a refractory material.

bay The longitudinal division of a foundry floor (Fig. B-9). The area between the bays is called the *gangway* or *gangways*. The various sizes of castings produced are usually divided into bays.

bayberry wax A wax made from bayberries—an old-timer in the foundry. It is used as a liquid pattern parting by dissolving it in white gasoline. The pattern is coated and when the gasoline evaporates, a hard thin coating of bayberry wax is left on the pattern. It is also used to coat cast iron castings to prevent rusting and as a molder's shovel coating to prevent sand from adhering to the shovel.

beam and sling The tackle arrangement used with a crane for turning over a cope or drag of a mold prior to assembly (Fig. B-10). Large flasks are fitted with *roll-over trunnions* over which the bails are placed to roll-over the flask section. The beam has notches to adjust the distance between bails for the various lengths of flasks.

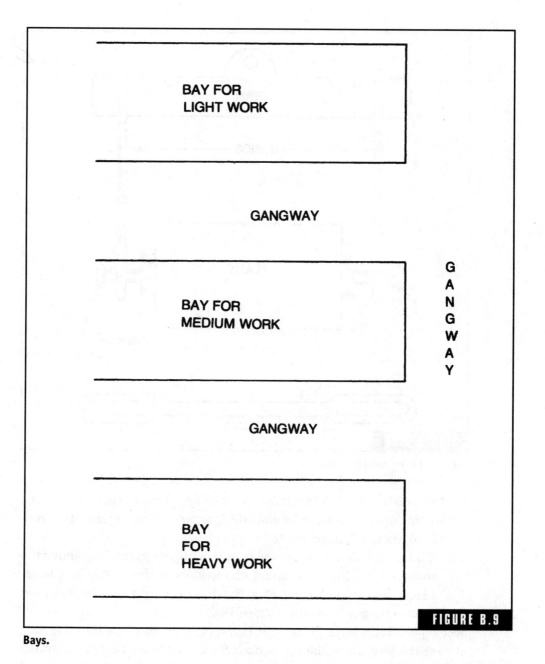

FIGURE B.9

Bays.

The beam should be constructed so that the slings cannot be jarred off the beam when in use. A hook on the ends of the beam adds to the safety factor.

Beam and sling arrangement.

bearing metals   Any metals used as bearings, ferrous and nonferrous. There are hundreds of metals designated as bearing metals—from babbitts to oil-impregnated coppers.

bed   The initial charge of coke placed in a cupola extending above the tuyeres on which the metal charges are melted. The bed is replaced and maintained at a fixed height by the coke between metal charges (continuous melting).

bedding in   With large patterns it is the practice to place the drag side of the pattern in the pit or drag flask on a bed of lightly rammed sand (Fig. B-11). Ram and tuck the sand under the pattern and around the sides, working up to drag parting line. The pattern is usually lifted out prior to making up the cope so that the drag mold can be checked for soft spots and also for the parting. When satisfied that the drag is right, the pattern is returned and the cope made up in the usual manner. This system eliminates the

FIGURE B.11

The process of bedding-in.

necessity of rolling over the drag—an advantage with the production of large heavy castings. In some cases the pattern is supported during the bedding-in operation with an *overcastle*. The overcastle holds the pattern in the correct position during ramming and it is then removed to make up the cone.

beeswax Beeswax is used in wax fillet formulas and various investment waxes. It is a long chain ester, myriad palmitate, and cerotic acid with a melting point of approximately 145 F.

bench lifter A simple steel tool with a right-angled square foot on one end of a flat bent blade (Fig. B-12).

This tool repairs sand molds and lifts out any tramp or loose sand that might have fallen into a pocket. To remove dirt from a

FIGURE B.12

Bench lifter.

FIGURE B.13

Bench rammer.

pocket that will not blow out with the bellows, you simply spit on the heel of the lifter, reach down, and pick it up, then wipe off the heel and go back and slick the spot down a bit.

bench molder A molder who produces small molds made on a molder's bench.

bench molds Small hand-rammed molds made on the molder's bench that can be handled by one man. When they get too large, they are made on the floor and called *floor molds*.

bench rammer Made of oiled maple. You can buy one or turn one on a lathe and bandsaw the peen end into a wedge shape (Fig. B-13). The butt end is used to ram the sand tightly around the inside perimeter of the flask to prevent the cope or drag mold from falling out when either half is moved, rolled over, or lifted.

bentonite A hydrous silicate of alumina, a colloidal clay derived from volcanic ash. It is employed as a binder in foundry sands and is added to naturally bonded sands to increase their green and dry strength. It is also used as an oil well mud and has numerous other commercial uses. A typical green sand formula uses bentonite as the principal binder. By composition it is 14 parts silica or heap sand, 6 parts bank sand, 1 part air float sea coal, and 1 part bentonite.

Bentonite is an unusual type of clay in that it swells 15 to 20 times its volume in water.

Two basic types are sold for foundry use—southern and western. The basic chemical difference between the two is that the western bentonite is higher in soda, alumina, and chemical water (combined H_2O) and lower in potash, lime, magnesia, and iron. Southern bentonite has less baked and hot strength. It collapses more readily, making it more suitable as a binder for light aluminum and bronze castings, where desirable. With steel and heavy castings, western bentonite will give the added hot strength and retard premature collapsibility where needed.

It is a common practice to use the two blended together to produce the desired results for a particular type and weight of castings. The most common blend appears to be 50/50.

TABLE B.1 Beryllium Pouring Range.

Per Cent Beryllium	Pouring Range
1.90 to 2.15	1900/2100°F.
2.50 to 2.75	1850/1900°F
.45 to .60	2050/2200°F.

beryllium bronze An alloy of copper and beryllium usually not more than 3 percent beryllium. Also called *beryllium copper*, it is used to produce strong mechanical parts, locomotive bearings, plastic molds, non-sparking tools, springs, etc. Beryllium bronze is defined as an alloy containing over 2 percent of beryllium or beryllium plus other metals other than copper (over 2 percent).

No flux is necessary in melting beryllium bronze. Beryllium itself is a good deoxidizer. Some melters use a dry charcoal cover when melting. The pouring range varies somewhat with the percent beryllium in the alloy being cast (Table B-1).

Beryllium bronze should be handled like aluminum bronze because it has a tendency to dross.

FIGURE B.14

Bessemer ladle.

BLAST
AIR

TUYERES

LINING

FIGURE B.15

SIDE BLOW CONVERTER

Bessemer process.

bessemer ladle A steel ladle lined with refractory material and having one or more stopper and nozzle systems for bottom pouring (Fig. B-14). The stopper is attached to the end of the stopper rod, which is insulated with refractory sleeves. The stopper plug is seated in the nozzle when closed. The nozzle is opened to pour or teem by raising the stopper rod by a lever attached to the outside of the ladle and the top of the stopper rod.

bessemer process A steel-making process that blows air through or over the molten pig iron in a converter, oxidizing the silicon and carbon (Fig. B-15). The carbon is reduced to carbon monoxide and liberated as gas and the oxides of maganese and silicon form with the slag. The reactions which take place are exothermic and no additional heat is necessary in the refining process, which is called the *blow*. It takes approximately 20 minutes to blow a heat. When the heat is finished it consists of some iron oxide, .03 percent silicon and manganese and approximately .06

percent carbon. The desired carbon content is adjusted by adding the proper amount of cupola iron and adjusting the composition with ferro alloys. The converter is mounted on trunnions so that it can be tipped for charging, blowing, and pouring. The air is fed to the tuyeres through one of the hollow trunnions. In the side-blow converter the air is blown across the top face of the charge and the angle is adjusted by the operator. In the bottom blow converter the air is blown in through the charge from the bottom.

binder   Any material used to hold a mold or core material together in the green or dry state such as cereal, pitch, resin, oil, sulphate, water glass, latex, etc. In an oil sand core, the oil is the binder. When baked, it cements or glues the sand grains together.

blacking or mold wash scab   A case where the blacking or wash on the mold or core, when heated, breaks away and lifts off the surface like a leaf and is retained in or on the metal. The cause is a poor binder in the wash, an improperly dried wash, a poor wash formula, or all of these possibilities.

blackstrap foundry molasses   A heavy, nonedible molasses which has been treated chemically to prevent it from souring or fermenting. It is used as a binder in core and mold washes, sprays, pastes, dough rolls, and core daubing. Also used in skin-dried work by tempering the facing sand with a mixture of 1 part molasses to 10 parts water. It is a good spray at 10 to 1 for green sand cores which have been dried at 350 to 400 F. Sprayed while hot, it gives the core a nice firm skin.

blacking scab   A casting defect. It is caused by mold blacking or wash flaking off the mold surface due to sand expansion and being retained in or on the surface of the casting. The cause is usually due to an excessively strong bond in the wash or not enough cushion material in the sand or wash. It is also related to *backing holes*, which are irregular-shaped surface cavities containing carbonaceous matter.

blast   The wind or air supplied to a cupola, converter, or furnace to support combustion.

blast cleaning   Cleaning (removing sand or oxide scale) by impinging action of sand, grit, or shot projected by air, water, or centrifugal force.

blast gate   A sliding metal gate used to adjust the flow of air to the cupola wind belt, and the air to burners on some types of nonfer-

FIGURE B.16

Blast gate.

rous furnaces (Fig. B-16). There are two schools of thought as to where it should go. The first school says in the blast pipe proper and the second school says in a dog leg from the blast pipe to spill the air from the blower. Thus when closed, the air flows fully through the blast pipe and when open, less flows through the blast pipe. With the second arrangement the blower operates at a constant speed and load. With the first, when it is closed or partially closed there is a back pressure on the blower.

bleeder A defect caused by shaking the casting out too soon when a portion of it is still liquid. The section runs out, leaving a defect. In extreme cases the entire center section will run out onto the shake-out man's feet.

blended sands Use the suggested sand blends in Table B-2 as a guide in selecting your own basic blends. Start with a good high grade silica, washed, dried, screened, and graded. Adjustments can be made to the base after sufficient tracking is done.

blind riser A blind riser is any feed riser which does not extend through the cope to the atmosphere.

blind risers (foam) Blind risers are formed in a sand mold by using preformed styrofoam spheres and pear shapes which are stuck

TABLE B.2 Suggested Blended Sands.

Substance	Fineness	Permeability
Heavy iron using green or dry sand	61 & 50	80 to 120
Medium iron using green sand	70 & 45	50 to 70
Light squeezer iron, green sand	110 & 80	20 to 30
Stove plate iron, green sand	200 & 160	9 to 17
Heavy green steel, green sand	60 & 35	140 to 290
Heavy steel, dry sand	55 & 40	90 to 250
Light squeezer malleable iron	130 & 95	20 to 40
Heavy malleable iron	80 & 70	40 to 70
Copper and monel	150 & 120	30 to 60
Aluminum	250 & 150	6 to 15
General brass	150 & 120	12 to 20

down on a locating pin on the pattern at the riser site (Fig. B-17). The spheres and pears have a preformed recess which fits down on the locating pin. In operation, the desired size of the sphere or pear is placed on the locator pin and the mold is rammed in the usual manner. When the cope is drawn, the styrofoam blind riser remains in the sand body. The metal poured into the mold vaporizes the styrofoam, forming the riser to feed the casting. It is a common practice to vent the riser form with a ⅛ to ³⁄₁₆ vent wire through the cope. The pin on the pattern should be taller than the depth of the retaining hole in the styrofoam riser form so that the styrofoam shape winds up above the

Foam blind riser.

pattern slightly. The pin length will vary depending upon whether the mold is hand rammed or rammed on a squeezer and how close the styrofoam form is to the top of the cope.

Spheres can be purchased in diameters from 2½ inches to 6 inches, or in pear shapes from 2½ inches to 6 inches. They may

FIGURE B.18

A positive pressure blower.

be purchased from Frostee Foam Co., Box L, Antioch, IL 60002. Or, you can fabricate your own.

blister A shallow blow covered over with a thin film of metal.

bloating The swelling of any refractory material due to excessive heat or carbon monoxide in the furnace.

blowers Blowers come in all sizes and shapes (Figs. B-18 and B-19). They are rated in cubic feet per minute at various delivery pressures. The most common type of blower is the *centrifugal fan type*—a cast or fabricated case which turns a paddle type of impellor. The design of these blowers varies considerably from manufacturer to manufacturer and also with the intended use for a particular blower. Blowers are often called *fans* in the foundry. In some blowers the impellor itself is *shrouded* on both sides with the idea that this increases its efficiency, both in pressure and volume. This question is up for grabs.

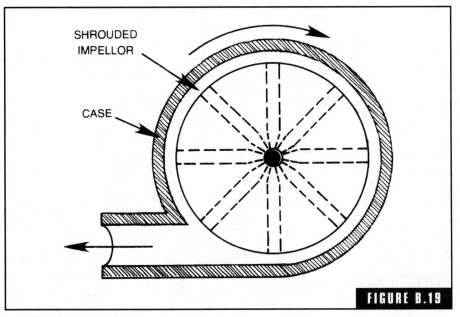

Centrifugal blower.

The shrouds are riveted or screwed to the edges of the blades. Some blowers are compound. One stage delivers air to another stage, upping the output.

The other common type of foundry blower is the *positive pressure blower*. This type of blower has two lobe-shaped impellors which are geared to each other to maintain an exact relation between them at all times. They do not touch each other or the case, but are fitted so closely that it is impossible for the air, once taken in, to pass back through the intake.

The positive pressure blower is superior to the centrifugal fan type for supplying air to a cupola because the pressure remains constant regardless of conditions in the cupola.

blowing of cores Cores are often produced on machines called *core blowers*, which vary greatly in size, capacity, and mechanization (Fig. B-20). However, regardless of the blower design and size, the principal is the same. The sand mix is blown into the core box by introducing air at high pressure on the sand in a reservoir, thus blowing the sand into the core box through blow holes in the top of the core box and through the blow plate on the sand

FIGURE B.20

Blowing of cores.

reservoir. The sand traveling at a high velocity is abruptly stopped by the cavity walls of the box, thus ramming itself. The air continues through the sand and out the vents in the core box.

The machine is provided with the mechanical arrangements for moving the reservoir to fill it and clamping the box vertically and horizontally as needed during the blow cycle. The controls are tied together in such a way that the blow cannot be made until the box is in position and properly clamped. The reservoir is exhausted prior to releasing the box.

blows   Round to elongated holes caused by the generation or accumulation of entrapped gas or air. The usual cause of blow holes is:

- sand rammed too hard (decreasing the permeability)
- permeability too low for the job
- sand and core too wet (excessive moisture)
- insufficient or closed-off core vent
- green core not properly dried
- incompletely dried core or mold wash

- insufficient mold venting

- insufficient hydrostatic pressure (cope too short)

- cope bars too close to mold cavity

- wet gagger or soldier too close to mold cavity

- poor grain distribution

Any combination of hot and cold materials leads to condensation as a hot core is set in a mold or vice versa. A cold chill or hot chill will cause blows, as well as wet or rusty chaplets.

blowy metal When a metal is gassed in melting to the point that it kicks and churns in the furnace or ladle, it is referred to as blowy metal and should not be poured unless it can be saved by degassing or deoxidizing. With most metals simply re-melting again under the correct conditions will correct the problem. Metal poured into a wet or incompletely dried ladle will kick and blow. Trying to dry a ladle with hot metal just won't work.

bobble The casting will resemble a cold shut or look like it was poured short. The problem was a slacked or interrupted pour. When pouring a casting, the metal must be poured at a constant choked velocity. If you slack off or reduce the velocity, you can cause this defect. If you interrupt the pour, start—stop—and start, only for a second you may cause a bobble. A great percentage of lost castings is caused by pouring improperly.

bolted cement A super fine *Portland cement* used for *print back* or *return facing*. In green sand casting where an exceptionally fine surface detail is required, as in casting art work, plaques, and grave markers the practice is to draw the pattern, dust the mold cavity lightly with bolted cement, and immediately return the pattern to the cavity and tap down. Then you redraw the pattern. This process sets the cement smoothly in the cavity. The mold is closed and poured in the usual manner. If done properly, you can produce some very fine work.

bolted charcoal Finely ground charcoal used in a *dust bag* as a shake-on mold facing and in print back work. Sometimes it is combined with graphite. It can be used as a parting dust. *Granulated charcoal* is used as a cover on the surface of molten metal, especially brass, to prevent metal oxidation from the products of combustion.

FIGURE B.21

Bolted cores.

bolted cores The practice of bolting cores together, when it is felt that pasting could fail due to the pressure involved in pouring a particular (design) casting (Fig. B-21). The cores are drilled and countersunk or provisions are made in the core box to form the bolt holes. After bolting, the countersink recess must be filled and mudded. Separate cores can be made and baked and simply glued in place. The joint is then mudded.

bolting pads A pad or boss-type projection on a casting, which if not properly designed or chilled, will produce a hot spot and localized shrinkage at that point due to the abrupt change of metal thickness (Fig. B-22). *Hot spots* are also caused by raised pattern letters and incorrect rib design. If the bolting pads are large enough they can be cored out to prevent localized shrinkage.

bonding action of clay in molding sand Although most clay is sticky when moist, the sand grains of the mold are held in place by clay wedges that hold the sand grains in place, as in a stone wall—the old wedge and block theory (Fig. B-23).

PREFERRED
DESIGN

FIGURE B.22

Bolting pads.

bonding clays A large family of clays used in bonding molding sands composed of one or more of the minerals kaolinite, illite, and montomorillonite (Bentonite).

Clays come about from the weathering of various types of volcanic ash. Clays are composed of minute crystalline flakes of constituent minerals. Generally the smaller the size of the particles of the clay minerals, the greater the bonding power.

The bonding action of clay in molding sand.

booking Booking refers to green and dry sand cores (Fig. B-24). Using a full-core box, ramming each half box with sand and striking both off level with the box and closing them together like a book brings the mating surfaces at the parting line together. Then remove one half box and place a *drier* in place of the half box that was removed. Roll the remaining half box and drier over and remove the box leaving the core resting in the drier for baking. In the case of a green sand core on a half arbor, remove the core from the box.

Flasks with *roll-off hinges,* where the cope is opened and closed like a book, are referred to as *booked molds.*

borax Hydrous sodium borate used in the foundry as a flux in melting metals.

boric acid Also called boracic acid $B_2O_3 \cdot 3H_2O$, made by adding hydrochloric acid or sulphuric acid to borax and crystallizing. Its

Booking process.

main foundry use is as a protective agent in magnesium molding sands usually in combination with sulphur or sulphur and fluoride salts. It works to inhibit the action of water vapor upon the hot metal (Magnesium).

Use 3 to 6 percent by weight depending upon the section thickness of the casting and the sand. The more massive the casting, the greater the amount needed. Also the injection of a small amount of sulphur dioxide gas into the mold just before pouring helps to prevent oxidation of the surface of the casting.

bott A blunt cone of clay used to stop off the flow of iron from the tap hole of a cupola or air furnace. There are many mixes formulated by the melter. One such mix is 5 parts molding sand, 5 parts clay, and 1 part wheat flour.

Some tenders, after forming the bott and placing it on the *bott rod*, sprinkle a coating of coal dust or graphite on the bott with a shake bag. This seems to help release the bott when tapping, providing there is a parting between the tap hole and bott.

bott stick More often called a *bott rod*. It is a rod ¾ inch in diameter 8 feet long with a 2-inch diameter plate welded to the business end and a loop handle on the other (Fig. B-25). It is used to place the bott firmly into the tap hole of a cupola or air furnace to shut off the flow of metal. The bott is stuck to the flat plate by wetting the

FIGURE B.25

A bolt rod.

plate and pressing it firmly into the tap hole, coming in at a slight angle above the metal stream. When in place, the bar is twisted and slid downward to release the bott from the rod.

The English bott rod is domed on the end. The theory is that a large surface area will hold the bott and there will be less likelihood of losing the bott (of it falling off).

bottom board   The board used to support the sand mold until the mold is poured. It is constructed like the molding board, but need not be smooth—only level and stiff. Bottom boards from 10 × 16 inches to 18 × 30 inches should be made of 1 inch thick lumber with two cleats made of 2 × 3 inch stock. Bottom boards 48 × 30 inches use 1½-inch thick lumber with three cleats made of 3 × 3 inch stock. Bottom boards 50 to 80 inches use 2-inch thick lumber with four to five cleats made of 3 × 4 inch stock.

bottom pouring   Filling the mold cavity from the bottom by simple displacement by means of gates entering the bottom of the mold from the runner.

bottom sand   The molding sand rammed against the bottom doors of a cupola to form the sloping hearth. Also called the *crucible bottom*.

Some brass melters ram a molding sand bottom in a brass furnace around the pedestal block. This makes it easy to clean out the bottom for maintenance or to remove a spill in the bottom.

bouyouzos   A hydrometer calibrated in grams per liter. The hydrometer shows the number of grams still in suspension at the time it is read. Used to determine the size distribution of small particles.

brads   Small, usually not headed, wire nails used in pattern and model work. When headed they are then called *flathead wire nails*. Brads run from ¼ inch long, 22 gauge to 3 inches long, 12 gauge.

brasses   Red brass, leaded red brass, semi-red brass, leaded semi-red brass, yellow brass, leaded yellow brass, high strength yellow brass, leaded high strength brass, silicon brass, tin brass, tin nickel brass, nickel brass (nickel silver), and leaded nickel brass.

brazing   When you join metals by fusion of a nonferrous alloy that has a melting point above 800 F. but at a lower fusion point than the metals being joined.

FIGURE B.26

The breast of the refractory portion of a cupola or air furnace.

The three basic types of brazing methods are *torch brazing, furnace brazing,* and *dip* or *flux brazing.* Torch brazing is done with a torch and rod (as filler metal). For furnace brazing and dip brazing, the parts are assembled and the filler metal applied as wire, washers, clips, and bands. Or they may be integrally bonded.

Silver soldering is actually silver brazing. When you get below 800 F. melting point (with your filler metal), you are soft soldering.

breast The refractory portion of a cupola or air furnace in which the *tap hole* is located (Fig. B-26). It is located in the front of the cupola and on each side of an air furnace usually equipped with a *pouring spout*, which extends outward from the furnace to direct the stream of metal from the furnace into the receiving ladle.

breeze Coke and coal screenings used to vent large cores and molds (Fig. B-27). Widely used in large sweep work and large skeleton (pattern) work.

bridge chaplet Bridge chaplets are made of 20 gauge cold rolled steel and hot dip tinned or copper plated (Fig. B-28). An economical chaplet for use in castings where the conditions under which the chaplets are used are not severe.

FIGURE B.27

A large core filled with breeze.

Brinnell hardness tester A device (press) which presses a 10mm diameter steel ball against a metal sample or casting at a known or given load—500 Kg for nonferrous, 3000 for ferrous. The diameter of the indention made on the specimen in question is measured and the hardness number is taken from a table computing the hardness.

FIGURE B.28

Bridge chaplet.

briquets Compact or cylindrical-shaped blocks formed of finely divided materials. They are formed under pressure with various binders in order to increase their density and reduce their loss due to oxidation and draft in melting or treating a bath. Includes borings, chips, ferro alloys, silicon carbide, charcoal dust, coal dust, etc.

broken casting Often caused by improper design or improper filleting along with improper handling anywhere along the line. Copper base castings, red brass, yellow brass, etc., are known as *hot short*—they break easily when hot. Thus, if the casting is shaken out of the mold before it has cooled sufficiently, it can break very easily. A mold or core which has a too high *hot strength* will not give or collapse to give the casting room to move as it shrinks. It will then break the casting.

bronzes Tin bronze, leaded tin bronze, high leaded tin bronze, leaded bronze, nickel bronze, leaded nickel bronze, aluminum bronze, silicon bronze, and beryllium bronze.

Brunelli strainer Invented by an Italian foundry engineer (Fig. B-29). His claim is that his pouring system does away with the necessity of risers or feeders on large castings. He also claims the metal entering the mold is oxidized in proportion to the volume of air with which it comes in contact.

buckle An expansion scab, an indentation on the face of the casting caused by the sand being rammed too hard or not containing sufficient combustible material such as wood flour or sea coal (Fig. B-30). The heat from the metal causes the sand to expand and it cannot do so without buckling. It is a very common defect in full-mold investment casting when insufficient gating is used and the mold fills too slowly, subjecting the mold walls to the heat for too long a period of time, causing excessive expansion and spalling.

FIGURE B.29

Brunelli strainer.

FIGURE B.30

A buckle.

bulb (paste)   A short-snouted rubber bulb used to apply core paste to the joints of cores for pasting them together (Fig. B-31). Used to run a paste line on the drag of small molds to help prevent a run-out at the joint and over the print on cores to stop metal from running over the ends and stopping off the core vent. Also used to put paste on the handle of the finishing trowel in the back pocket of the molder. When he reaches for his trowel, he will get a good grip.

FIGURE B.31

A short-snouted rubber bulb.

bulb sponge The bulb sponge consists of a rubber bulb with a hollow brass stem terminating in a soft brush (Fig. B-32). The stem is pulled out and the bulb filled about three-fourths full of water. The stem is then replaced. The bulb sponge is used to swab around the pattern prior to drawing it, in the way the flax swab is used for floor molding. The bulb is gently squeezed to keep the brush wet while swabbing.

bull ladle A two-man ladle for carrying and pouring metal. It has a shank with two handles. When ladles get much over 200 pounds capacity, they become *crane* or *trolley ladles*.

bungs A section of a removable arch roof. In large air furnaces and kilns the roof is very often made by using cast iron frames that carry a section of the arched roof. The frames have eyes for lifting them off with a crane for maintenance, charging, etc.

burned sand Molding sand in which the clay portion has been destroyed by the heat of the metal.

button head chaplet Round-headed chaplet with a forged or upset head.

butt ramming Ramming the cope or drag with a butt-shape rammer, either by hand or pneumaticly. The butt rammer is the flat circular end of the rammer.

Bulb sponge.

Bull ladle.

Butt raming is done with a butt-shaped rammer.

cabbage head A puffed riser head caused by badly gassed metal (Fig. C-1). In copper casting the molder usually pours what is known as a *text cock*—a sprue cut into a box rammed with sand. If a cabbage head forms, the metal is deoxidized again and a second cock is poured. This process is repeated until the cock pulls (shrinks); then and only then is the mold poured. Very good insurance when pouring a large mold. A good practice with any metal which is subjected to gassing.

calcium boride An alloy of calcium and boron CaB_6 used as a deoxidizer of nonferrous metals. Often the prime ingredient in a commercial deoxidizer.

calcium carbide Produced by fusing lime and coke in the electric furnace. When calcium carbide is put into water (or gets wet) it produces acetylene gas and a residue of slaked lime. Widely used as a welding and cutting gas when combined with an oxygen oxy/acetylene torch.

calcium manganese-silicon An alloy used as a scavenger for oxides, gasses, and nonmetallic impurities in steel.

calcium molybdate A crushed product of lime, molybdenum, iron, and silica used to add molybdenum to iron and steel heats.

calcium silicon An alloy of calcium, silicon, and iron used as a deoxidizer and degassifier for steel. Also known as *calcium silicide*.

calcium sulfate The principal binder used in full investment molds for casting nonferrous metals. Gypsum, when calcined, is called *plaster of paris*. Typical formula for plaster bonded investment is 2 parts plaster, 3 parts silicon flour, olivine flour or crushed red bricks.

camber As a defect, a warped casting. It is caused by any number of problems: incorrect number and size of ribs; a design which contributes to differential stress; flask bars too close to the pattern; sand too strong in green, dry, or hot strength; or insufficient combustibles in the sand (wood flour etc.).

FIGURE C.1

Cabbage head.

camber (pattern)   A pattern is intentionally bowed, sprung, or faked to prevent a camber defect (warp) (Fig. C-2). The pattern is cambered in the opposite direction of the anticipated warp. If done correctly the casting will come out true.

   In patterns for cast iron oil pans and sumps for tractor engines, the pattern is often cambered in order to produce a straight flat surface where the pan mates up with the engine.

compound camber   A camber which is both bent and twisted.

captive foundry   A foundry that is part of a manufacturing company or operation which consumes its entire output and produces no castings for outside customers.

carbide   A compound of carbon with one or more metallic elements such as silicon carbide, aluminum carbide, etc.

carbon dioxide   A colorless, odorless gas, CO_2. Also called *carbonic anhydride* when solid; dry ice. It is used to cure (set the binder) when making molds and cores using silicate of soda (water glass)

CASTING PRODUCED
FROM CAMBERED
PATTERN

CAMBERED PATTERN

EXAGGERATED CAMBER

FIGURE C.2

Chamber patterns are internationally bowed or cambeed to prevent defects.

as the binder by passing the gas through the sand and silicate of soda mix.

carbon equivalent The relationship of the total carbon, silicon, and phosphorous content in a gray iron expressed by the formula:

$$\frac{C.E. = T.C. + Si\ percent + P\ percent}{3}$$

T.C. = Total carbon - Si = Silicon - P = Phosphorous

carbon (in gray iron) Carbon in gray iron is in two forms, combined (in solution) and free (graphite flakes). The ratio of combined to free carbon is controlled by the charge make up and silicon content. Silicon throws the combined carbon out into the iron in the form of free carbon. Strength properties are improved by the reduction of free carbon flakes and their uniform distribution. The smaller the flake size the better. The silicon lowers the solvent power of iron for carbon.

carbon steel Steel that owes its properties chiefly to its carbon content. It is without substantial amounts of other alloying elements. Also called *ordinary steel*, *straight carbon steel*, and *plain carbon steel*.

card pattern A number of small patterns fastened together by gates or to themselves (Fig. C-3). Bearing caps and clutch dog patterns are

FIGURE C.3

CORE PRINT

BREAK AWAY

CORE PRINT

PATTERN

Card pattern.

often carded and cast as a unit and sawed apart to produce the upper and lower member.

Bearing cap carded patterns have the advantage that the bore is machined before the castings are parted. In this way the radius of the upper and lower member is exactly the same as being machined at the same time on the same center.

card of patterns When several different loosely gated patterns are assembled as a unit to be molded in the same flask.

car oven A large core or mold drying oven with tracks on which a large car (containing the cores or molds) can be pushed (rolled) into the oven for drying.

cast gate The gate through which the metal enters the mold cavity. Also a gate cast to a metal pattern as part of the pattern.

cast steel Any object made by pouring molten steel into molds.

casting design An item to be cast must be designed with the selected casting method in mind. This requires a good working knowledge of casting methods and practices. If not, the foundry and pattern maker should be consulted; this will result in a great saving to the designer. It involves many, many factors such as metal selection, pattern equipment, casting method, finishing, etc. The casting cost can often be greatly increased by overlooking some simple element.

casting ladle Any device used to transfer molten metal into a mold, as opposed to a *transfer ladle*, which is used to feed the casting ladles.

casting strains Internal strains resulting from the cooling of a casting plus residual stresses. Strains in castings can be removed by various heat treating and stress relieving techniques. The design, along with the particular metal poured, plays a great part in strains and stresses in a casting.

cast structure   The structure of a cast alloy consisting of cored dendrites and, in some alloys, a network of other constituents. The structure is on a microscopic scale. A micrograph structural study.

cast weldments   The reduction of a complicated casting into two or more simple castings, welded together to produce the desired part.

caustic dip   A solution of sodium hydroxide (lye) and water used to clean the surface of a metal. Bright dip for aluminum castings. Also used as an etch with aluminum alloys to reveal the microstructure.

cavitation erosion   Erosion of a material due to the formation and collapsing of cavities in a liquid at the solid-liquid interface. The principal of ultrasonic cleaning in a liquid.

cement bonded sands   Molds and cores produced by bonding silica sand with HI early cement and air drying for a minimum of 72 hours. Also known as *72 hour sand*. The first cement sand mix was patented by John Smith of Verona, Pennsylvania over 70 years ago. It consisted of 10 parts silica sand and 1 part portland cement moistened to 6 percent moisture with molasses water. It was used to cast both ferrous and nonferrous metals. Still used to some extent today, but largely replaced by furan no-bake mixes.

cementite   The structure with the compound Fe_3C which forms when austenite changes on cooling. The combined carbon structure of cast iron is known as *austenite*.

center line   A well defined gauge line placed on the work or layout to serve as a basis from which dimensions are to be measured.

centrifugal casting   The production of castings by centrifugal force (true centrifugal) where the molten metal is poured into a rotating mold at the axis of rotation and is conveyed by centrifugal force out to the peripheral extremities leaving a hollow casting with the impurities in the center or bore (Fig. C-4). Cast iron and steel pipe are produced by this method, as are bronze bushing stocks.

centrifuging   The process of casting whereby the metal is driven into mold cavities which are located off the center of rotation (Fig. C-5). These can be single or multiple cavities. The mold material

FIGURE C.4

Centrifugal casting.

FIGURE C.5

Centrifuging.

can be metal, rubber, green sand, investment, carbon, etc. Often mistakenly called centrifugal casting.

center line shrinkage A defect which can occur in any metal (Fig. C-6). It is most often found in steel in thin sections, although it is not relegated solely to thin sections. A shrinkage cavity in the center of the casing wall due to the stopping of feed metal.

This shrinkage can be eliminated by tapering the casting to promote directional solidification toward the feed metal or padding. It can be removed by machining or grinding.

The author has seen cases of railroad trucks with centerline shrinkage to the point that they were hollow as if they were

FIGURE C.6

Centerline shrinkage.

cored. They are not scrapped as it is a fact that a casting with centerline shrinkage is serviceable if the load is flexual.

The author cast a very large plaque 6 × 4 feet, which was perfect in all respects except for it is completely hollow centerline shrinkage.

That was some 25 or 26 years ago and it's still hanging on the building. The metal was 88 percent Cu, 10 percent Sn, and 2 percent Zn.

cereal   A bonding material and a cushion material. The most widely used in the foundry is corn flour produced from wet milling of corn starch. The effectiveness of corn flour depends entirely on how it is used. In synthetic sands it works well from ½ percent to 2½ percent by weight. It is widely used in steel sands. The author uses corn flour in nonferrous sands to impart resilience. Corn flour increases dry compression strength, baked permeability, toughness, mulling time, moisture pick up, mold hardness and deformation. It decreases the green permeability, sand expansion, hot compressive strength, and flowability. Cereals are replaced with wood flour to some extent; however, each has its distinct use. Corn flour is very beneficial when you have weak sands and no other additive can eliminate or reduce scabs, rattails, buckles, and similar defects quite as well as 1 per cent to 1½ per cent corn flour added to the facing. It also keeps spalling to a minimum.

chamfer   To bevel a sharp edge (Fig. C-7).

FIGURE C.7

Chamfer.

chamotte   A refractory produced from high alumina clays that have been calcined to a temperature above their softening point.

chaplet clips   Clips used to attach two or more chaplets together when the proper size is not available in your chaplet stock (Fig. C-8).

chaplets   A large family of metal devices, supports, or spacers used to support cores in molds long enough for the metal to solidify without moving or breaking a core during pouring (Fig. C-9.) They burn in and become part of the parent metal. Chaplets are not used when the pattern has sufficient core prints, which serve the same purpose.

charcoal   A highly amorphous carbon fuel produced by heating wood in the absence of oxygen; used widely to melt in the cupola at one time and as a cover material on metal baths, in core and mold washes, etc. At one time all iron was melted using charcoal as a fuel.

charge   The metal placed in a cupola or furnace for melting.

cheek   A section of flask between the cope and the drag sections of a flask to decrease the difficulty of molding an unusual shape or to fill the need for more than one parting line (Fig. C-10).

FIGURE C.8

Chaplet chips.

FIGURE C.9

Chaplets.

Cheek is the section of flask between the cope and drag section.

chill Metallic inserts (usually cast iron) located in the mold to promote rapid cooling at a desired point to make the casting harder at this point or to promote directional solidification and prevent shrinkage at a hot spot which cannot be fed from a riser (Fig. C-11). They can be internal as well as external.

chilled edges A condition (defect) in thin cast iron where the edges of the casting are hard (white iron). (Fig. C-12). The major cause is that the carbon equivalent is too low for the section being cast. If the CE is too high for the section it will *kish* (excessive free graphite at the edges and thin sections).

chill nails Large-headed nails used as internal and external chills (Fig. C-13). Horseshoe nails are widely used due to the head mass. The

Chills are metallic inserts.

FIGURE C.12

Chilled edge.

FIGURE C.13

Chill nails.

nails are pushed into the sand at the point to be chilled. *Fanner chips* are a specially manufactured nail for internal chilling.

chill wash A wash coating applied to external chills to prevent them from kicking and blowing, causing a defect at their point of contact with the casting. These wash coatings include washes of lube oil and graphite, lard oil, red lead and water (dry thoroughly), shellac, and alcohol and resin.

chloration The process of passing chlorine gas through molten magnesium to remove dissolved gasses and trapped oxides (a degassing and refining process).

choking Keeping the pouring basin brimming full from start to finish when pouring a casting.

Christmas tree A single sprue containing many castings formed by a stacked mold.

chrome pickle A pickling solution for dipping magnesium castings; it produces a protective film on the casting and provides a base for painting. It consists of a solution of nitric acid and sodium dichromate.

chromium An elementary metal, Cr, used as an alloy in stainless steels, heat resistant steels, and high strength steels for plating, hard facing ferrous alloys, cast iron, etc.

churning Also called *feeding* or *pumping*. A molder churns the liquid metal in a riser with a wrought iron bar to keep it open and to assist in feeding the casting.

cinder mill A revolving tumbler used to wash, cool, and retrieve good coke and iron from the cupola drop. When the day's heat is over, the bottom doors on the cupola are dropped and the coke and iron remaining drop out. It is quenched with water and sent to the cinder mill.

clamp off A defect caused by the displacement of sand in a mold due to clamping or improper handling of weights. It results in an indentation in the casting surface.

clay tile gates The use of pre-formed gate tiles of ceramic materials with large iron and steel castings to prevent the washing and eroding of the mold and its gating system during pouring. It is basically a plumbing system of ceramic piping, elbows, tees, and splash tiles. These tiles can be purchased in a wide variety of sizes just like plumbing ware.

cleaning castings Removing the sand and oxide scale and shaking out the cores by hand, sand blasting, shot blasting, chemical pickling, etc.

This often represents a good chunk of the cost of producing the casting.

cleavage plane The junction where two independent planes of crystal growth meet and interfere with each other (Fig. C-14). This con-

ELIMINATED
PROPER
DESIGN

FIGURE C.14

Cleavage plane.

dition produces a weak point at the junction. Its primary cause is a sharp edge or junction which is not filleted.

cohesion The force by which various particles are held together. Factors are hot or cold workings of the material and the molecular arrangement due to heat treatment or chemical action.

coke The residue or product left—mainly fixed carbon and ash—produced by heating-heating bituminous coal in the absence of air to 1200 to 1400 C and expelling the volatile matter.

A good grade coal will produce from 1 ton of coal, .7 tons of coke, 11,5000 cubic feet of gas, 12 gallons of tar, 27 pounds ammonium sulphate, 50 gallons of benzol, and .9 gallon of tolluol and naphtha.

Foundry coke should have an ignition point of 1000 F; sulphur, maximum .7 percent; and be strong enough to carry the charges in the cupola. Coke is widely used as the fuel in the blast furnace.

cold chamber die casting In the cold chamber machine the metal is ladled into the shot chamber, not submerged in the molten bath as the hot chamber machines (Fig. C-15).

cold shortness Metals that are brittle at room or low temperatures are called cold short metals.

cold shot Where two streams of metal in a mold fail to weld together. This defect is usually caused by a metal too cold poured too slowly or a gating system improperly designed so that the mold cannot be filled fast enough.

collapsibility A measurement of the ease or resistance of a sand mixture or core to breaking down under castings conditions.

FIGURE C.15

Cold chamber die casting.

A core in a casting must collapse as the casting cools and shrinks to prevent hot tearing and to facilitate the removal of the core. The degree of collapsibility, a factor of hot strength, varies depending on the pouring temperature, casting design, metal, and the size of the casting.

The mold and core must collapse at the right time. A core in an aluminum casting must collapse at a fairly low temperature and much faster than one for a steel casting. It is controlled by the type, kind, and amount of binder used.

colloids Materials less than .0002 inches in size, gelatinous, highly absorbent, and sticky when wet.

combination core box A core box that may be altered with a plug or stop off to produce a core of another shape. Such a box is built so that a left- and right-hand core can be made from the same box.

combined carbon Carbon chemically combined in iron and steel.

combined water Water chemically combined in a mineral matter and can be driven off only by temperatures above the boiling point of water. The removal of combined water is called *calcining*.

combustibility The ability of a substance to burn or combust. Combustion is the chemical change resulting from the combination of combustible constituents of a matter with oxygen, producing heat energy.

compressive strength The maximum stress that a material can stand without a predefined amount of deformation when subjected to compression.

Compound skimmer.

compound skimmer   A skimmer and pouring head arrangement combined (Fig. C-16).

condensation   Moisture formed from placing a hot core in a cold mold or a cold chill in a hot mold and causing a blow defect.

contraction   The reduction in size of material as it cools from an elevated heat to room temperature. The contraction of most bronze alloys from molten to room temperature is ³⁄₁₆ of an inch per foot.

cope   The upper or topmost section of a flask, mold, or pattern.

cope and drag mounts   Two separate pattern mounts, one fitted with female guides for the drag and one fitted with pins for the cope. These must match up with the flask used (Fig. C-17).

   The cope half of the pattern is attached to the cope mount and the drag pattern is attached to the drag mount. The cope and drag molds are produced separately and put together for pouring. The usual practice is for one molder to make copes and another to make the drags. Cope and drag mounts are quite common when

FIGURE C.17

Cope and drag mounts.

making large castings where a matchplate would be out of the question due to its bulk and weight. Cope and drag mounts are sometimes called *tubs*.

coping out   Extending the sand of the cope downward into the drag by cutting away a portion of the sand in the drag. This is done prior to ramming the cope to facilitate mold making and removal of the pattern by establishing the correct mold parting. It also eliminates back draft (Fig. C-18).

copper   Yellowish red in color, tough, ductile, and malleable metal. Found native in a large number of ores. Melting point, 1083 C; boiling point, 2310 C; specific gravity 8.91; and weight .321 pounds per cubic inch.

Sound copper castings are difficult to produce due to the affinity to oxygen when melting. Melt on the oxidizing side with a charcoal cover and deoxidize with phos-copper 1½ to 2 ounces per 100 pounds. In the south we never melted and poured copper on a rainy day or one with high humidity. Large risers are required due to its high shrinkage. Dry sand molds, cement sand molds, and furan no-bake molds are your best bet for medium-to-heavy copper castings.

copper base alloy   Any alloy where the main constituent is copper. Copper is alloyed with lead, zinc, nickel, tin, silicon, etc.

85 percent copper, 5 percent tin, 5 percent lead, and 5 percent zinc is called *ounce metal* or *red brass*.

Coping out cuts away a portion of the sand in the drag.

copper phosphorous Also known as *phos copper*. It is a metal deoxidizer made of copper containing various percentages of phosphorous sold in shot and wafer form. The two most popular percentages are 10 and 15 percent. The phosphorous is combined with the copper to make it stable so it can be handled safely. The usual amount used in a red brass heat is 1 to 2 ounces of 15 percent phos copper per 100 pounds of metal (15 percent phosphorous; 85 percent copper).

  The copper melts, releasing the phosphorous which combines with the copper oxides in the melt and releases the copper as oxide-free copper.

core A pre-formed baked sand or green sand aggregate inserted in a mold to shape the interior part of a casting which cannot be shaped by the pattern (Fig. C-19).

  When a pattern requires a core, a projection must be made on the pattern. This projection forms an impression in the sand of the mold in which to locate the core and hold it during the casting. These projections are called *core prints* and are part of the pattern.

  Sometimes it is possible to make a pattern in such a way that a core will remain in the sand when the pattern is removed. The pattern for a simple shoring washer is made in this way.

core assembly When cores are too complicated to produce with ease as a single unit, a core assembly is made. It is made up of a series

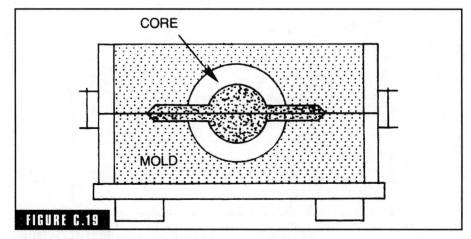

FIGURE C.19

A core is often inserted in the mold.

of cores (parts) and assembled by pasting, leading, bolting, etc. An example of this is the coring for a water-cooled engine block, which is quite complicated but consists of an assembly of simpler cores.

core binders Materials used alone or in combination to bind sand grains together to form a core; the grains are set by chemical action, heat, microwaves, etc. Linseed oil, fish oil, water glass, urea, wheat flour, cement, dextrin, molasses, hydrol, sulfite, latex, furan, and pitch, are common binders.

core box Wood, metal, or plastic structure that has the shape of the desired core to be produced—the female shape of the desired core (male).

core box drawing machine A machine that mechanically draws the rolled over core box from the core. There is a wide variety of machines built. Some roll the box plate and core over and draw the box upward; in others the core plate is lowered from the box. Some are completely automatic and blow the core in the box and draw it. Others are semiautomatic, while some are operated completely manually.

core daubing Also called *core mudding*. The joints of glued cores are daubed or mudded to make a smooth joint and to prevent metal from finning at the junction. Like paste, daubing can be purchased or homemade.

Red talc or graphite moistened with water to a soft mud works well, as does 3 percent bentonite, 3 percent dextrin or molasses, and 94 percent silica flour mixed with water to a soft mud.

Core drier.

core driers   Metal plates that have the shape of the core to support it and keep it in shape during the baking cycle (Fig. C-20).

core, green sand   A core made of molding sand (not baked) with a core box formed by the pattern during molding and used in the green state (Fig. C-21).

core grinding   With close work, such as engine cores, where precision is needed, the cores are made oversize at the joint and ground to the height desired (Fig. C-22). The core grinder consists of a table on which the core holding fixture and an adjustable swing arm grinding wheel are attached. When adjusted to the desired height, the grinding wheel is swung across the core in the jig, grinding it to size and at the same time producing a true and level surface.

Green sand core.

FIGURE C.22

Core grinding.

core hardness The measure of hardness with a core hardness scratch gauge (Fig. C-23). A spring-loaded dial indicator device similar to a mold hardness gauge. It measures the depth of penetration of a steel knife edge as it is drawn across the core with the instrument pressed against the core. The shoe rests on the core. Typical readings:

■ Dry sand molds: Soft—20

■ Baked cores: Soft—35

■ Baked cores: Hard—75

■ Dry sand molds: Hard—40

■ Baked cores: Medium—50

■ Baked cores: Very Hard—90

FIGURE C.23

Core hardness.

core hooks Hooks or pat eyes placed in a core; used to lift or handle the core (Fig. C-24).

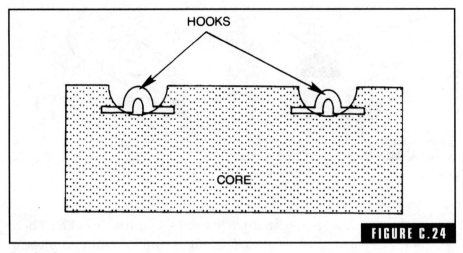

FIGURE C.24

Core hooks.

core maker's trowel   The core maker's trowel is exactly like a finishing trowel except that the blade is parallel its entire length and the nose is perfectly square (Fig. C-25). They come in widths of from 1 to 2 inches in ¼-inch steps; blade lengths of 4½ to 7 inches long in ½-inch steps. This trowel is used to strike off core boxes. Because it is parallel and square ended, a core can be easily trimmed or repaired and sides can be squared up.

core marker   The print on a core which is so shaped that it can be set in the mold only one way, matching a corresponding shaped print on the pattern (Fig. C-26). Also known as a *keeper* or *key*.

core molds   A mold made entirely of cores; the no-bake molding system is essentially core molds.

core paste   A prepared adhesive used to glue and join sections of cores together. You can make your own from water glass and talc, dextrin, flour, graphite, and molasses; however, it is more economi-

CORE MAKERS TROWEL

FIGURE C.25

Core maker's trowel.

FIGURE C.26

Core marker.

cal to purchase a prepared paste from a foundry supplier. There is a hot paste, sold in stick form. It is applied with an electric paste gun, which heats the paste and applies it with a trigger action.

core plug   A wood or metal form that is an exact reproduction of a desired core and its print (Fig. C-27). The purpose is to see exactly

FIGURE C.27

Core plugs.

what the core will look like to determine the construction of the core box, boxes, or driers.

In many cases the core plug is used to produce a plaster cast core box, then lagged to produce a pattern. This is a good quick method where only a few castings are required or a prototype piece.

core print An extension on a pattern which makes a print in the mold cavity used to hold and locate the core in the proper position and alignment in the mold during casting (Fig. C-28). The core print on a core is that part of the core that rests in a print in the mold.

The so-called soft plugs or freeze plugs on the side of your auto engine are in reality cores extended through into prints in the mold to support the core during pouring.

core rise This defect is caused by a core rising from its intended position toward the cope surface. It causes a variation in wall thickness or, when touching the cope, there is no metal at that point.

The core has shifted from its position. A *green sand core rise* is when a green sand core in the drag is cracked at its base (caused when drawing the pattern) and floats toward the cope. Dry sand cores will float if the unsupported span of a thin insufficiently rodded core is too great. It will bend upward by the buoyancy of the metal. Insufficient core prints in number and de-

FIGURE C.28

Core print.

sign, insufficient chaplets, slipped chaplet, chaplets left out by molder, or poor design of the core are causes. This defect is easy to spot and remedy.

core rods Rods and/or wires incorporated in the core during the core-making. They are used to give the necessary strength to the core to prevent it from breaking from the forces it is subjected to during the casting operation. It can be a small wire in some cases or large rods and wires in combination, as one would use to reinforce concrete in building a wall, etc. The size, amount, and complexity are determined by the size of the casting and design of the cored cavity.

core sand Sand free from clay, a nearly pure silica, any sharp sea sand used to make dry sand cores. Core sand is usually purchased as washed, dried, and graded. When core sand is bonded with clay or bentonite, tempered and used to mold with, it becomes molding sand.

core shift Distortion or variation of a cored cavity in a casting due to the core moving (shifting) position, or the misalignment of cores in assembling (Fig. C-29).

core sizing Checking a core with a template or other gauge to determine its go/no-go tolerance limits (Fig. C-30).

core sweeps Cores produced from a sweep or sweep box in place of a full core box. Large cores are often swept to cut down on the pattern cost (core boxes) (Fig. C-31).

core venting Because more often than not the core is almost totally surrounded by metal, the natural venting properties of the core (sand) must be supplemented by creating additional passages

FIGURE C.29

Core shift.

Core sizing.

Core sweep.

leading from the interior of the core through the prints to the outside of the mold.

core vent wax A specially formulated wax used to vent dry sand cores (Fig. C-32). The wax is rammed in place during the coremaking and melts during the baking of the core, leaving a clean hole or vent in its place. It is sold in spools in sizes from $\frac{1}{32}$ to $\frac{5}{8}$ round solid, from $\frac{1}{8}$ to $\frac{3}{8}$ round hollow, and $\frac{1}{32} \times \frac{1}{8}$ to $\frac{1}{4} \times \frac{3}{4}$ flat oval.

cores baking dielectric Baking cores bonded with urea binders by passing them through dielectric oven (microwave oven). Typical core mix suitable for dielectric baking: 500 pounds sharp sand; 11 pounds urea formaldehyde base binder; 4½ pounds cereal; 1¼ pounds boric acid; 2½ quarts kerosene; and 8 quarts water.

corrosion The oxidization of a material, like rusting, which is increased with the presence of heat and oxygen or materials which contain oxygen such as H_2SO_4, sulphuric acid.

cover core A core that essentially covers the entire mold cavity with the exception of the gate entrance and is held down by the cope and in place by its print (Fig. C-33). In many cases the cope can be elimi-

Core vent wax.

Cover lifts.

nated and a weight set on the cover core. A core sand pouring cup should be used to pour the casting—a great saving in labor.

cover lifts Tin forms used to cast the lifter bridge on stove covers (Fig. C-34). However, the clever engineer or inventor can find many other uses for them.

The tin is dropped into a socket in the pattern and the sand is sucked under the tin. Then the mold is finished. When the pattern is removed, the tin remains in the mold. The metal flows through the inside of the tin forming the crossbar or lifter bridge, performing a task which would be difficult to do with a core.

cracked molds Molds that are cracked due to improper handling—flasks too weak, weak and rotten bottom boards, mold sitting on an uneven surface, loose flask bars. The defects caused by cracked molds are scabs, run outs, and finning.

FIGURE C.34

Cover lifts.

creep The slow or gradual distortion of metal under a constant stress.

cribbing Also called curbing (Fig. C-35). A large mold is surrounded with heavy planks or steel beams and the space between the cribbing is rammed with floor sand to back and strengthen the mold. In solid investment molds this practice is widespread due to the fragile characteristics of a calcined mold. Cribbing will also prevent a run out should the mold crack during pouring. Should the mold be lowered into a pit and then supported by rammed sand, the term is *pitting*. The end results are the same.

crucible A large family of ceramic pots or receptacles made of graphite and clay or clay and other materials such as silicon car-

FIGURE C.35

Cribbing.

bide, etc. Used primarily in the foundry to melt steel, iron, bronze, aluminum, etc. Pots made of iron, steel, and wrought steel when used to melt in are also referred to as crucibles. Crucibles cover a size range of a few ounces capacity to 2395 pounds (A #700) and up. Foundry crucibles are standardized by size and number. The rule of thumb is a crucible's capacity is one times its size number in aluminum and three times in red brass. A number 10 crucible will hold 10 pounds of molten aluminum or 30 pounds of molten brass.

crush This defect is caused by the actual crushing of the mold, causing indentations in the casting surface. It is caused by flask equipment, such as bottom boards or cores, that are too tall or too large for the prints or jackets. Also caused by rough handling.

crush strip A strip around a large pattern that prevents the matching edges of a mold cavity from crushing when they meet (Fig. C-36). An intentional flash around the casting. Used on large castings where the cope, due to its weight, could twist or sag, preventing the cope from coming down on the drag evenly at all points.

The crush strip is removed from the casting by chipping or grinding. Any damage done by crushing will occur away from the casting and not into the cavity.

crystobalite A form of quartz with a melting point of 3140 F. crushed and ground to flour. It is widely used in prepared investments.

Crush strip.

cupola A continuous melting device primarily for (but not limited to) cast iron, which is in fact and operation a small type of blast furnace lined with refractories for melting the metal in direct contact with the fuel (coke or charcoal) by forcing blast air under pressure through openings (tuyeres) near its base. The cupola resembles a smoke stack and is often called a *stack*.

cupping The tendency of flat sawed pattern lumber to curl away from the heart of the tree (Fig. C-37). This is one reason why you should buy quarter-sawn pattern lumber.

cut Defects in a casting caused by the erosion of the sand by the molten metal flowing over the mold or cored surface.

cutting over Working over floor or heap sand with a molders' shovel to distribute the moisture, areate, and otherwise obtain a uniform mixture.

Cupping.

cutting shellac Diluting shellac with alcohol to the desired consistency. Dissolving flake shellac with alcohol. Always add a pinch of *oxalic acid* to cut shellac to prevent it from oxidizing and turning black.

D

dam gate   A gate constructed with a dam to effect a ready choke and skimmer (Fig. D-1). It is usually made with a triangular core which sets in a suitable print.

damper screw shells   Screw shells are drawn tin shells with a roller thread used for casting a threaded hole (Fig. D-2). They eliminate the cost of drilling and tapping. Because these threads are rolled, they are not satisfactory for a pressure-tight fitting.

    The shell is dropped into a hole in the pattern before molding and the inside fills with green sand when the mold is rammed. The hole in the pattern must be large enough for the shell to draw freely. They can also be used on a core to produce a threaded hole.

daub   Refractory material used to build up and replace the burned back section of the cupola at the melting zone. It consists of fire clay and ganister or a commercial product such as plastic fire brick. After each run of the cupola, this area must be chipped back to a fresh slag-free lining, and the cupola daubed back to its original diameter at the melting zone. Also used to repair ladles, lips, and furnace linings. The area requiring the repair must be thoroughly cleaned and wetted down and the daubing material rammed firmly in place. The daubing mix must be only wet enough to work. Excessive moisture will cause the daubing to steam and blow off when the bed is ignited or when the cupola is put under blast. Daubing repairs should be dried with a torch or in a core oven. If wet, they will fail or gas the metal in the ladle. It must be done correctly and carefully without rushing.

decarbonization   The loss of carbon from the surface of a ferrous alloy as the result of heating in a medium that reacts with the carbon.

decrepitation   The property of a material or substance to fly apart on being heated (explode).

FIGURE D.1

Dam gate.

FIGURE D.2

Damper screw shell.

deformation (sand) The change of the linear dimension of a sand mixture when put under stress.

degassing The removal of absorbed gasses from a metal bath by chemical or mechanical action. Deoxidizing red brass with phosphorous copper is a chemical action. Removing gas from an aluminum bath by bubbling dry nitrogen through it is a mechanical action because the nitrogen has no chemical action with the aluminum or dissolved gasses but creates a mechanical vehicle (bubbles) to which the gasses attach themselves and ride to the surface and out.

dendrite The crystals formed during solidification (Fig. D-3). As a casting starts to freeze in the mold, the metal in immediate contact with the walls of the mold will freeze first, forming a thin layer of equi-axed crystals. Dendrite crystals then grow or shoot

SOLIDIFIED SKIN

DENTRITE
CRYSTAL GROWTH

FIGURE D.3

Dentrite.

out from this face into the remaining liquid, forming crystals
which look like pine trees.

deoxidize The removal of oxygen from metal oxides in a bath. When
you rob them of their oxygen, they then revert back to metal. Is
done by introducing a substance that has a greater affinity for
oxygen than the substance which is oxidized (combined with
oxygen) such as lithium or phosphorous for copper, aluminum
for steel.

density The mass of a unit volume of a material at different temperatures, measured as specific gravity.

desulphurizing compounds Compounds used to remove or lower the
sulphur in molten cast iron prior to pouring. Sulphur is primarily an undesirable element in iron.

The active desulphurizing agent in both caustic soda (76 percent) and soda ash (58 percent) is sodium oxide. Eighty to 85 percent or more of the sulphur present in cupola iron can be
removed by a single ladle treatment.

Of the two reagents used to remove sulphur, sodium carbonate (soda ash) is the most used. A good commercially pure soda
ash is best and is sold under various trade names.

desulphurizing ladle A U-shaped ladle usually mounted in front of the
cupola on trunnions with a tilting mechanism; used to treat the
iron with soda ash to remove the sulphur (Fig. D-4). The iron is
tapped into the ladle, the stream of iron from the cupola spout
goes into the ladle through a slot-shaped opening on one end of
its insulated cover, and is then treated. Iron is poured into the receiving ladles from a tea pot spout on the opposite end by tilting

FIGURE D.4

Desulphurizing ladle.

the U ladle. The slot arrangement gives access to the iron coming from the cupola regardless of the angle of tilt. Some loss of temperature results but is usually offset by the increase in fluidity of the desulphurized iron.

dextrin   Also called *amylin*. It is a compound having strong adhesive properties; a white powder, odorless with a sweetish taste, water soluble. It is made by the action of dilute nitric and hydrochloric acids on starch, then heating to 100 to 125 C. It is used as a binder in skin dried, dry sand molds, core washes, etc.

dezincification   The loss of zinc from the surface of a zinc-bearing alloy such as brass; or zinc corrosion. It is accompanied by the deposit of a residue of one or more active components—usually copper.

diffusion   The movement of atoms within a solution in a direction from a region of high concentration to one of low concentration in order to achieve homogenity of a solution which may be a liquid, solid, or gas.

die casting Casting into a permanent mold (metal or graphite) by forcing the metal into the mold cavity under high pressure. A rapid method of casting which is highly mechanized and only used where a large volume of castings are needed due to the high cost of dies and machines. It is limited by design and metal selection. The most used metal in this case is zinc and zinc alloys.

dirty castings Dirty castings can come from many causes; however, most are caused by poor pouring practices, gating, and sloppy molding. Additional causes include:

- Not skimming properly.
- Gates too large to choke properly.
- Not establishing and maintaining a choke.
- Mold cavity not blown out completely and properly.
- Excessive use of dry parting.
- Weak sand.
- Soft molding.
- Wild metal.
- Carbon too high for casting section (in iron).
- Gates nozzling (spraying) the metal into the cavity.

discs Chaplet shims, plain or perforated tin plates used to provide a shim or to provide an additional bearing surface to rest the chaplet on in the case where the core is very heavy or subjected to excessive lift when the mold is poured (Fig. D-5).

On the cope side of the core the plates are simply laid in position prior to setting the cope. On the drag side they are usually pasted to the core with core paste. The paste is either oven- or torch-dried.

dispersion Separation or scattering of fine particles in a liquid medium (deflocculation) used in connection with the fineness test of clay.

dissolved gasses Gasses dissolved by a metal when heated and/or melted. In most cases they come from the products of combustion and must be removed by the proper degassing treatment.

dolomite A type of limestone used in making cement and lime; used as a flux in melting iron in the cupola.

FIGURE D.5

Discs.

double head chaplets Mild steel double headed chaplets, tinned or
copper plated, round or square heads.

dough roll A roll made of flour and molasses water and rolled out on
a flat board, like clay snakes or large macaroni (Fig. D-6). The
dough roll is placed on the drag around the cavity prior to closing
the mold. It acts as a gasket or seal to prevent a run out during
pouring by taking up any unevenness between the cope and the
drag mating surfaces.

dovetails Tin forms which permit the accurate casting of dovetailed
grooves, either straight or tapered (Fig. D-7).

FIGURE D.6

Dough roll.

Dovetails.

A brass lock strip is attached to the pattern, which sticks up through a groove in the tin to locate it and hold it in position during molding.

dowel A pin used to join sections of parted patterns and core boxes to assure the correct registry.

draft Pattern draft is defined as the taper on vertical elements in a pattern which allows easy withdrawal of the pattern from the mold (Fig. D-8). The amount of draft required will vary with the depth of the pattern. The general rule is ⅛-inch taper to the foot, which comes out to about 1 degree; on shallow patterns, such as a disc, a ¹⁄₁₆-inch taper of 0.5 degree is sufficient.

drag The lower or bottom section of a mold or pattern.

draw back A section of a mold that must be lifted away on an arbor or plate to facilitate the removal of the pattern (Fig. D-9).

draw bolt A threaded eye which fits a matching thread in a plate (*draw plate*). It is let into a pattern and used to lift (draw) the pattern from the mold or otherwise handle it (Fig. D-10).

drawing Removing the pattern from the mold. Removing a core box from core.

FIGURE D.8

A draft.

FIGURE D.9

A draw back.

draw pins, screw, and hooks   These items are used to remove or draw the pattern from the mold (Fig. D-11). The draw pin is driven into the wooden pattern and used to lift it out as a handle. On a short small pattern one pin in the center will do it. If the pattern is long, use one on each end for a two-hand straight lift. The draw hook is used the same way. The draw screw is screwed into the pattern for a better purchase on heavier patterns and prevents the pattern from accidentally coming loose prematurely and falling, damaging the mold, pattern, or both. In large patterns, plates are let into the pattern at its parting face. This has a tapped hole into which a draw pin with a matching thread is screwed for lifting by hand or with a sling from a crane. Two or more are used.

FIGURE D.10

Draw bolt.

A. Draw screw; B. draw pin; and C. draw hook.

Metal patterns, if loose, are drilled and tapped to receive a draw pin.

draw plate　A plate or device sometimes attached to the pattern to assist or facilitate the drawing of the pattern from the sand (Fig. D-12). A vibrating guide plate used to draw a core box from the core. In some cases it is a simple cutout in a plate through which the pattern is drawn.

draws　A shrinkage or draw at the point where the gate joins the casting (Fig. D-13). A common form of defect on chunky yellow brass castings. By adjusting the gating and filleting, it can usually be overcome.

draw stick　A pointed hardwood stick used to draw small light patterns from a mold.

driers (ladle)　Heating devices used to dry ladle linings and preheat them (Fig. D-14). They can be electric or gas and oil fired. The lining must be dry and if the ladle is not heated high enough prior to tapping metal into it, a great loss of metal temperature will occur and the ladle will scull over or freeze.

driers (sand)　Any device used to dry wet sand; these may be fired with coal, gas, oil, or electricity (Fig. D-15). Some are continuous driers. The sand tumbles through a heated and inclined revolving cylinder. Others have a simple coal- or coke-fired pot belly stove arrangement with a drying jacket around its circumference.

drops　A portion of the cope sand drops into the mold cavity before or during pouring. The causes are bumping with weights, rough

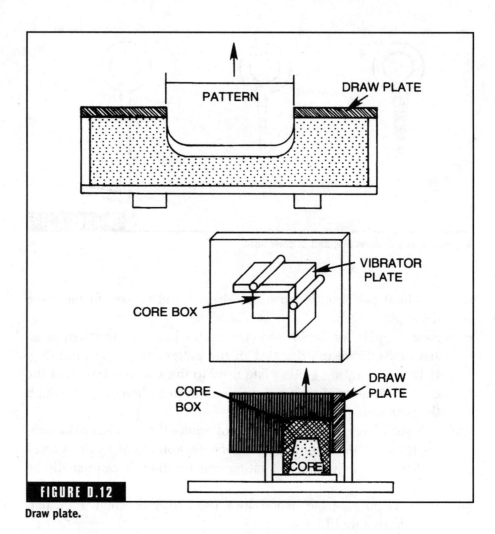

FIGURE D.12

Draw plate.

clamping, weak molding sand (low green strength), rough closing, and jackets placed on roughly, etc.

dross Metal oxides on a molten metal bath or as a defect found in and
on the surface of a casting due to improper gating, melting practice, or deoxidizing treatment.

dry binders Binders used in core and mold making. They are dry.
Includes a wide variety of prepared dry binders such as lion
binder, truline binder, flour, rosin, wheat flour, corn flour, clay,
pitch, goulac, etc.

dry sand molds Any mold that has been dried (baked) prior to pouring. Core molds and furan no-bake are also sometimes called dry sand molds. Although they are dry (no free moisture), they should be called by their respective names.

Dry sand molds are produced from green sand (system sand) or bonded crude silica sand or a combination of the two to which a baking type binder is added to provide a bond when the mold is dried. This bond can be pitch, oil, cereal, etc., alone or in various combinations.

Draws.

The molds are placed (open) in a mold drying oven and dried at 350 to 450 F. overnight. They are allowed to cool, cored, closed up, and poured.

Typical dry sand mixes:

■ Heavy brass—system sand tempered with glutrin water (1 pint glutrin to 5 gallons water), 5 percent pitch by weight, baked until dry.

Driers dry ladle linings.

WET SAND

FLAME

DRY SAND

WET SAND

FIRE BOX

ASH PIT

DRY SAND

FIGURE D.15

Driers also dry wet sand.

- Medium to heavy grey iron—60 gallons dry heap sand (floor or system sand); 30 gallons crude dry silica sand; 4 gallons bentonite; 3 gallons pitch.

- Heavy phosphor bronze—naturally bonded molding sand, 25 gallons; river sand, 10 gallons; wheat flour, 1 gallon; blue clay water, 30 to 40 baume. Bake at 450 F. until dry.

dry strength   A mold must not only hold its shape in the green state, but it must also hold its shape in the dry state. This is an important property and is measured as dry compression by allowing the test specimen to dry out before testing, the testing is then carried out in the same manner as for green strength. A good average figure is 30 pounds per square inch. Dry strength should be no higher than necessary. Excessive dry strength results in a critical sand. If the molding sand has a too high dry strength it will not give or break down as the casting shrinks during solidification.

ductile iron   Also called *nodular iron*. A cast iron where the graphite distributed through a ferritic matrix is spheroid or nodular in shape instead of flat flakes in a matrix of pearlite and ferrite. It is produced by adding (treating) the molten iron with an alloy of magnesium, copper-ferrosilicon, or a nodulizing alloy marketed by various firms for the introduction of magnesium into iron. The treatment leaves up to .08 percent residual magnesium in the iron. The free graphite in ductile iron in spheroid (ball) shapes gives the iron its ductile characteristics.

ductility   The measure of the degree of permanent deformation (elongation) a metal or material will take before fracturing or breaking.

dune sand   Wind blown deposits of sand—90 percent silica, usually located near large bodies of water, but not necessarily.

durability   The measure of the sand's ability to withstand repeated usage without losing its properties and to recover its bond strength after repeated usage. The sand's fineness and the type and amount of clay bond determines the sand's durability. The ability of the bonding clay to retain its moisture is also an important factor.

dust bag   Pourous cotton cloth bags used to apply dry parting and facing materials to a sand mold.

![E](letter E in box)

electric riddle   An electrically powered riddle. See also gyratory riddle.

electrodes   Welding rods used for electric welding and carbon rods used in the arc furnace for melting.

elongation   The amount of extension in the vicinity of the fracture in the tensile test. It is expressed in percents of the standard gauge length of 2 inches (Fig. E-1). The coupon sample used to test the tensile strength is first marked off with two center punch marks 2 inches apart. The coupon is pulled (stretched) until it breaks on the tensile strength machine, giving the tensile strength. The two ends of the sample are then fitted together at the point of fracture and the distance between the punch marks measured to determine the percent of elongation.

ethyl silicate   A silicic acid used as the principal binder for ceramic investment molds. The normal content of ethyl silicate is 25 percent available silica. Water hydrolyzes ethyl silicate to alcohol and silicic acid which dehydrates to an adhesive amorphous silica.

etching   Attacking a highly polished metal sample surface with a weak acid or other corrosive agent (caustic soda for aluminum). The etching agent attacks the various constituents of the metal unequally so that when the etchant is removed by washing and drying, it can be examined under a microscope or, in some cases, by eye.

eutectic   The alloy structure of two or more solid phases formed from a liquid eutectically.

A pure metal's solidification temperature may be lowered by adding another metal. The reduction of the solidification temperature is proportional to the amount added, up to a point. The solidification range of a high copper alloy such as 95 percent copper would run somewhere in the neighborhood of 1850 to 1700 F. against 1600 to 1580 F. for a similar alloy with only 58 percent copper.

FIGURE E.1

Elongation is the amount of extension of the vicinity of the fracture.

If we add sodium chloride (salt) to water we lower the freezing point of the water. Then as the freezing point is reached, the ice crystals (salt free) make the remaining unfrozen portion higher in salt content, reducing the freezing point still further down the scale. When we reach this point by lowering the temperature when ice crystals start to form again, the same thing happens until we finally reach the point where the water and salt freezes. This final frozen mass of frozen ice and salt crystals is the eutectic. The *eutectic temperature* is the point where this freezing happens.

It is the basis of equipment used today to determine the carbon, silicon, and total carbon of a sample. You pour a sample of molten iron in a special cup containing a thermocouple and plot the solidification curve. The curve is displayed on a digital LED readout in percents of carbon, silicon, and total carbon of cast iron. This method is called *thermal analysis*. It is the measurement of the cooling curve of a solidifying iron sample and the electronic interpretation of the curve in terms of carbon, silicon, and total carbon.

exoband A sodium silicate (water glass) binder used in the carbon dioxide mold and core bonding system.

expansion The dilation or increase of size that sand or matter undergoes when heated.

expendable pattern As in lost wax casting, the pattern is lost. Expendable patterns for sand casting are styrofoam and shaped to the desired form with attached styrofoam gates, runners, and risers. The styrofoam pattern is molded with dry, clay-free sharp silica sand in a box or steel frame. The pattern is vaporized by the metal poured into the mold, leaving the casting.

facing   The layer of sand surrounding the mold cavity. When a mold is made using a specially prepared molding sand in the mold immediately over the pattern to produce a smoother casting surface or a more refractory surface for the metal to lie against. It is then backed with system or floor sand. It can be simply new or finer sand or sand containing a bond such as flour or pitch (Fig. F-1).

false cheek   Making a mold from a pattern which would require a cheek only if done in a two-part flask by double rolling the mold (Fig. F-2). The cope half of the mold is made first, rolled over and the portion of sand which would normally be in the cheek is formed. The drag is rammed against the cope and false cheek, removed, and the drag half of the pattern is then drawn. The drag replaces the false cheek. The mold is then rolled over and the cope removed. The cope section of the pattern is removed from the false cheek and the mold is closed.

false core   A core made of green or dry sand to take care of an undercut on a pattern; it is removed and glued or wired in position in the mold proper.

   The core is made by tucking the sand into the undercut (back draft) and forming a print on the core. When the mold is rammed, the false core will leave a corresponding female print into which it is secured.

fasteners, corrugated   Corrugated (nails) fasteners used in pattern construction to secure stock together when turning a split pattern (Fig. F-3).

fatigue   The tendency for a metal to crack or break under conditions of repeated cyclic stressing—bending back and forth, vibrating, continuously working.

FIGURE F.1

Facing sand.

FIGURE F.2

False cheek.

FIGURE F.3

Corrugated fasteners.

feeder   A reservoir of molten metal to make up for the contraction of metal as it solidifies. To prevent shrinkage cavities in the casting (voids caused by lack of feed metal) as a riser or head.

feeding   Pouring additional molten metal into a freshly poured mold to compensate for volume shrinkage while the casting is setting. Also referred to as *topping off* or *hot topping*.

feel of molding sand   Tempering a molding sand to the point that it feels correct. Regardless of the amount of instrument checks, a good feeling sand usually rams easier and better. This skill of telling when a molding sand is right comes only with experience and practice.

ferrite   Pure iron consists of ferrite crystals, which are only slightly attached by the usual etching agents except at the grain boundaries.

ferro alloys   Alloys of iron and another element or elements (other than carbon) when used as a raw material in the manufacture of ferrous metals.

ferro boron   An alloy that is 10 percent boron and 90 percent iron.

ferro chromium   An alloy of iron and chromium containing from 66 to 72 percent chromium and .06 to 7 percent carbon. Used to add chromium to a metal bath.

ferro manganese   Iron manganese alloy containing over 30 percent manganese; used to introduce manganese in a metal bath.

ferro molybdenum   An alloy that is 58 to 64 percent molybdenum and the balance iron.

ferro phosphorous   An alloy of iron and phosphorous used to add phosphorous to steel to make phosphorous steel.

ferro silicon   An alloy of iron and silicon used for the addition of silicon in iron and steel baths.

ferro titanium   An alloy that is 17 to 38 percent titanium, with the balance iron.

ferro vanadium   An alloy that is 35 to 40 percent vanadium, with the balance iron.

ferrostatic pressure   The pressure of the liquid steel poured into a mold. As long as the metal remains liquid this pressure is equal in all directions.

ferrous   Alloys in which the predominant metal or solvent is iron.

fillet irons   Steel or brass tools with each end being ball shaped. The ball is used to apply wax fillets to patterns (Fig. F-4). They are

FIGURE F.4

Fillet iron.

sold singularly or in sets from ⅟₁₆-inch ball to ⅝-inch ball. Each tool consists of two different size balls. A number 2 tool has a ¼-inch ball on one end and a ³⁄₁₆-inch ball on the other end. The tool is warmed over an alcohol lamp and the fillet is rubbed into place, using the tool with the radius corresponding to the selected fillet.

fillets   Patternmaker's fillets are made of wax, wood, paper, or leather and are used to form a radius on a pattern or core box (Fig. F-5). Wax fillets are applied with a fillet iron. Paper, wood, and leather fillets are glued in place. The choice of which type of fillets to use depends upon the end use of the pattern. For a pattern used only for a limited run now and again, wax is fine; if it is a master from which metal production patterns are to be made, where if the pattern is large or to be used quite often, wood or leather might be the better choice. For small to medium patterns of jobbing work, 90 percent are filleted with wax. Paper fillets went out of use some time back but are available. Wood fillets can be used for straight runs only. They are cut slightly over 90 degrees with the back relieved so that they will form a good tight fit when installed.

One-half to 1-inch leather fillets are shaped like wood fillets with a relief at the 90-degree junction. Wood fillets are, in some cases, glued and bradded into place. Never use brads on leather fillets as they draw the leather and make an uneven surface.

Fillets can be made of wax, wood, paper or leather.

When applying fillets to a pattern or core box there is a tendency to rush it—*don't*. You should apply the fillets with the same care as in building the pattern.

film on metal   When metal falling from a single gate has to climb a hill to fill the other side of the mold, oftentimes a film is formed when the metal in the first valley stops momentarily then spills over into the second valley (Fig. F-6). This temporary halt will cause a reflected cold-shut and in some instances a sufficient film will form on the halted metal to separate part of the casting into layers. Two or more gates should be provided so that none of the metal has to rise over a hill and then run down into the valley on the other side. A gate leading into each valley will allow the mold to fill uniformly.

filters   A pad of coarse steel wool placed at the bottom of the sprue when casting magnesium to eliminate vortex action of the metal stream and assist in filtering out oxide skins (Fig. F-7). Slot sprues are used in casting magnesium to prevent vortex.

fin   This defect is a fin of metal on the casting caused by a crack in the cope or drag. It is caused by wracked flasks, bad jackets, uneven warped bottom boards, uneven strike off, insufficient cope or drag depth, bottom board not properly rubbed, or drag mold sitting unevenly (rocking).

fineness   A measure of the actual grain sizes of a sand mixture. It is made by passing a standard sample, usually 100 grams, through a series of graded sieves. About 10 different sieve sizes are used. Because most sands are composed of a mixture of various size

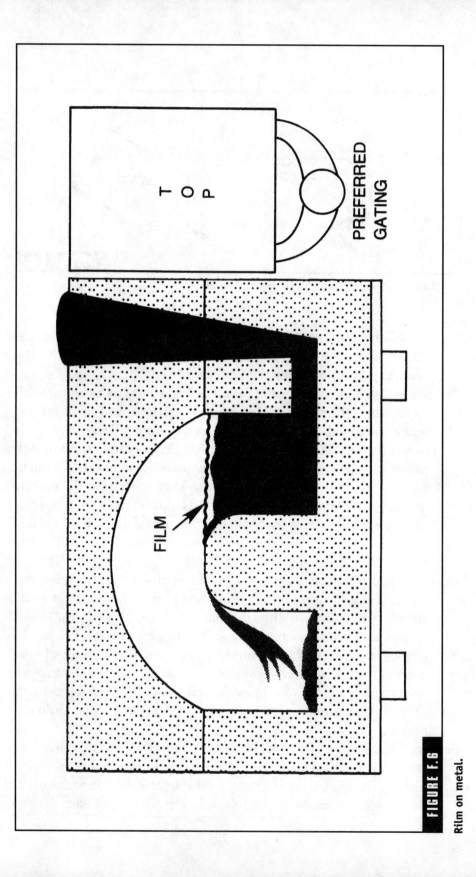

TOP

PREFERRED GATING

FILM

FIGURE F.6

Rilm on metal.

A filter.

grains there is a distribution of sands remaining on the measuring sieves.

The fineness number assigned to the sample is the number of the sieve through which the largest amount of sand passed.

finger gates Multiple gates into a casting from a single runner (Fig. F-8).

Finger gates.

finish allowance The amount of extra stock left on the surface of a casting for machining plus shrinkage compensation.

finish mark The symbol in the form of an *f* appearing on a line of a print or drawing indicating that the marked edge of the surface of the casting is to be machined finished. It indicates the need for additional stock at the point or surface indicated.

finishing trowel The finishing trowel is used for general trowel of the molding sand to sleek down a surface, to repair a surface, or cut away the sand around the cope of a snap flask (Fig. F-9).

fire brick Bricks made of clay with a fusion point no less than 1580 C. or 2876 F.

fire clay Any clay with a fusion point not less than 2768 F.

fitted head chaplets A stem chaplet in which the head is fitted or shaped to fit a particular shape (on the core) (Fig. F-10).

flange A stiffening member or a means of attachment to another object (Fig. F-11).

flat back patterns Patterns that are flat on the side presented to the cope and do not extend into the cope of the mold. The entire mold cavity is in the drag (Fig. F-12).

flame annealing The process of softening a metal by heat from a high-temperature flame.

flame hardening The application of heat to a metal from a high-temperature flame to quenching (cooling as required).

flare point The temperature of a metal such as yellow brass and high strength yellow brass (manganese bronze) where the zinc flares send little pips of zinc oxide from the metal surface. Low tensile

FIGURE F.9

A finishing trowel.

FIGURE F.10

Fitted head chaplet.

FIGURE F.11

Flange.

FIGURE F.12

Flat back patterns.

strength manganese will flare at about 1850 F. and high tensile Mg. Br. at or close to 1950 F.

flax swab Also called a *horse tail*, it is used to swab the sand around the pattern at the junction of pattern and sand (Fig. F-13). To prevent it from breaking away when the pattern is rapped and lifted from the sand, it is dampened by dipping it into a pail of water and shaking it out well. Used on floor work where the pattern presents a fair-sized perimeter.

The swab is also used by some molders to apply wet mold wash or blacking to a mold surface. This requires great dexterity.

flint shot Flint rock ground, crushed, and graded for use in place of sand for sand blasting. Flint nodules look like pearls and are free from cleavage lines. It is hard and clean and outlasts sand 3 to 1.

floor flasks Flasks that are too large to be handled on the bench (Fig. F-14). These can be of wood or metal. The wood flasks are constructed in such a manner that the long sides provide the lifting handles for two man lifting and handling.

In floor flasks, unlike bench flasks, when you reach a size of 18 × 18 inches to 30 × 30 inches, members called *bars* are put in the cope. These bars help support the weight of the sand in the cope and prevent it from dropping out. Bars are required in the drag half of the flask only when it is necessary to roll the job over and lift the drag instead of the cope. In this case they are called *grids*.

FIGURE F.13

A flax swab.

Floor flask.

The bars do not come all the way to the parting but clear the parting and portion of the pattern that is in the cope by a minimum of ½ inch. These bars in many cases have to be contoured to conform with the portion of pattern that is in the cope.

In all cases the bars are brought to a dull point along their lower edge to make it possible to tuck and ram the sand firmly under the bars.

The inside surfaces of both the flask and the bars in the cope section are often covered with large-headed roofing nails with the head projecting ⅛ to ¼ of an inch. This gives the entire inner surface an excellent tooth and a good purchase on the sand.

Of course the floor flask, like all others, must be provided with suitable points and guides on both ends.

floor rammer Same purpose and design as a bench rammer only the butt and peen ends are made of cast iron and attached to each end of a piece of pipe or a hickory handle. The average length is 42 inches.

flowability The ability of a molding sand to flow and be easily rammed around a pattern. The ability of a sand to pack in and around a pattern with a uniform density.

flow rate The relationship of pouring rate, height of sprue, area and diameter of the sprue. For example, a round sprue ¾ inch in diameter 5 inches tall will deliver 1 pound of molten aluminum per second. A sprue the same size, only 15 inches tall will deliver 1¾ pounds per second. A 2-inch sprue 5 inches tall will deliver 5¾ inches per second, and at 15 inches tall, 2 inches in diameter it will deliver 10 pounds per second.

fluidity The ability of molten metal to flow readily, as measured by the length of a standard spiral casting.

flushing of metal Bubbling an inert gas through a metal bath with a metal or carbon lance to remove hydrogen, oxygen, etc., from the molten metal.

flux Applying a solid or gaseous material to molten metal in order to remove oxide dross and other materials. Sometimes referred to as refining.

flux inclusions Flux and/or slag poured down the sprue and winding up on or in the casting. Caused by improper ladle or crucible skimming, not choking, improper gates, or completely emptying a ladle or crucible during pouring.

fluorspar A commercial grade of calcium fluoride CaF_2 used as a flux in ferrous melting.

fly ash A finely divided product of combustion, sometimes found as inclusions in metal melted in an open hearth furnace.

foaming metal Manganese bronze and aluminum bronze have a tendency to foam like beer. This foam solidifies and appears as dross in or under the surface of the casting.

   The least agitation in handling causes foaming. The metal must enter the mold quietly at the bottom and fill the mold by simple displacement.

follow board A board with a cavity or socket in it which conforms to the form of the pattern and defines the parting surface of the drag (Fig. F-15). It can be made of wood, plaster, or metal. When made of sand it is called a *dry sand match*.

FIGURE F.15

Follow board.

The pattern rests in the follow board while making up the drag half of the mold and, in doing so, establishes the correct sand parting. The follow board is removed, leaving the pattern rammed in the drag up to the parting. The cope then takes the place of the follow board and is rammed in the usual manner. A simple follow board might consist of a molding board with a hole in it to allow the pattern to rest firmly on the board while the drag is rammed.

forehearth   A refractory-lined reservoir in front of a cupola connected to the cupola by a trough. It is used to collect the metal from the cupola (Fig. F-16). The cupola runs continuously and the metal is tapped from the forehearth. It may be treated in the forehearth. A large quantity of metal can be accumulated in the forehearth for a large casting.

formaldehyde   Also called *methylene oxide*. It is produced by the oxidation of methyl alcohol. Its composition is HCHO.

By condensing *urea* with formaldehyde you produce *urea-formaldehyde* resins, which are widely used in the foundry industry as binders for cores and shell molding (sand shell, not ceramic shell).

CUPOLA

FOREHEARTH

FIGURE F.16

Forehearth.

foundry   An establishment or works where the production of castings is the principal endeavor.

foundry sprinklers   Sprinkler cans used by molders to add moisture to molding sand to keep it in condition.

foundry torches   Kerosene- or oil-fired torches used in the foundry for skin drying molds. They produce an easily controlled flame. Also used to dry small hand ladles which have been daubed.

freezing range of alloys   This refers to the temperature range over which a given alloy freezes. In most cases the wider this range is the greater chance of segregation, a problem with some alloys. Silicon bronze solidifies over a range of 160 F., while copper 90 percent and tin 10 percent solidifies over a 300 F. range. With copper 90 percent and zinc 10 percent, the range of solidification is negligible.

freezing ratio

$$\frac{\text{Surface Area of the Casting}}{\text{Volume of the Casting}}$$

$$\frac{\text{Surface Area of Riser}}{\text{Volume of the Riser}}$$

If the two are equal, the freezing ratio is unity, and the riser and the casting will solidify at the same rate.

French gates   The system of pouring flat plates on end rather than horizontally. The French gate is attached to the casting its entire length (Fig. F-17).

French rammer   The French rammer is a piece of 1 inch diameter cold roll steel turned to an eye on one end and slightly tapered on the other (Fig. F-18). The bulk of the ramming is done with the eye.

French sand   For many years French sand was considered the finest naturally bonded molding sand for fine art work, plaques, statuary, etc. Many of Rodin's pieces were cast in French sand. This sand comes from Fontenay des Roses near Paris. I have been told that they have been digging sand from this pit for some 400 plus years. It was common practice for many foundries to keep a ½ ton or more of French sand in the shop for that special job or a gravemarker casting. Use it as a facing, riddled against the pattern ¼-inch thick, then backed with regular or system sand.

FIGURE F.17

French gates.

FIGURE F.18

French rammer.

Ten random samples of French sand showed the following test average:

- Clay, 17.2 percent

- Permeability, 18 at 7.2 percent moisture

- Grain fineness, 176

- Green strength, 10.5

- Shear, 3.1

Yankee sand, which replaced French sand during World War I, comes from around Albany, N.Y. An average of 10 samples showed:

- Clay, 19.8

- Permeability, 18.4 at 6.5 percent moisture

- Green compression, 16.7

- Shear, 3.8

fuels for melting   Any fuel used to melt metal—solid, gaseous, liquid, or electrical, coal, coke, natural gas, oil, etc.

fuller's earth   A clay closely related to bentonite. Has also been used as a sand binder.

full pattern   A pattern that is constructed in one piece and not requiring that it be split in order to mold the job (Fig. F-19).

FIGURE F.19

Full pattern.

fuming bronze   Flaring manganese bronze. It is believed by some that a few minutes of fuming, then replacing the lost zinc gives you higher tensile strength in the casting.This school is very much divided. Some say under no conditions flare the heat.

furans   Various derivatives of furfural produced from formaldehyde and acetylene are known collectively as furans. They are used to produce resins and plastics. The furans most widely used in the foundry are furfural alcohol resins. These resins are the basic of the furan no-bake process of molding and core making, which has grown in leaps and bounds in the last several years because of the following advantages:

- Simple sand mix—resin, sand, and activator
- Excellent flowability
- Reduced rodding
- Reduction of skilled personnel
- Less core and mold finishing
- Uniform hardness
- Closer tolerance and smoother casting
- No ovens required, self curing
- Easy shake out
- Smaller molds due to its strength
- Cores and molds do not develop thermal cracks when poured
- Molds can be used for ferrous or nonferrous molding
- No flasks required
- Less weighting

The normal formula for furan no-bake system is 2 percent binder against the weight of the sand—100 pounds sand, 2 pounds furan binder. The activator or catalyst to set the binder is phosphoric acid (85 percent). The amount of binder required is 25 to 30 percent of the weight of the binder. The average formula is 100 pounds sharp sand, 2 pounds binder, and ½-pound phosphoric acid (85 percent).

The activator is mixed with the dry sand, then the binder. The time the sand takes to set up is varied with the amount (percent) of activator used. Most pattern coatings are soluble in furfural alcohol. Heat is generated by the polymerization of the resin. You must use uncoated patterns, dry parting, or wipe the pattern or core box with kerosene and rub the surface with graphite or mica. (The kerosene parting system works best.) There are some commercial pattern coatings available for the no-bake system.

furnace, induction The induction furnace operates by the process of induction (Fig. F-20). The metal charge is made the secondary of a high frequency transformer, 1000 to 3000 cycles. Eddy currents are induced in the metal charge in much the same way a transformer introduces them in the secondary winding. The winding in this case (secondary) is the metal charge, which acts like a short circuited secondary.

furnace, passive A charcoal- or coal-fired nonferrous furnace which depends upon its blast air for combustion by the draft created by a chimney or stack (Fig. F-21). The fuel and crucible rest on a grate.

furnace, pit A furnace usually placed in a pit with the cover at floor level.

furnace, tilting A furnace which can be tipped in order to pour the molten metal bath into a receiving or pouring ladle by hand wheel, lever, hydraulic or air cylinders.

fused silica Silica that has been fused at a high temperature and ground into various meshes (particle sizes). Used as a refractory and as a stucco for ceramic shell molds.

fusion This defect is a rough glassy surface of fused melted sand on the casting surface, either on the outside or on a cored surface. The cause is a too-low sintering or melting point of the sand or core. It is quite common when a small diameter core runs through an exceptionally heavy section of great heat which actually melts the core. This can also be caused by pouring hotter

FIGURE F.20

An induction furnace.

A passive furnace.

than necessary for the sand or cores. A mold or core wash can prevent this in some cases but if the sintering point of your sand is too low for the class of work, you need a more refractory sand; zircon, etc.

gaggers   L-shaped metal rods, square or twisted, used to assist in the supporting of the sand in the cope of a floor or larger mold (Fig. G-1).

ganister   A highly siliceous sand stone used as a refractory, particularly for furnace linings; crushed and sized, it is used as a grog in refractory clays.

garnet paper   Sandpaper covered with crushed garnets in place of sand. A high grade sandpaper preferred by patternmakers because of its long life and superior sanding ability.

gas generated   The gas generated by a core or mold when heated by the molten metal.

gas porosity   Widely dispersed bright round holes which appear on fractured and machined surfaces. It is caused by gasses being absorbed in the metal during melting. The gas is released during solidification of the casting. The cause is poor melting practices (oxidizing conditions) and poor deoxidizing practices.

gate cutter   The best gate cutter is made from a section of a tobacco can (Fig. G-2).

To cut a gate or runner in green sand, the tab is held between the thumb and first finger and the gate or runner is cut just as you would cut a groove or channel in wood with a gouge. The width is controlled by bending the cutters' sides in and out. The depth is controlled by the operator.

gated matchplate   A matchplate where the gates and runners are attached permanently to the plate and patterns (Fig. G-3). In a pressure cast matchplate, the gates, patterns, and runners are all one casting (unit).

gated pattern   The gate is the channel or channels in a sand mold through which the molten metal enters the cavity left by the pattern (Fig. G-4). This channel can be made in two ways. One way is by cutting

FIGURE G.1

Gaggers.

FIGURE G.2

Gate cutter.

the channel or channels with a gate cutter. The other is by forming the pattern with a projection attached to it which will form this gate or gates during the process of ramming up the mold.

gates and risers The plumbing system used to fill a mold cavity (Fig. G-5).

geared ladles Large or small ladles equipped with a hand wheel and gearing mechanism, used to tip the ladle.

Geneva chaplets A tin-plated sheet steel strong chaplet with a good bearing surface and unrestricted metal flow (Fig. G-6).

FIGURE G.3

Gated matchplate.

FIGURE G.4

Gated patterns.

German crucible clay A high grade clay used in the making of crucibles. It is sold bolted and used as a shake-on facing and a print back. See also *bolted cement*.

German silver A white alloy of copper, nickel, and zinc. The highest grade is extra white: 50 percent copper, 30 percent nickel, and 20

FIGURE G.5

Gates and riser.

FIGURE G.6

Geneva chaplets.

percent zinc. The cheap grade, called *fifths*, has a yellowish color and is used where the finished part to be plated is 57 percent copper, 7 percent nickel, and 36 percent zinc.

germination The condition where you have abnormal grain growth. A few grains may grow at the expense of neighboring grains during solidification.

glue patternmakers Glue used to glue up stock and pattern members. Animal hide hot glue, cooked in a double boiler, was the standard for years. However, it has been replaced by various liquid glues in the past several years.

glutrin A lignin sulphite liquid core binder also used as a mold spray and in washes, glues, and muds as binders, etc. When dried to a powder it is called *goulac.*

goulac A dry water soluble powder made from lignin sulphite liquor. It is a by-product of the paper pulp industry and used as a dry core binder in facing sand mixes. When mixed with water, it is used as a mold, core spray, and wash binder, and in core pastes as dough rolls. It is a replacement for molasses in the foundry.

grab hook A grab hook differs from a sling chain hook in shape (Fig. G-7). The opening is much wider so that it can be hooked into the rollover pad eyes on large flasks. Also used to lift large copes.

GRAB-HOOK   CHAIN HOOK   **FIGURE G.7**

A grab hook and chain hook.

graphite A crystalline or amorphous carbon used in the foundry as a mold coating and core wash. It is an additive to some molding sands and crucibles. It goes by many names including *blacking, plumbago, silver lead*, and *ceylon lead*. By whatever name used, it is a form of carbon which can differ greatly in its physical properties. The finest grain is a crystalline graphite from ceylon. The chief action, when used as a facing for a sand mold, is that it fills in the spaces between the sand grains and provides a smooth highly refractory surface upon which the metal can lie. This coating allows the sand to peel cleanly from the casting and prevents burning in—sand melting on to the casting surface. It is amorphous graphite when used for cast iron. A carbide iron surface is formed on the casting due to it being dissolved by the molten iron; this produces a dirty hard surface. When crystalline graphite is used, it is not dissolved and imparts a smooth easy-to-machine surface that is bluish in color.

A lead pencil is graphite (not lead). However, lead will make a mark very much like graphite when rubbed on paper. This is probably how graphite got one of its many names, *black lead*.

As a wet mold and core wash, it is combined with a suitable binder and sold under many trade names. Some companies put out graphite washes which contain graphite with a binder which you mix with a volatile liquid as a vehicle. Alcohol and naptha are the most common. These washes are sprayed or brushed on to a mold or core surface and then ignited. The vehicle burns and the resulting heat sets the binder to form a firm, baked on coating. When the vehicle is water with a water soluble binder such as lignin sulphite, the coated mold or core must be dried with a torch or in an oven to remove the water and set the wash. As a dry mold facing it can be used as is or with a small amount of wheat flour as a binder.

It is applied to the mold by shaking it on the mold cavity through a porous cloth bag (*blacking bag*) or brushed on with a fine camel hairbrush. The excess is blown out with the bellows.

It is also sold in graded flat plates or crystals used to form a cover on melting bronze to prevent oxidization. When the metal is melted, the plates float on the metal to form a shingle-like cover that prevents the products of combustion (burner) from coming in contact with the metal surface. They are skimmed back to pour and used over and over. Graphite crucibles are made of German fire clay and graphite and fired in a kiln like pottery. Graphite can be purchased in many grades of fineness from air float to fairly coarse. Super fine collodial graphite is used as a coating for die cast dies and permanent molds (metal molds) by suspending it in water and spraying the hot die or cavity. The water evaporates, leaving a fine coat on the mold surface. It prevents the casting from sticking in the cavity or soldering itself to the cavity. This coat usually lasts for several castings. I have found over the years that anything short of the finest grade (most costly) is foolish finance.

The higher percentage of pure carbon the better; look for high carbon that is free from grit and foreign material. There are quite a few prepared graphite-based washes and facings on the market containing various synthetic and natural binders, additives, and vehicles. They can be purchased dry (you mix it to suit yourself) or pre-mixed. One of the best all around commercial products I have found for both a mold and core wash is sold under the trade name of Zirc-O-Graph™ A. It is a paste-like form of graphite and zircon flour with a binder which you mix with isopropol alcohol to the desired *baume*—a measure of specific gravity of liquids and solutions reduced to a simple scale of numbers.

Graphite can be produced artificially by passing an alternating current through a mixture of petroleum coke and coal tar pitch.

Each foundry supply manufacturer markets various types of washes and facings designed for molds, cores, ladle liners, etc.

graphite stopper The stopper attached to the stopper rod of a bottom pour ladle (Bessemer ladle). A stopper attached to a rod used in a large reservoir used to pour a mold.

gravel Gravel refers to any granular material. An appreciable portion would pass through a sieve with ½-inch openings but be retained on a No. 6 sieve (six openings per square inch).

green bond strength The strength of a tempered sand expressed by its ability to hold a mold in shape. Sand molds are subjected to compressive, tensile, shearing, and transverse stresses. Which of these stresses is more important to the sands' molding properties is a point of controversy.

The green compressive strength test is the most used test in the foundry. A rammed specimen of tempered molding sand is produced that is 2 inches in diameter and 2 inches in height. The rammed sample is then subjected to a load which is gradually increased until the sample breaks. The point where the sample breaks is taken as the green compression strength.

green compression The measure of compressive strength of a green sand sample—tenacity.

green permeability The measure of the ability to pass gasses through a sample of tempered molding sand.

green sand molds A mold composed of prepared molding sand in the moist or as mixed condition.

grid bars and grids Large flasks where the drag is rolled over and a bottom board would be cumbersome or impractical (Fig. G-8). The drag is fitted with cast iron or steel grids. The drag is rammed part way, the grid bolted in place and finished through the openings in the grid.

gyratory electric riddle This piece of equipment is inexpensive by comparison to all other mechanical sand conditioners available (Fig. G-9). The comb electric riddles have been manufactured for many, many years. I have one that was built in 1925 and it is still going strong. That company is still in business and a new one can be bought today. The comb riddle is simply an electric riddle or sifter which, by its gyratory actions, tempers and aerates the sand in one operation. The term *riddle* means to sift through a screen.

The operation of a comb riddle is simplicity itself. A one-sixth horsepower, low speed motor drives a shaft which is attached to

BOTTOM VIEW
GRIDDED DRAG

FIGURE G.8

Grid bars and grids.

a flywheel directly above the riddle. This flywheel is out of balance by virtue of a lead weight attached to one side of the flywheel's inner rim. When the flywheel is rotated, it imparts a gyratory or shaking motion to the lower screen, causing the sand shoveled into the riddle to mix and go through. The screens are easily removed by a quick clamp arrangement for cleaning or changing. The screens can be purchased in a wide variety of openings from 8 to the inch to the ½ inch. The ¼ mesh or four squares per inch is most commonly used screen to condition sand.

MOTOR

FLY WHEEL

RIDDLE

(COMBS)

FIGURE G.9

Gyratory electric riddle.

hanging core A core which is hung from the cope by tie wires (Fig. H-1).

hardener Any metallic or nonmetallic element added to a base metal or alloy to increase its hardness. Antimony added to lead will increase its hardness.

hard spots A problem with metallic iron castings. Wherever there is a shrink it will cause a hard spot and, as a result, machining difficulties.

hay rope A loose rope made of hay used to wind around core arbors. When making large loam or dry sand molds the rope provides a cushion to aid in the core collapse and ample venting.

head strainer A strainer core (ceramic or core sand) placed in a riser or head when the casting is poured directly into the head (Fig. H-2).

heap sand The sand used in the foundry to produce the bulk of the work, also called system or floor sand. Exclusive of special facing sands.

heart trowel The heart trowel is a handy little trowel for general molding and, as its name implies, has a heart-shaped blade. They run in size from 2 inches wide to 3 inches wide in ¼-inch steps (Fig. H-3).

heat treating The physical properties of some metals such as hardness, ductility, and strength may be altered by various methods of heating and cooling.

high lead tin bronze These alloys are traditionally the bearing and bushing bronzes. A typical high lead bronze would be 80 percent copper; 10 percent tin; 10 percent lead; .32 pounds per cubic inch; patternmakers' shrinkage, ⅛ inches per foot; pouring temperature light castings 2,000 to 2250 F.; heavy castings, 1850 to 2100 F.

high strength yellow brass Another name for manganese bronze. Typical composition: 63 percent copper; 25 percent zinc; 3 percent iron; 6 percent aluminum; and 3 percent manganese.

FIGURE H.1

Hanging core.

FIGURE H.2

Head strainer.

hinge tubes Tin forms used to core holes through ribs and lugs. They extend into the mold perpendicular to the parting (Fig. H-4). The hinge tube is placed in a properly fitted notch in the pattern before the sand is rammed. It remains in the mold after the pattern is drawn. Clean holes, accurate for size and location, are assured.

HEART
TROWEL

FIGURE H.3

Heart trowel.

Hinge tubes come in sizes from ⅛ to 1 inch round and oval from
¾₁₆ × ⁹⁄₃₂ to ½ × ¾ inches. They come ready to use with the pin tube
filled with baked core sand.

holding furnace An electric or fuel fired furnace for maintaining
molten metal from a larger furnace at the right casting tempera-

PATTERN

HINGE TUBE

PATTERN

MOLD

HINGE TUBE

CLEAN HOLE

CASTING

FIGURE H.4

Hinge tubes.

ture. The holding furnace is not a melting furnace and is able only to maintain the temperature of a metal bath. It is used to collect and hold.

hot box process   Accelerating the curing of a furan type binder with heat. This is done by ovens, infrared lamps, dielectric ovens, or by heating the core box itself.

The application of heat greatly enhances the resin reaction. Originally furan binders were the same used in the no-bake system (cured at room temperature). However, phenol has greatly replaced or substituted all or part of the furfural alcohol. Phenol urea-formaldehyde or modified furan, phenol, furfural alcohol urea-formaldehyde are all used.

hot chamber die casting   A die casting machine where the shot chamber is immersed under the casting metal and is self-filling. When the shot piston, on its return stroke, passes a port, the liquid metal fills the shot chamber through this port for the next shot.

hot spruing   Removing castings from gates before the metal has completely solidified. Hot spruing of light section casting and intricate castings is widely practiced. The gates must be designed so that they will not break back into the casting. Small and medium gray iron casings can be cold sprued in most cases, leaving only a nub to grind.

hot tears   This defect is actuary a tear or separation fracture due to the physical restriction of the mold and/or the core upon the shrinking casting. The biggest cause is too high a hot strength of the core or molding sand. These defects can be external or internal. A core that is overly reinforced with rods or an arbor will not collapse.

If you restrict the movement of the casting during its shrinking from solidification to room temperature, it will literary tear itself apart.

humectant   Any material added to foundry sand to retain moisture.

hydroblast   Cleaning castings with a high pressure stream of water and abrasive (usually sand).

hydrogen   Hydrogen is a colorless, odorless, tasteless elementary gas. It is easily produced by the disassociation of water or from any hydrides.

hydrogen absorption   The absorption of hydrogen by molten metal. The hydrogen usually comes from the products of combustion cracking hydrides as water vapor H_2O. Some metals have a great affinity for hydrogen when heated, aluminum in particular. Care must be exercised when melting with gaseous fuels so that the flame is properly controlled. With aluminum it should be neutral or slightly oxidizing.

hydrometer An instrument used to check the *baume*, the specific gravity of liquids (Fig. H-5).

hypereutectoid steel Steel containing more than the eutectoid percentage of carbon.

DEGREES BAUME

FIGURE H.5

Hydrometer.

I

infrared heat The use of infrared heat to bake cores with water soluble binders and those that soften on heating and harden on cooling (such as rosin).

illites A type of bonding clay. Not all illite clays are suitable but those with high bonding power have good dispersion and are quite satisfactory.

impact test The test given to a material with a pendulum in which the specimen is supported at one end as a cantilever beam (Fig. I-1). Measures the energy required to break off the free end. Called *Izod test*.

impoverishment The loss of any constituent from an alloy or localized area of an alloy by oxidation, liquidation, volatilization, or changes in the solid state. Also called *depletion*.

inclusions Dirt, slag, etc. This defect is caused by failure to maintain a choke when pouring, dirty molding, failure to blow out mold properly prior to closing, sloppy core setting causing edges of the print in the mold to break away and fall into the mold. The drag should be blown out, the cores set, and blown out again. Dirt falling down the sprue prior to the mold being poured or knocked in during the weighting and jacketing are also causes.

inconel A high nickel metal used for furnace fixtures, dairy, and food equipment. 79.5 percent nickel, 13 percent chromium, 6.5 percent iron, 0.08 carbon, developed by International Nickel Co.

in gates The gate leading directly into the mold cavity.

inhibitor A material such as fluoride, boric acid, or sulphur added to the molding sand for casting magnesium alloys to prevent burning of the molten magnesium. Restraining an undesirable chemical action i.e., oxidation. Any addition to a solution or substance to prevent or minimize corrosion.

GAUGE

PENDULUM

HAMMER

TEST
PIECE

CLAMP

FIGURE I.1

Impact test.

ingot molds   Cast iron or steel molds for casting ingots; also used to pig or ingot the metal left over in a ladle or the day's melt.

innoculant   Any material added to a molten metal which will modify the structure and change the physical and mechanical properties.

irregular draw   A pattern or portion of a pattern so constructed that it must be removed from the mold in other than a straight vertical lift (Fig. I-2).

irregular parting   A parting plane between the cope and drag that lies on more than one plane (Fig. I-3).

inserts   Parts formed of a second material, usually a metal. They are placed in a mold and cast into the body of the casting and appear as integral structural parts of the final casting (Fig. I-4).

inverse chill   A defect found in gray iron castings. It is hard or chilled iron. The cause may be incorrect carbon equivalent for the job or the presence of nonferrous metals in the charge, like lead, antimony, or tellurium. They are detrimental impurities.

An irregular draw.

Irregular parting.

investment casting wax Any wax used for expendable wax patterns and
gates. It runs from a hard carving wax to extremely soft. Over
2,000 formulas are available in natural or synthetic waxes.

investment molds Molds constructed of a refractory material around
wax or other expendable patterns such as plastic, mercury, etc.

FIGURE I.4

Inserts appears as integral structural parts of the final casting.

jacket A wood or metal frame placed around a mold made in a snap flask during pouring to support the mold and to prevent a run out between the cope and drag.

The common practice is to have as many jackets (for each size snap mold) as can be poured at one time. When the molds have solidified sufficiently the jackets are removed and placed on the next set of molds to be poured. It is called *jumping jackets*. Jackets must be carefully placed on the molds so as not to shift the cope and drag. The jackets must be kept in good shape and fit the molds like a glove. A tapered snap flask and tapered jackets work best due to the taper.

jack stars Jack stars are white cast iron stars similar to the jacks children play, except that they are pointed (Fig. J-1). These stars come in various numbers of points and sizes and are used to clean castings in a tumbler. The castings and stars are charged into the tumbler and the tumbler is rotated. The rotation causes the stars to rub and clean the castings. The points of the stars pick and rub sand loose from the castings. They can be purchased, but most iron foundries have a matchplate of star patterns and cast them as needed.

jar ramming Also called *jolt ramming*. The packing or ramming of the sand in a mold or core box by raising and dropping upon an anvil, the sand itself being the ramming medium (Fig. J-2). Jolt machines come in various sizes

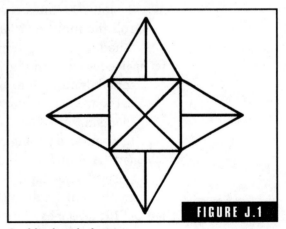

FIGURE J.1

A white iron jack star.

FIGURE J.2

The process of jar ramming.

from small bench jolt machines to large machines that will handle an extremely large burden (weight). These machines are pneumatic in operation. The air enters the cylinder under the piston, raising the table and mold when the piston passes the exhaust port. The air behind the piston exhausts, and the table and mold fall, striking the anvil.

The abrupt stopping of the table, mold, and sand upon striking the anvil does the ramming as the sand that is free to move continues its trip downward. The cycle is repeated until the desired density of the ram is reached.

Jolt machines can be purchased with various features which roll the mold over and draw the pattern when the jolting is finished.

jet engine bronze   An alloy of 68 to 62 percent nickel, 21 to 24 percent molybdenum, 7 to 8.2 percent aluminum (less than .1 percent carbon, .25 percent silicon, .15 percent iron, and .30 percent manganese). This alloy is called *kinsalloy* and is used for high-temperature jet engine parts.

job shop   A foundry which engages in casting for all comers, as opposed to the captive shop that manufactures numerous types of castings in small quantities.

jolt pin lift machines   Operated by the same principal as the stripper. The foundrymen lift the rammed flask from the pattern. The only difference is that it is done by four pins engaging the four corners of the flask. The pins are carried on a yoke, which is lifted by suitable cylinders.

jolt squeeze pin lift machine   A jolt squeeze machine equipped with a
pin lift to draw the mold from the pattern which is fixed to the
table.

A jolt squeeze molding machine. A. squeeze cylinder; B. squeeze piston; C. jolt piston;
E. vibrator knee valve; and F. jolt knee valve.

Unlike the jolt squeeze machine on which the entire mold is produced (cope and drag), the jolt squeeze pin lift, jolt stripper, jolt rollover, jolt rollover and draw, and the jolt pin lift machines produce half molds. The molders work in pairs. One operator makes drags and one makes the matching copes.

The usual combination is a jolt rollover draw or jolt squeeze rollover, a draw machine for the drag (which must be rolled over), and a jolt pin lift or jolt squeeze pin lift for the cope.

Completely mechanized machines can be had to make the mold completely ready to pour.

jolt squeeze molding machine A molding machine which is equipped with two cylinders and two positions—one for jolting the mold and one for squeezing the mold (Fig. J-3).

The machine is equipped with a molding table and a movable squeeze plate. The machine is designed to produce molds from matchplates. In operation, with the platen swung aside, the flask—complete with pattern between cope and drag—is placed on the table, drag side up. Sand is riddled onto the pattern, the drag is filled with molding sand, and a bottom board is placed inside the drag. The mold is jolted (see *jar ramming*) by the molder operating the jar air valve with his knee. When jolted sufficiently, the mold is rolled over with the cope upward. Sand is riddled on

FIGURE J.4

Jolt stripper machine.

the patterns in the cope, the cope filled and peen rammed, and a squeezer board is placed inside the cope. The platen is swung into position and the squeeze cylinder actuated. This procedure raises the mold against the platen and squeezes the entire mold between the bottom board and squeezer board, finishing the ramming of the cope and drag. The platen is swung aside the squeezer board, removed, and the sprue is cut. The pattern is vibrated, the cope drawn and set off. The pattern (matchplate) is again vibrated and drawn from the drag. The cope is then placed on the drag and the completed mold is set off for pouring.

jolt stripper machine   See *jar ramming*. The jolt stripper machine is a jolt machine with an air-operated lifting plate on which the flask bearing sets (Fig. J-4). This plate is raised drawing the mold half from the pattern, which is fixed to the jolt table.

K

kaolinite A hydrated aluminum-silicate clay also known as *fire clay*. It is one of a family of three distinct minerals having a similar composition—kaolinite, nacrite, and dicite. It is a sedimentary clay of low flux content. Its prime use in molding sands is in facing for very heavy work and also in dry sand work when excellent hot strength is required. It is often blended with western bentonite for this purpose. It comes closer than any other type of bonding clay to producing a sand which approximates the properties of naturally bonded sands. It's tough, durable, and easy to use.

killed steel Steel that has been completely deoxidized with silicon or aluminum to reduce the oxygen content to a minimum.

kiln dried The artificial air drying of pattern lumber in place of drying naturally.

kish (cast iron) If the carbon equivalent of the iron is too high for the section poured and its cooling rate is slow, free graphite will form on the cope surface in black shiny flakes free from the casting. It causes rough, holey defects, usually widespread. The carbon equivalent is the relationship of the total carbon to the silicon and phosphorous content of the iron. It is controlled by the make-up charge. Silicon is added at the spout. It is called carbon equivalent because the addition of silicon or phosphorous is only one third as effective as carbon, therefore the carbon equivalent of the three additives is equal to the total percentage of pure carbon plus one third the percentage of the silicon and phosphorous combined. The carbon equivalent is varied by the foundryman depending on what type of iron he is producing and what he is pouring.

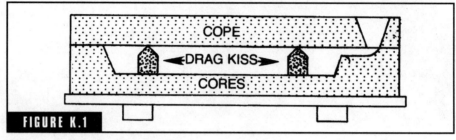

A kiss core does not set in a print.

kiss core   Kiss core is a small core which does not set in a print, but is held in place by the pressure of the cope surface of the mold (Fig. K-1).

knock out   The operation of removing sand cores from a casting.

ladle additions See innoculant.

ladle bowls Hand shank bowls which are shaped more like a bowl than a bucket (Fig. L-1).

ladle shanks The device by which a ladle is carried for transporting and pouring.

ladles Steel, refractory-lined containers used to receive and pour molten metal. They range in size from small hand ladles to crane ladles of 100 tons and over in capacity.

lagging of patterns Increasing the size and dimension of a pattern by applying strips of wood, plastic, or sheet wax to the area you wish to increase in dimension.

lake sand Another name for river sand, sharp sand, bank sand, white sand, core sand, and sugar sand. Usually defined as clay-free high silica sand.

lamp black A practically pure carbon (soot) produced by burning carbonaceous substances in an insufficient supply of air (reducing atmosphere). It is used in core and mold washes and blackings.

large skim gates Skimmer tins (Fig. L-2). Round and perforated tins or mica used as a skimmer under the pouring basin or elsewhere in the gating system.

latent heat of fusion When a molten mass of pure metal starts to cool the temperature drops at a definite ratio. A point of solidification is reached where the temperature remains constant until the entire mass is solidified. This point is called the *latent heat of fusion*.

lathe dog A forged or cast L-shaped device used to drive work in the lathe when turning between centers (Fig. L-3). The work is clamped in the dog jaw with a set screw or cap screws. The drive leg fits loosely into a slot in the faceplate.

launder An old term used to designate a channel for conducting molten metal.

FIGURE L.1

Ladle bowl.

FIGURE L.2

Large skin gates.

FIGURE L.3

Lathe dog.

layout board A smooth board with two sides square upon which the pattern layout is made. The dimensions are taken from this layout when making the pattern. A blueprint is used only to make the layout because they never show core prints, core boxes, etc., which the patternmaker must determine himself and put on the layout board.

lead A soft heavy bluish metal, Pb, obtained chiefly from the mineral galena. Melting point 621 F., boiling point 2777 F. When remelted from scrap, it is called secondary lead. It is widely used in alloying with other metals.

leaded cores A cousin of bolted cores (Fig. L-4). In place of bolting a core together you can lead them together by pouring molten lead into the attachment holes and then covering the top counter sink with a cap core. The cores must fit very closely to prevent lead from running out at the joint.

FIGURE L.4

Leaded cores.

lead dispersement The amount of lead that will go into solution with another metal. For example, pure molten copper will dissolve approximately 35 percent lead. If 2½ percent nickel is added, it jumps up to 70 percent.

lead effect The effect of lead as a defect. The presence of lead in a heat of aluminum bronze can cause a defect called *blue*. These are blue to purple stains on the surface of the casting, usually from cores or chills as little as .005 to .01 percent of lead amounts. Over .03 will cause gray to black stains.

It has little effect in regard to physical properties other than to contribute to hot shortness at elevated temperatures. Lead in the amount of .40 percent and above in manganese bronze (high strength yellow brass) has a deleterious effect on the mechanical properties and should be kept to .20 percent or lower. Lead in silicon bronze combines with the silicon to form lead silicate (glass). The problem is in distinguishing some red brasses (leaded) from silicon bronze. A small chunk of a leaded red brass in a silicon bronze heat will spoil the entire heat.

leaded nickel brass An alloy of copper, tin, lead, nickel, zinc, and iron. Also called nickel silver. When the alloy contains from 11 to 17.5 percent nickel in its composition it is called *leaded nickel brass*. When the nickel content is from 19.5 percent to 27 percent, it is called *leaded nickel bronze*.

Leaded nickel brass—typical:

- Copper, 58 percent
- Tin, 3 percent
- Lead, 11 percent
- Nickel, 14 percent
- Iron, 1.5 percent
- Zinc, balance

Leaded nickel bronze—typical:

- Copper, 67 percent
- Tin, 4.5 percent
- Lead, 5 percent

- Nickel, 21.5 percent

- Zinc, 10 percent

- Iron, 1 percent

- Manganese, 1 percent

As the nickel increases, the melting and pouring temperature increases. For 14 percent nickel, the pouring temperature for medium size castings would be 2200 F. For 17.5 percent nickel, 2260 F.; 21.5 percent nickel, 2300 F.; and for 24 percent nickel, 2400 F.

leaded red brass The most common leaded red brass is called ounce metal or 85 three 5's: 85 percent copper, 5 percent tin, 5 percent lead and 5 percent zinc. It is .318 pounds per cubic inch and has a 3⁄16 patternmaker's shrinkage per foot. The pouring temperature for light work is 2100 F. to 2300 F., for heavy work, 1950 F. to 2150 F. It can be deoxidized with 15 percent phosphorous copper, 1 to 2 ounces per 100 pounds.

An easy alloy to cast for general work. When the tin content is below 4 percent and the zinc increases it is called *semi-red brass*.

Semi-red brass-typical:

- 78 percent copper

- 3 percent tin

- 7 percent lead

- 12 percent zinc

leakers Castings, when subjected to hydraulic pressure, leak through the casting walls. This can be caused by many factors such as pouring temperature, gas porosity, wet molds, design, shrinkage porosity, or a chaplet which did not fuse or burn in properly. In short, it is an unsound casting. More often than not the fault lies in the casting design.

lead sweat High lead tin bronzes containing 15 to 27 percent lead are inclined to bleed or sweat lead. Also they have lead segregation. Excess gas absorption during melting will accelerate this condition. It cannot always be cured with excessive phosphorous copper additions (to deoxidize). It helps to add a small amount of lead oxide or copper oxide to melt 3 to 5 minutes before pulling the pot.

Remember that these alloys start to melt at 620 F., the melting point of lead. If you shake the casting out of the mold before it gets down below 620 F., it is going to bleed all the lead out from between the copper crystals and leave you with a lead-coated copper sponge. It is best to leave these high lead castings in the sand until they are at room temperature.

leaves in core   Strange as this may seem, blowing and gas porosity in a casting are often traced to leaves, roots, coke, and coal in the core sand. When using a raw beach or lake sand, if you do not buy washed and dried silica sand, check your sand for organic matter. It might be so very finely divided that it can escape detection. Check using the loss to ignition test to determine how much trash is present in the sand other than silica.

lifting force   The lifting or buoyant force on the cope is the product of the horizontal area of the cavity in the cope, the height of the head of metal above this area, and the density of the metal. This lifting force on the cope has to be reckoned with. If the force is greater than the weight of the cope, the cope will be lifted by this force when the mold is poured and run out at the joint, resulting in a lost casting plus a mess. In order to determine how much weight has to be placed on the cope, if any, to prevent a lift of the cope we multiply the area of the surface of the metal pressing against the cope by the depth of the cope above the casting and the product by 0.26 for iron, 0.30 for brass, and 0.09 for aluminum. These figures represent the weight in pounds of 1 cubic inch of iron, brass, and aluminum respectively.

If you are casting a flat plate 12 × 12 inches, the surface area against the cope would be 144 square inches. If this was molded in a flask which measured 18 × 18 inches with a 5-inch cope and the metal you are casting is red brass, you have 144 × 5 inches (the height of the cope), times 0.30 (the weight of 1 cubic inch of brass). You wind up with a lifting force of 216 pounds. One cubic inch of rammed molding sand weighs 0.06 pounds. So with that factor, the cope weight would be 18 × 18 × 5 inches times 0.06 or 97.2 pounds. If you subtract the cope weight from the lifting force of 216 pounds minus 97.2 pounds, you are still short by about 119 pounds. This is the weight you must add to the cope to prevent it from lifting with no safety factor. With a 20 percent safety factor, add 24 more pounds. You should put 150 pounds on the cope.

lifting hook (flasks)   See also *grab hook*. A hook or pad eye attached to a large flask for lifting or rolling over (Fig. L-5). A flask trunnion is sometimes called an *open lifting hook*.

lifting plates   Metal plates let into a pattern with a tapped hole in which a lifting screw (eye) with mating thread is screwed into to lift the pattern (Fig. L-6).

light metals   Metals that have a low specific gravity such as beryllium, magnesium, and aluminum.

light metal gate tubes   Perforated tin tubes used as skimmers in pouring aluminum and magnesium—strainer tubes (Fig. L-7).

lime in molding sand   The presence of excessive lime in a molding sand is often the hidden cause of gas holes, porosity, pin holes, and blisters in a casting.

liquid contraction   The shrinkage occurring in metal in the liquid state as it cools. Volumetric shrinkage.

liquid parting   A liquid used as a parting material in place of a dry or dust type parting, brushed or sprayed on the pattern. Old time liquid parting was bayberry wax dissolved in gasoline. When the gasoline dissolved, the pattern was lightly coated with wax.

FIGURE L.5

Lifting hook.

FIGURE L.6

Lifting plate.

SPURE

COPE

RUNNER

RUNNER

FIGURE L.7

Light metal gate tubes.

There are numerous commercial liquid partings on the market, ground mica, graphite, waxes, etc. They are dissolved or dispersed in various vehicles.

liquidus The temperature at which freezing begins during cooling, or melting ends during heating.

litharge Lead monoxide, PbO, also called *massicot*. It is a yellow-to-orange powder used in the foundry to make oil sand followers (oil match) (Fig. L-8). The most used formula is ½ dry naturally bonded molding sand and ½ dry sharp (core sad). Temper the sand with linseed oil and mix in a small handful of litharge.

When dry, a litharge match or follower is rock hard and will take a lot of abuse, lasting for years.

loam molding The production of large molds built up with bricks, plates, and various arbors which are covered with loam and dried to give the form of the casting desired. Great skill is required, covering a large variety of foundry knowledge, molding, pattern making, melting, etc.

Litharge.

loam sand A mixture of sand, silt, and clay in such proportions as to exhibit sand and clay particles in about equal proportions: 50 percent sand and 50 percent clay and silt.

lock buttons Aluminum buttons riveted to a matchplate directly over a corresponding counterbore recess (Fig. L-9). When the mold is made and the plate removed, you have sand projections on one face of the mold and corresponding female depressions directly opposite on the other face. When the mold is closed, these male and female sand members provide a sand-to-sand lock to help prevent the mold halves from shifting during handling, jacketing, pouring, etc.

loose patterns Unmounted patterns.

loose piece A part of a pattern so attached that it remains in the mold and is removed after the main body of the pattern is drawn (Fig.

Lock button.

FIGURE L.10

Loose piece.

L-10). The loose piece might be dovetailed to the pattern or pinned on with dowels. If by dowels, the sand is packed (rammed) tightly around the dowels and the loose piece to hold it in position. The dowels are withdrawn and the mold finished in the usual manner.

loss and gain in the cupola   The loss or gain of various elements when melting with a cupola varies depending upon its operation or who is operating it; the average, when melting iron, is loss of silicon, 10 percent; loss of manganese, 20 percent; and a gain of sulphur, .03 to .05.

When melting brass; the loss of copper, nil; loss of tin, negligible; loss of lead, 15 to 25 percent depending upon the percent of lead in the alloy. The higher the percent, the greater the percent loss and loss of zinc, 50 to 60 percent.

When melting brass or bronze in the cupola, it is best to melt the copper and tap it into a hot ladle containing the tin, lead, and zinc in the form of shot or small preheated chunks.

loss of ignition   The test to determine the percent of material in a molding sand which is lost or burned away during casting. Five grams of the sample sand are placed in a porcelain crucible and heated at 1610 F. for one hour and reweighed:

$$\frac{\text{Loss in Weight}}{\text{Weight of Sample}} \times 100 = \text{Percent of Loss}$$

Too high a percent of carbonous or gas-producing materials in a molding sand will cause gas holes, porosity, and pin holes in the castings. The percent is checked by ignition test.

lug   An ear-like projection, frequently split as a clamping lug on a tailstock.

lugs, matchplate   Metal lugs attached to the ears of a matchplate that match the flask pin shape (Fig. L-11). The lugs follow the drag pins as the plate is lifted (drawn), guiding the plate straight up.

lumber, diamond pattern   Pattern lumber with a carved face in various diamond designs. This lumber is used to make patterns with a

FIGURE L.11

Matchplate lug.

non-skid surface such as treads, sewer covers, catch basins, and similar industrial and street castings. Five different diamond designs are available from most patternmaker's supply houses, in thicknesses of ½, ⅝, and ¾ inch thick, 8, 10, and 12 inches wide and in various lengths. The design is machine carved and clean with ample draft.

lute A mixture of fire clay used to seal cracks such as the crack between a crucible and a crucible cover.

lycopodium A fine yellow powder obtained from a plant known as club moss, cultivated in Russia. It is regarded as the finest and perfect dry parting material, used when casting highly ornamental bronze work (as a dry parting). It is expensive, therefore, is used only for special jobs. It can be purchased in some drugstores.

M

machinability A measure of the ease of machining a metal. The easiest material to machine and that which offers the least resistance to machining would be rated 100. As a material becomes tougher to machine the rating lowers. Where a leaded red brass has a machinability rating of 90, an alloy of 90 percent copper and 10 percent nickel has a machinability rating of 10 or less; white iron 0 to 1.

machine ramming The term used to refer to a mold on a molding machine, slinger, etc., other than hand ramming. The use of pneumatic rammers is considered hand molding.

magnesium A silver-white metal, Mg, 64 percent the weight of aluminum with the specific gravity of 1.74. The melting point of magnesium is 651 C., 1202 F., and the boiling point 1120 C. (Fig. M-1).

Magnesium and magnesium alloys are melted and poured from crucibles made of welded boiler plate in sizes from 60 to 1000 pounds capacity. Small shops melt in the ladle. The ladle simply sits down through a hole in the furnace cover.

Sand used for magnesium casting must be low in moisture and contain inhibitors to prevent oxidization of the magnesium from water vapor. (See inhibitor.)

Multiple gates should be used in place of one or two large gates in order to fill the mold as rapidly as possible to prevent the sand from getting too hot and causing excessive steam. A typical magnesium base alloy for sand casting is composed of aluminum, 9 to 11 percent; zinc, .3 percent maximum; silicon, .3 percent maximum; copper, .10 percent maximum; nickel, .01 maximum; and magnesium, the balance. The tensile strength as cast is 23,000 PSI, when heat treated, it is 32,000 PSI.

FIGURE M.1

Magnesium.

magnetic brad set A pattern and model maker's tool used to set (drive) small wire brads with ease and in hard-to-reach places (Fig. M-2). It is a wooden handled tool equipped with a hollow tube which is spring loaded into the handle. The brad is held in the tube by the magnetic tipped plunger. The nose of the tube containing the brad is placed where you want to set the brad. Force is applied to the handle, pushing the magnetic plunger forward as the tube goes back against its spring thus pushing the brad into place.

The brad is pressed in place with a steady firm pressure. Never strike or drive the tool. This results in a bent brad and marred surface.

magnetic pulley A pulley used on a sand conveyor belt in ferrous foundries to remove tramp metal such as lost gates and shot metal from the sand (Fig. M-3). Because it is a permanent magnet,

FIGURE M.2

Magnetic brad set.

Magnetic pulley.

the sand will discharge from the belt and the tramp iron or steel will continue part way around the pulley due to magnetic attraction. It will discharge when the belt carries it away from the magnetic bond or attraction, dropping it off under the belt. Eriez of Canada produces a magnetic pulley with a unique magnetic field which is criss-crossing, radial, axial, and diagonal. It eliminates dead spots.

manganese copper   An alloy of manganese and copper used for the introduction of manganese into an alloy.

marine animal oils   A class of marine oils such as menhaden oil, sardine oil, whale oil, etc. These oils are used in conjunction with a vegetable oil such as linseed oil to produce core oils. (Menhaden oil is made from boiling porgy fish. Also called white fish.)

mass hardness   A condition in which the entire casting is too hard and unmachinable.

master dowels   Male and female dowels used in pattern to ensure a correct and precise register of pattern components while at the same time allowing the components to be freely taken apart or put together for molding (Fig. M-4). Maintains correct register with repeated use, which is not the case with wooden dowels.

FIGURE M.4

Master dowels.

Master dowels can be purchased in a large variety of sizes, designs, and lengths in brass or steel with the special tools required to install them.

master pattern A pattern used to cast the production patterns or equipment.

master sheet wax A sheet wax which can be purchased in a wide variety of thicknesses. It can be purchased with or without pressure sensitive adhesive on back. Its uses are too numerous to list. The limit depends upon the ingenuity of the user. The wax can be purchased with melting temperatures from 100 F. to 300 F. in sizes from 8 × 12 sheets to 12 × 24 inch sheets with a thickness of from 1/64 inches to 3/8 inches. Its use in the pattern shop is to *lag* up a pattern, make a core box pattern from a *core plug*, drier patterns from plugs, or a master pattern from a plug.

In the event only a few castings are required, a plug can be lagged up with sheet wax to the desired metal thickness and shape, shellacked and used as a pattern.

matched partings Forming of a projection upon the mating surface of the cope half of a pattern and a corresponding depression in the surface of the drag.

Matchplate.

matchplate The matchplate is the same as the mounted pattern with the exception that when you have part of the casting in the cope and part in the drag (split pattern), these parts are attached to the board or plate opposite each other and in the correct location so that when the plate is removed and the mold is closed, the cavities in the cope and drag match up correctly (Fig. M-5).

matchplate flask A large steel flask (very accurate) fitted with lifting screws to make a perfect draw; used to cast matchplates (Fig. M-6).

matchplate inserts Steel buttons cast in aluminum matchplates. When they are produced, these buttons are located where the cope and drag flask rest on the plate during molding (Fig. M-7). Their purpose is to prevent the flask from wearing the relatively soft aluminum plate at its point of contact.

Matchplate flask.

FIGURE M.7

Matchplate inserts.

medium pattern   A pattern that is used only occasionally or for casting a one-time piece. It is usually constructed as cheaply as possible. If it is a split pattern, wooden dowels are used for pins and fit it into holes drilled into the matching half.

melamine   A trimmer of cyanide used to produce a resin by reacting melamine and formaldehyde. A core binder.

melting atmosphere   The atmosphere in the melting furnace which is reducing (short on oxygen), oxidizing (rich on oxygen), neutral (neither oxidizing nor reducing), or inert by the introduction of an insert gas into the melting chamber.

melting loss   The loss of metal in the charge during the melting operation; it is kept to a minimum with good sound melting practice.

melting rate   The weight of metal in pounds or tons melted in one hour. If a cupola has a rate of 5, it should melt 5 tons of iron per hour at the tap.

melting ratio   The proportion of the weight of metal to the weight of fuel in a cupola melting. A cupola melting at a 7 to 1 ratio is melting 7 pounds of iron for each pound of coke.

metallic filler   Iron, aluminum, copper, or brass powder mixed with an epoxy or resin used to repair minor defects in a casting face or surface.

metal penetration   This defect should not be confused with an expansion scab, which is attached to the casting by a thin vein of metal. A penetration defect is a rough unsightly mixture of sand and metal caused by the metal penetrating into the mold wall or the surfaces of a core (not fused).

The defect is basically caused by a too-soft and uneven ramming of the mold or core, making the sand too open or porous. A too-high pouring temperature or a corner too sharp (insufficient filleting) makes it impossible to ram the sand tight enough, localization of the overheating of the sand due to poor gating practice, or a mold with a sand that is too open for the job, also cause penetration.

Penetration in brass castings is sometimes traced to excessive phosphorous used in deoxidizing the metal which makes it excessively fluid.

misrun   A portion of the casting fails to run due to cold metal, slow pouring, insufficient hydrostatic pressure, or sluggish metal (nonfluid due to badly gassed or oxidized metal).

micro shrinkage   The reference to extremely fine micro porosity caused by shrinkage.

moisture   The percent of moisture (water) in a molding sand.

mold and core washes   These washes coat the internal sand mold cavity and the surface of the core which comes in contact with the hot metal with a *refractory* coating in order to prevent the metal from burning-in. They produce smoother surfaces on the castings and facilitate the separation of the castings from the sand. This process is known as *peel*. In low melting metals and alloys this is not much of a problem due to the relatively low temperature involved.

Aluminum can be cast in molding sand which is quite fine and with a low refractiveness. It produces a clean smooth surface and excellent peel. However, because sand cores used in aluminum casting are usually quite open (high permeability), the cored cavity will not be nearly as smooth as the surface of the casting in contact with the green sand. The usual practice is to coat the core with a *wash* to fill in the spaces between the sand grains and present a smooth surface of the metal to lay against. Lead, zinc, and very fluid metals, which will actually seek their way between the grains of sand due to a low surface tension, are examples of where you would use a mold or core wash.

As a general practice it is wise to coat the portion of all dry sand cores with a core wash. As the temperature of the metal being cast rises, the permeability of the sand must be increased to allow for the greater volume of gas and steam being generated to pass through the mold walls and not back through the molten metal (coarser sand). These conditions increase the need for mold and core washes.

Also, when the metal section is quite heavy and subjects the sand to a longer period of heating during solidification, you need a wash. A ¼-inch brass casting poured at 2150 F. would present no problem as to burning or peel, but the same metal, poured at a lower temperature of 1950 F. and 1- to 2-inches thick in section, would burn-in badly with poor peel. This also applies to pouring the metal at an excessive temperature.

Another cause for rough surface, poor peel, and burn-in would be a casting poured with an excessively tall sprue and risers above the highest point of the casting. Here we have increased the *hydrostatic pressure* greatly against the cope surface, causing the metal to penetrate the cope and give a rough surface.

Where you have a casting which is quite large in size and requires a longer time to pour the section of sand directly below, the pouring sprue must take the impact and passage of hot metal for a longer interval of time and can be burned and eroded away, washing into the casting. Here again is where a good wash would be used at the gates into the cavity.

When you have an internal core which is necked down and passes through a wall, even though you are not concerned with the appearance or smoothness of the internal cavity, you have what is known as a *hot spot*. The core has to be washed at this point or the core could be badly eroded or come completely apart.

Learning when, where, and how much to apply a core wash is learned by experience and commonsense.

A mold facing or wash will overcome some of the problems of a poor sand that has insufficient refractories, but this is foolish finance.

Dry mold facings are also known as *shake-on facings*. Graphite is the most widely used.

Core and mold washes are carbonaceous and carbon free (Table M-1). Binders are organic and inorganic (Table M-2).

In the proper selection of a mold or core wash, dry or wet, you are better off with a simple compound. *Skin dried* molds come under the same category.

There are two ways of accomplishing this treatment. One way is to spray the mold cavity with a wet binder with or without a carbonaceous or carbon-free ingredient.

On light-to-medium size castings usually the mold can be simply sprayed (fine spray) with a mixture of 1 part molasses or lignin sulphite to 10 parts of water. Then carefully dry this with a soft flame torch moving continuously to prevent localizing heat and burning. The mold will then have a dry firm skin upon which the metal can lie. The

TABLE M.1 Carbonaceous and Carbon-Free Molds.

Carbonaceous	Carbon Free
Graphite	Silica Flour
Carbon Black	Talc
Ground Hard or Soft Coal	Magnesite
Petroleum Pitch	Alumina
	Asbestos
	Mica
	Zircon

trick here is to dry without burning the binder (molasses or lignin sulphite) and the mold must be poured shortly after skin drying to prevent the moisture in the mold behind this skin from migrating back to the surface. If this migration occurred, it would defeat the purpose. For heavier work or higher melting metals you can add graphite, talc, or any one of the bases and proceed just as described.

TABLE M.2 Binders.	
Organic	**Inorganic**
Starches	Clays
Dextrin	Bentonites
Sugar	Silicates
Molasses	Oxychloride
Rubber Cement	
Linglin Sulphite	
Glucose, etc.	

A very good method when using green sand cores made of the same sand the mold is made from is to dry the core completely. Dry it in a core oven 350 to 400 F. until dry through and through or overnight. When the cores are removed from the oven they are very fragile, crumbly, and cannot be handled at all. If sprayed while hot with molasses, or lignin sulphite when cold, they have a nice firm skin and can be set in the mold. Here again you should pour the mold shortly after closing to prevent moisture in the mold from migrating to the core.

The cores must be cold. A hot core set in a cold mold will cause condensation and blow.

This system is not cheap but does a very excellent job. The cores shake out easily, leaving a clean smooth defect-free surface. On thin wall castings, they can't be beat.

In place of skin drying the mold by spraying and torch drying, you can mix the binder with enough sand to cover the pattern with a layer ½-to 1-inch thick. Finish the mold with floor backing sand and then dry the mold face with a torch.

The binder can be molasses, lignin sulphite water, dry goulac, dry lignin sulphite, glucose, rosin, etc.

It is common practice to use a facing sand in many cases that is not skin dried but can consist of merely new sand, or sand mixed with sea coal, pitch flour, wheat flour, etc., and backed with flour or system sand.

A typical facing sand mix consists of 3 parts air float sea coal; 1 part goulac; and 10 parts molding sand. Another mix consists of 15 parts sharp sand; ½ part bentonite; and 3 parts system sand.

In some classes of work, the molder works with two sands, one for facing and a coarser sand for backing. This can cause trouble as the two eventually become so mixed together in the system that it all becomes useless.

moldability This characteristic is related to the nature of the bonding clay and the fineness of the sand.

Because the base sand determines the resulting finish of the casting, it should be selected with care, keeping in mind the type, weight, and class of casting desired. The three or four types of screened sands formerly used for a base have given way to the practice of blending one coarse sand with a fine one, which results in a better grain distribution. It has been found to produce a better finish and texture. Each of the two sands selected should have a good grain distribution within itself. Contrary to popular belief, additives of an organic or carbonaceous nature do not improve the finish but only furnish combustibles resulting in better peel.

mold clamps Floor molds are always clamped to pour. Sometimes they are weighted, sometimes not, but always clamped (Fig. M-8). There are two basic types of clamps used.

The *C clamp* is cast iron or square steel stock. In operation the bottom foot is placed under the bottom board and a wedge (wood or steel) is tapped between the top foot and the top of the flask side.

A better practice is to place two wedges between the clamp foot and flask by hand, then tighten them with a small pinch bar.

FIGURE M.8

Mold clamps.

Driving them tight jolts the mold and could cause internal damage, such as a drop.

The jack clamp is the preferred, but most expensive clamp. Its operation is simple. The foot is placed under the bottom board and the clamping foot is slid down against the cope flask. A bar is placed in the cam lever and pushed down until the clamp is snug and tight.

molder's bellows There are two types of bellows—one a short snout or bench bellow and one a long snout floor bellows (Fig. M-9). The theory is that a molder can wreck a bench mold blowing it out with a long snout floor bellows by hitting the sand with the snout. This theory is true due to the different stance and angle when blowing a mold bench high or on the ground. With care one only needs a 9- or 10-inch floor bellow to blow out cope and drag molds, sprue hole, and gates.

molder's blow can The blow can is a simple mouth spray can used to apply liquid mold coats and washes to molds and cores, or to ap-

VALVE

FIGURE M.9

Molder's bellows.

FIGURE M.10

Molder's blow can.

ply water to dampen a large area (Fig. M-10). It can also be operated with the air hose like the sucker.

molder's shovel   A shovel 38 inches long with a 9 × 12-inch flat blade. The handle is wedge shaped into a peen and a rubber piece is dovetailed into a cast handle (Fig. M-11).

mold anchor   Mold anchors are used to prevent shifting between the cope and the drag of molds made in slip or snap flasks (Fig. M-12). After the pattern has been drawn, but before the mold is closed, one end of the mold anchor is pressed into the sand of the drag and the cope is closed on the other end, securely locking the cope and drag in perfect alignment. Mold anchors can be purchased or made. They are made of sheet steel or tin plate.

PEEN

HANDLE

FIGURE M.11

Molder's shovel.

USE 4 OR MORE

DRAG MOLD

FIGURE M.12

Mold anchor.

mold hardness gauge A spring-loaded dial indicator gauge used to determine the mold hardness (Fig. M-13). The gauge is marked off from 0 to 100. The gauge measures the depth or amount of depression a convex shaped plunger makes when pressed down on a mold surface.

In operation the gauge is pressed down until the base anvil is level with the sand and the reading taken from the dial. The mold hardness gauge has a brake button which freezes its action. Readings may be taken in a deep pocket by applying then withdrawing the gauge. An excellent tool to not only gauge mold hardness but locate soft spots and uneven ramming.

molding board The molding board is a smooth board on which to rest the pattern and flask when starting to make a mold (Fig. M-14). The board should be as large as the outside of the flask and stiff enough to support the sand and pattern without springing when the sand is rammed. One is needed for each size of flask. Suitable cleats are nailed to the underside of the board. Their purpose is to stiffen the board and to raise it from the bench or floor to allow you to get your fingers under the board to roll over the mold.

PLUNGER

FIGURE M.13

Mold hardness gauge.

FIGURE M.14

Molding board.

mold shift A shift or misalignment between the cope cheek and/or drag sections of a mold causing a likewise shift in the casting.

mold weights All snap flask work is weighted before molding. In most cases all that is needed is a standard snap weight, which is usually cast by the foundry to suit their own snap sizes (Fig. M-15).

  The snap flask mold weights are from 1½ to 2 inches thick cast iron and weigh from 35 to 50 pounds for a 12 × 16-inch mold.

FIGURE M.15

Mold weights.

The rounded cross-shaped opening through the weight is to accommodate pouring the metal into the mold. The weights are always set so that the pouring basin is easy to see and pour. It should not be too close to the weight.

In some cases two or more stacked weights are used per mold.

Another type of mold weight which I favor for snap and small rigid flask bench work is the *sad iron* type of weight. They look like irons heated on the stove for pressing clothes, except that they are quite a bit heavier.

molybdenum A silvery-white metal, Mo, occurring chiefly in the mineral molybdenite and as a by product from copper ores. Its widest foundry use is in steel to reduce grain growth. In cast iron, it inhibits the decomposition of austenite to produce a strong fine-grained iron. In both steel and iron it is commonly alloyed with other elements such as nickel, chromium, manganese, copper, and vanadium.

monel A natural alloy produced directly from Canadian Bessemer Matte by the reduction of nickel ore, or produced by alloying. The average composition is 67 percent nickel, 28 percent copper, with the remaining balance of 5 percent iron, manganese, and silicon. Its melting point is approximately 2460 F. It can be cast, rolled, or forged. 65,000 PSI tensile up to 100,000 PSI (cast); 50 percent elongation.

motor chaplets A riveted head. Round or square-headed chaplet. Some have a round head on one end and square head on the other end. Others have a sprig or peg on one end to locate it in a hole in a core (Fig. M-16).

mottled cast iron Cast iron consisting of a mixture of variable proportions of gray cast iron and white cast iron. It has a mottled white and gray fracture.

mounted pattern When a pattern is mounted to a board to facilitate molding, it is called a mounted pattern. In this case the mount guides on each end match up with the flask used to make the mold. The plate is placed between the cope and drag flask. The drag is then rammed and rolled over. The cope is now rammed and lifted off. The plate with the attached pattern is lifted off the drag half. The mold is then finished and closed.

muller A sand mixing machine which conditions and mixes the sand by the mulling action of one or more large flat-face wheels rotating in a tub, but not touching the bottom (Fig. M-17). Plows direct or

FIGURE M.16

Motor chaplets.

windrow the sand in front of the mulling wheels, which mull the sand with a smearing action as they roll over the sand. Some mullers are constructed so that the tub rotates and the wheels are stationary. Others have the tub stationary but the wheels travel in a circle.

multiple molds   A composite mold made up of stacked sections. Each produces a complete gate of castings and is poured from a single sprue (Fig. M-18). The top of one section forms the drag of the section above it and the cope of the section below it.

FIGURE M.17

Muller machine.

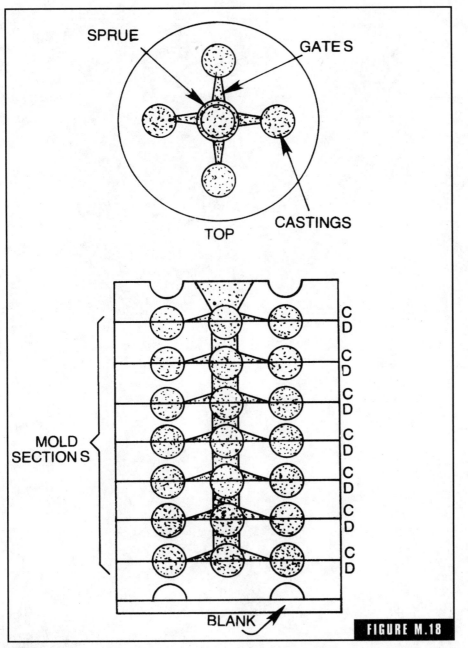

SPRUE

GATES

CASTINGS

TOP

C
D
C
D
C
D
C
D
C
D
C
D
C
D
C
D
C
D
C
D
C
D
C
D

MOLD
SECTIONS

BLANK

FIGURE M.18

Multiple molds.

N

natural molding sands Contains from 8 to 20 percent natural clay. The remaining material consists of a refractory aggregate, usually silica grains.

Any natural sand containing less than 5 percent natural clay is called a *bank sand* and is used for cores or as a base for synthetic molding sand.

Commercial molding sands mined by various companies usually acquire the name of the area where they are mined. The most popular naturally bonded molding sand is called Albany. It is mined in several different grades by the Albany Sand & Supply Co., Albany, N.Y. The origin of this sand is from the Pleistocene ice sheet of approximately 20,000 years ago which swept down from the north and completely overran what is now known as the Albany District. The result, after eons, is a seam of fine molding sand approximately 15 inches thick directly under an overburden of 8 inches of top soil.

neck down cores A core used to neck down a riser at its point of contact with the casting to aid in its removal. In turn, it defeats the action of the riser to some extent because the neck is first to freeze (Fig. N-1). Long skinny necks on risers render the riser useless.

neutral refractories A refractory which is neither definitely acid or definitely basic. Chrome refractories are the most nearly neutral of all commonly used refractories. Of course you have changes at high temperature due to chemical reaction, thus the use of the term *neither definitely*.

nichrome An alloy of nickel and chrome used to produce electric heating elements and parts subjected to high temperatures, kiln furniture, etc.

nickel A silvery-white metal with a yellowish cast isolated in the year 1751. It has been used in alloy with copper since ancient times. Specific gravity of 8.84, melts at 2646 F. Widely used as an alloy in

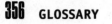

FIGURE N.1

Neck down core.

both ferrous and nonferrous metals. The uses of nickel could fill many a volume: nickel brass, nickel cast iron, nickel steel, nickel bronze, nickel chrome alloys, nickel plating, etc.

nitriding   The process of case hardening, where a ferrous metal is heated in contact with a nitrogenous material or in an atmosphere of ammonia. It produces surface hardening by the absorption of nitrogen.

nodular graphite   Free graphite in cast iron in the form of nodules or spheroids (nodular iron).

nonsilica parting compound   A dry parting containing no free silica, usually made of a high melting wax powder.

normalizing   Heating a ferrous alloy casting to above its transformation temperature and allowing it to cool slowly at room temperature in still air. Reduces internal stresses. Also called *stress relieving*.

normal segregation   Concentration of alloying constituents that have low melting points in the portion of the casting that solidifies last.

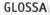

FIGURE N.2

Notch bar facilitates breakage.

notch bar Small-size ingots with notches to facilitate breakage (Fig. N-2).

nowel A colloquial term for the drag mold, not often used except by old timers.

nozzle opening The opening in the bottom of a Bessemer ladle through which the metal is teemed when the nozzle stopper is lifted.

nugget A small mass of metal, such as silver and gold, found in nature.

odd side   A flask or frame used to support a loose pattern to establish an approximate parting during the ramming of a cope or drag. Afterward, the mold being made is rolled over and the odd side is removed and shaken out. It is replaced with a cope or drag section and the mold is completed as usual. The odd side is often referred to as a *false cope* or *false drag*.

offset matchplate   The area inside of the flask is offset which produces a matching male and female offset in the completed mold which by its locking or mating nature helps to eliminate mold shift when producing snap work (Fig. O-1).

   The sure lock matchplate by Kindt Collins, Cleveland, Ohio, accomplishes the same thing as an offset plate only much more accurately by producing a series of male and female matching projections and sockets around the inside perimeter of the flask.

oil no-bake core and mold process   A synthetic oil binder mixed with basic sands and chemically activated to produce dri-sand cores and molds at room temperature. It is an acid dehydration or condensation reaction. The oxidation reaction is accomplished chemically rather than by heat and oxygen.

oil oxygen process   Used to produce dri-sand cores and molds by the principle of auto-oxidation. The system utilizes both oxidation and polymerization mechanics on a combination of oils containing chemical additives so that the final product is activated with oxygen-bearing materials. It will set (harden) in a predetermined time.

old casting for pattern   In some cases a broken or old casting can be used as a pattern to produce a new or additional casting. In the case of a simple casting which leaves its own core and has ample draft, like a cast iron frying pan, this can be a cinch. Large gear wheels have been cast from a broken gear as a pattern by waxing draft on the teeth,

Offset matchplate.

plugging the bore through the hub with a core print, and rapping the gear heavily in the mold to take care of the shrinkage. Old machinery replacement parts are often produced this way.

olivine foundry sand A translucent mineral $Mg.Fe. 2.SiO_4$ A solid solution of forsterite and fayalite. Also called *chrysolite*. The clearer green stones are used as gems, peridot. Olivine sand is highly refractory. The melting point of forsterite is 3470 F. It is expensive, but an excellent molding sand (when bonded with bentonite) and a great core sand for the tough jobs. *Olivine flour;* olivine sand ground to a flour makes an excellent investment mix—2 parts plaster of paris, 3 parts olivine flour. Also excellent core and mold washes bonded with molasses water or goulac water.

omission of a core Results and cause obvious.

open grain structure A defect where the grain is too coarse when machined or fractured. The causes are many, including carbon equivalent too high for the section, lack of carbide stabilizers, pouring too hot (in iron), or pouring too cold. This defect can be throughout the casting or in random spots.

open hearth   A furnace for melting metal in which the bath is heated by the convection of hot gasses over the surface of the metal and by radiation from the roof.

open sand casting   Casting in an open sand mold with no cope. This process is used to cast plates for rigging and where large weights are needed. The big trick in open sand work is in the ramming. The sand must be rammed hard enough to support the weight of the metal; otherwise, without the hydrostatic pressure provided with a cope and sprue height, the metal will kick badly and you wind up with a dangerous mess.

It is very tricky to say the least. It requires much greater skill than molding with a cope. Pouring an open sand mold is also tricky. The trick is to pour from one side, starting a wave of metal across the mold, slacking off and then pouring again in such a way that you catch the returning wave (rebound) with a second wave. You repeat this action until the mold is poured.

optical pyrometer   A temperature measuring device through which the observer sights the heated object and compares its incandescence with that of an electrically heated filament whose brightness can be regulated. The operator regulates the brightness of the filament until it matches by disappearing from the screen. The temperature is read on the side of the instrument.

optimum moisture   That moisture content which results in the maximum development of any property of a sand mixture.

organic material in melting   The gassing and inferior properties of castings (mainly nonferrous) where the scrap, chips, borings, etc., are not completely cleaned of cutting compounds and oils.

over hand   The extension of the end surface of the cope half of a core print beyond that of the drag in order to provide clearance for closing the mold (Fig. O-2). It prevents the cope from shaving if not closed completely level.

over iron   The amount of iron left in a ladle or excess melted for the floor. This over iron must be kept to a minimum but at the same time it must be short with the heat. In a ladle it can be more costly. It is similar to pouring a 500-pound casting with 450 pounds of metal in the ladle.

oxidation   Any reaction whereby an element reacts with oxygen. Combustion by-products and rust are both forms of oxidation.

FIGURE 0.2

The over hand provides clearance for closing the mold.

oxygen lance   A length of ⅛- to ¼-inch steel pipe connected by a flexible hose to a regulator and oxygen bottle. It is used to burn through steel or burn through a frozen tape hole on a cupola.

pad   A shallow projection on a casting distinguished from a boss or lug by shape and size only (Fig. P-1).

paddle mixer   A sand mixer which mixes the sand with a series of offset metal paddles in a churning action, as a plaster mixer.

parted pattern   A pattern made in two or more parts (Fig. P-2).

parting   The zone of separation between the cope and drag portions of a mold, flask, or pattern. Also called *parting plane*. The word parting also refers to any material used to effect a parting: parting powder, PVC, parting compounds, etc.

parting compound   A material dusted or sprayed on patterns to prevent adherence of sand and to prevent the sand-to-sand joint of a mold from adhering together.

parting line   A line on a pattern or casting corresponding to the separation between the cope and drag portions of a sand mold (Fig. P-3).

pasted cores   Cores which are made in halves and after they are dried, glued together to make the complete core. If the core is symmetrical, a half box is all that is needed.

FIGURE P.1

Pad.

FIGURE P.2

Parted pattern.

After the two halves of the core are dried, a vent is scratched along the centerline of one half and the sections are glued together with core paste. The seam is then mudded with a material known as *core daubing*. Both core paste and daubing can be purchased or made. For homemade core paste, use enough wheat flour dissolved in cold water to produce a creamy consistency.

For a good core daubing, mix fine graphite with molasses water—1 part molasses to 10 parts water. Enough graphite is added to the molasses water to make a stiff mud.

Another good daubing mix is graphite and linseed oil mixed to a stiff mud.

After a core has been pasted and daubed, it is a good idea to return the core to the core oven for a short period to dry the paste and daubing.

pattern board A true surface smooth board reinforced with cleats upon which a loose pattern is laid for ramming the drag.

pattern coating Coating material, like shellac, applied to wood patterns to protect them against moisture and abrasion.

FIGURE P.3

Parting line.

Stopping off.

pattern colors (wood patterns) Patterns are colored to indicate the following:

- Black—Surface to be left as cast (unfinished)
- Red—Surfaces of the casting to be machined
- Yellow—Core prints and seats of and for loose core prints
- Red stripes on a yellow background—Seats of and for loose pattern parts
- Black stripes diagonally on a yellow background—Stop-offs (Fig. P-4)

By looking at a properly colored pattern the molder can determine if he has all the parts, cores, and exactly how to proceed with the mold making.

pattern letters White metal, brass, or aluminum letters and figures for attaching to wood or metal patterns for identification, name, directions, etc. (Fig. P-5). The letters can be purchased in a wide variety of letter styles and sizes from as small as $\frac{3}{32}$ inch to 4 inches in size. They can be plain back, with sprigs, drilled, or with reverse letters for making branding irons. They are used widely to make grave markers, plaques, signs, etc.

Pattern letters.

Plain back letters are usually glued to the pattern or shellacked. Sprigged letters are attached to wood patterns by tapping them down in place with a soft hammer. The sprigs act as brads. Drilled letters are pinned or screwed on to the pattern. The letters are all drafted correctly for molding.

pattern lumber Although patterns can be made of many kinds of woods, most wood patterns are made of mahogany or sugar pine. Mahogany is usually used for fine delicate wood patterns but is not confined to small patterns. Philippine, African, Mexican, Honduran, Peruvian, and Cuban mahoganies are available for use to the patternmaking trade; however, Mexican, Honduran, and the Peruvian grades are by far the most used for pattern work. It is a hard wood, easily carved and worked and will withstand the hard use and abrasion encountered in the foundry exceptionally well. It weighs approximately 3 pounds per board foot and can be purchased in random lengths and widths from ¼ (1 inch thick) to ¹⁶⁄₄ (4 inch thick) in various grades. The better select grades are used for pattern work.

Sugar pine, a native wood of California and southern Oregon, weighs 2.3 pounds per board foot. It is a softer and lighter wood than mahogany. It is widely used and holds up extremely well under use in the foundry. It's also available in a wide range of widths, lengths, and thicknesses. The select grades are the most used for patterns. Basswood also is good.

For years Jelutong wood was used throughout the rest of the world for pattern work and it is now becoming popular in the western hemisphere. It is a white or straw colored wood with no differential between heart wood and sapwood, a moderately fine even texture, straight grain, and low luster with the weight of pine.

penetration   A casting rough surface defect which appears as if the metal has filled the voids between the sand grains without displacing them. It is caused by a too-coarse molding sand for the metal and casting weight.

perforated chaplets   Tin coated sheet steel chaplets made from perforated stock (Fig. P-6).

perforated tin sheets   Perforated tin plated sheets of steel used to form various types of skimmers and gates, sold in a wide variety of thicknesses and perforations.

permeability   The ability of the mold material to allow steam to pass through the walls. Permeability can be measured with a meter which measures the volume of air that will pass through a test specimen per minute under a standard pressure. Some instruments are designed to measure a pressure differential, which is indicated on a water tube gauge expressed in permeability units.

permanent molds   A mold made of metal or graphite. It is used repeatedly for the production of many castings of the same form, not an ingot mold. It is usually gravity poured. Ninety-nine percent of all automotive pistons are cast in permanent molds.

Petro Bond   Petro Bond is a patented oil bonding system of NL Baroid Industries. Petro Bonded sand consists of fine silica and a maximum of ½ percent of clay (preferably clay-free) mulled with Petro Bond oil, Petro Bond powder, and P-1 catalyst. Typical green sand properties using a GFN are 140 sand, compression strength 12 PSI, permeability 15, flowability 87, rammed hardness (mold hardness gauge) 84, and a green deformation in inches .010 to .014. It is basically used as nonferrous green sand and with excellent results up to and including a 4500-pound bronze casting. Two pounds of iron oxide per 100 pounds sand is beneficial to the correct balance between fine and coarser sand. If Petro Bonded sand is used as a facing sand, it will mix in readily with flour or system sand with no problem.

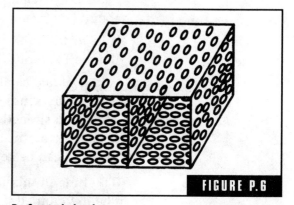

FIGURE P.6

Perforated chaplet.

It has been my personal experience with Petro-Bonded sand that if just sufficient graphite is added to give it a gray color (2 percent to 3 percent), the results are superior to those with just the iron oxide. It is not nearly as sticky, has excellent lifts, smoother casting surface, the flowability is increased 100 percent, and the mold hardness is improved. Although you need a mutter to prepare the initial batch I find it can be kept in shape for months on end by simply riddling it with a *gyratory riddle*. Most foundry supply houses will supply you with Petro Bonded sand ready to use (mulled by them).

Although it is no panacea for small hobby shops, for schools with little or no sand conditioning equipment, it is great. Because of the absence of moisture, a finer sand can be used and the problems caused by moisture are eliminated. Liquid parting cannot be used. Use a good grade of commercial dry parting or use Petro Bond (the dry binder) as a parting.

Some large commercial foundries have converted to complete Petro Bonded systems. A typical Petro Bond mix consists of 100 pounds dried silica sand, 5 pounds Petro Bond binder, 2 pounds Petro Bond oil, 1 ounce catalyst P-1 or 100 pounds dried silica sand, 5 pounds Petro Bond binder, 2 pints metro 20 (oil) from Mobile Oil Co., and 1 ounce methanol alcohol.

Petro Bond™ is a registered trademark of NL Industries Inc.

The mixing procedure for Petro Bond sand is divided into three phases:

1. Weigh out 100 pounds of sand and mix into it 5 pound of Petro Bond. Dump the load into the muller and mix dry for about one minute.

2. Add to the mix in the muller 2 pounds or 2 pints of Petro Bond oil and mull for about 10 minutes.

3. Add 1 ounce catalyst P-1 and mix for 3 to 5 minutes longer. With many sands the green strength will be at least 8.5 psi. The green strength required will depend on the type of metal to be cast and the size of the casting to be made. After mixing, the sand can be kept indefinitely.

The time of mixing varies with the type of muller used and can be determined by varying the mixing time until the desired strength is obtained.

In a slow muller the dry ingredients should be mixed for a minimum of one minute. Subsequently, the oil can be added slowly while the muller is in motion and mulled for a period of 10 minutes. The P-1 catalyst is then added and mixed for 3 to 5 minutes. The mix can then be stored indefinitely and will be usable at any time without further treatment.

If this mix results in a stronger sand than desired, it may be cut with clean sand.

As the sand is used it may become contaminated with coarse particles of core sand. If this contamination proceeds to the point where the over-all percentage of fines in the sand is noticeably reduced, it is advisable to add iron oxide during one of the remulling cycles. Such additions help restore the correct balance between fine and coarse sand. The usual procedure is to add the iron oxide at the rate of from 1 to 2 pounds per 100 pounds of sand. This addition will also result in a tougher but drier sand. It may then be necessary to add additional oil to restore proper moldability.

When it is used for the entire mold, after the casting has solidified and is *shaken out*, it is only necessary to *aerate* or *riddle* the sand before re-using. This sand can be used without remulling until the green strength has been reduced sufficiently to cause scabbing or washing.

Petro Bond sand may be used as a facing for green sand molds. When Petro Bond sand is used as a facing, the burned sand readily mixes with the green backing sand.

For both types of use, best finishes are obtained when the mold hardness is 80 or higher.

Patterns made of wood, plaster, aluminum, brass, steel, etc., can all be used. Bear in mind that the accuracy and finish of the casting produced can be no better than the pattern. Waxed patterns should not be used until they have been coated with a hard resin or paint.

The following difficulties usually can be eliminated by using the procedures described. If the trouble continues, carefully check all materials, equipment, and process cures being used.

■ Low Green Strength

The minimum green strength of 8½ pounds should be obtained if the mix is adequately mulled.

Improper milling. The formula may be correct and the ingredients good, but the actual mulling achieved may be inadequate. The muller must be clean and dry and have a rough enough surface to provide intensive mixing. The wheels of the muller should be lowered to the pan to give the proper mulling action. Plows that are too worn will not provide proper mixing. If portable mulling equipment is being used, the time of mulling should be greatly increased (above the time required for mulling by heavier stationary equipment) in order to get a mix of proper green strength.

Petro Bond content too low. Make sure you have used the amounts and the ratio of Petro Bond to oil that is prescribed in the foregoing mixing procedures. Be sure the Petro Bond is uniformly dry mixed and the oil is added slowly to avoid leakage.

Too much moisture in sand. Check the sand to make certain that the moisture content is less than ¼ percent.

Oil is not of the proper type. Recheck the oil being used. Make certain that the oil is of the proper specifications. If the finished mix has a glossy appearance, it indicates that the oil is probably not of the proper specifications.

■ Poor Finish of Castings

Incorrect mold hardness. Check your mold hardness. Make sure that its hardness is 80 or better. If you are using a very high green strength in your mix, make certain that the mold is rammed properly to give you a minimum mold hardness of 80.

Wrong parting agent. Do not use a liquid parting agent with Petro Bond. A dry parting is necessary if loose patterns are used, especially if they are wooden patterns that have been shellacked. Petro Bond can be used as a dry parting.

■ Turbulent Metal Flow or Lack of Effective Choke Feeding

To assure smooth metal flow and adequate filling of the cavity, choke the flow of metal to eliminate turbulence. Most metals can be poured at lower temperatures due to the absence of the chilling effect of water and the lower heat conductivity of the oil.

■ Cutting and Washing in Molds

Improper ramming of the mold. Make certain that the mold is rammed hard. Check the in gates and sprues to make sure they are properly cut. If the gates and risers are cut after the mold has been made, it is advisable to lightly swab the surface of the cut with the same oil used in the Petro Bond mix. This helps to bind the grains of sand and minimize any washing into the casting. In gates and sprues should be smaller in the Petro Bond molds than in conventional sand molds.

Improper pouring of molds. Petro Bond sand molds can be poured at considerably lower temperatures. If the surface of the Petro Bond mold is very smooth, the flow of metal should be reduced or restricted. This can be accomplished by using strainer cores or by changing the gating system so that the metal enters the mold without turbulence.

■ Non-Uniform Reproduction of Pattern

Improper mold hardness. If it is found that the cope and drag surfaces of the castings are smooth but the side walls are not, it is an indication that the mold has not been rammed hard enough. The mold hardness should be uniform on all the mold surfaces. Cope, drag, and matchplate equipment give the best reproduction.

■ Out of Dimension Castings

Insufficient cooling time. When castings are removed from the mold too soon there is a tendency of the casting to warp because of non-uniform solidification. It is essential to leave the casting in the sand long enough to have it properly solidified.

■ Gas Problems—Blows, Cold Shuts, Etc.

Too much oil in the mix—When excessive amounts of oil are used in Petro Bond mixes, the surface of the metal may show slight imperfections. To eliminate this condition, mull 2 percent iron oxide into the mix to absorb the excess oil. Another method is to rebalance the formula by the addition of clean silica sand and Petro Bond to bring the mix to the proper green strength.

Check permeability. Molds made with Petro Bond are poured at considerably lower permeability than molds made with water-bonded sand. There is, however, a minimum level of permeability. This is particularly true when pouring high temperature alloys. The optimum must be established to give proper castings.

■ Poor Castings Finish

Excessive contamination by core sand. Result of using same sand over a period of several months. Check your system and see if excessive amounts of core sand are being introduced.

phosphorous A nonmetallic element, P, widely diffused in nature and found in many rock materials and ores. In the foundry it is used as a deoxidizer combined with copper or other alloys to stabilize it so that it can be handled.

phosphoric acid H_3PO_4 used in pickling and rust proofing. Widely used as the catalyst in the furan no-bake sand system.

pickle To clean metal by chemicals or electro-chemicals. To remove surface oxides, etc. An acid or caustic solution.

pig bed Small scooped-out pig-shaped excavations made in an open sand mold or bed to pour off the excess metal from a heat.

pig iron Cast iron produced by the reduction of iron ore in a blast furnace.

pinch dog A steel C-shaped device with sharp points tapered on their inner face to give a clamping effect when driven into wood (Fig. P-7). The further in, the tighter the clamp (pinching) effect. Used in pattern work to hold one member to another while gluing, nailing, or drilling. The prime use is in gluing up stock. Some

PINCH DOG

FIGURE P.7

Pinch dog.

patternmakers use them to hold the two halves of stock together when turning a split pattern. This is a very dangerous practice. If they become loose while turning, the centrifugal force will throw them with great impact. You could be seriously injured or killed.

Pinch dogs come in sizes from ½ to 3 inches between points. Purchased from any pattern supply or foundry supply company, they can be used for a variety of tasks.

pin holes Surface pitted with pin holes; may also be an indicator of subsurface blow holes.

pine tree structure The appearance of dentrites crystal growth in a solidifying metal.

pitch and gilsonite Both of these materials are used to produce dry and hot strength along with good hot deformation and as expansion controls. Also used as a binder for dry sand work and black sand cores. It is a baking type of binder. Most prepared black core binders sold today under various trade names are usually a mixture of pitch, destrin, lignin sulphite, and resin. To use these correctly you should know the percentage of pitch. Light work pitch is used by percent by weight. When using pitch in dry sand work it must be worked well on the wet side. It is used in skin dry and dry sand work for large aluminum bronze work and dried overnight. Sometimes it is used in combination with 50:50 with sea coal and also with southern bentonite. When used as a replacement for sea coal, it can be used as low as ½ percent to as high as 4 percent by weight. The mold hardness, toughness, and green strength increases as does the hot and dry strength. The permeability decreases somewhat and little or no effect on the flowability is encountered. It should be noted that other materials are also used as ingredients in facings such as lignin sulphite, rosin, graphite, coke, and fuel oil. Gilsonite is a natural pitch much more potent than coal tar pitch and usually is used sparingly in the order of ½ to 1 percent in green sand facing mixes. It is also used in the manufacture of some mold and core washes.

porosity Unsoundness of a casting due to the presence of blow holes, gas holes, or shrinkage cavities.

poured short Casting incomplete due to not filling the mold. Going back and touching up the mold will not correct it.

pouring basin A basin on or in the cope to hold the metal prior to its entrance into the sprue.

pouring devices Any device that is used to handle ladles or crucibles for pouring molten metal. They vary from simple shanks to complex apparatus and automatic robotic devices.

pressure Too low a pressure (hydrostatic) by having too shallow a cope flask. Thus a short sprue will cause scars, seams, and plates as a casting defect.

pressure tight A casting that does not leak under pressure. It is free from porosity and unsoundness.

primary crystals The first dentritic crystals formed in an alloy during cooling below the liquidus temperature.

print back The pattern is removed from the mold and the sand cavity dusted with cement or plumbago. The pattern is returned and rapped to set the surface and redrawn. This system is used to produce an extremely smooth casting surface. It is widely used when casting plaques and grave markers.

progressive solidification The solidification of a casting from the thin sections the farthest away from the sprue toward the sprue or riser (Fig. P-8). It is accomplished by correct design, chills, correct gating, and risering.

FIGURE P.8

Progressive solidification.

prop   The iron post that holds the cupola bottom doors closed.

protein binders   Core and mold binders which are organic compounds containing nitrogen.

pull cracks   Hot tear.

pull down   A sand buckle in the cope due to excessive expansion of the cope sand. Insufficient combustibles in the sand (wood flour, etc.).

push-up   An indentation in a casting usually on the drag side due to the displacement of the sand in the mold. Often caused by improperly seated bottom boards, poor clamping practice, or too shallow a drag for the job.

quenching Heating a casting to a specified temperature and rapidly cooling it in water, oil, etc., to create a heat treatment.

R

radiant heat The heat radiated from a furnace arch and walls. Also the heat radiated from the molten metal poured into a mold. The cause is often metal penetration due to the improper location of gates and risers; this promotes localized overheating of the sand. Pouring a mold with an insufficient number of gates will subject the mold surfaces to radiant heat for too long a period and will cause the mold surface to break down. A very common problem with investment castings which are undergated and prevent the mold from filling fast enough.

radiator chaplets Differ from most other chaplets in that they are set before the mold is rammed (Fig. R-1). The practice is to drill a hole in the pattern corresponding to the diameter of the wire used in the chaplet. The chaplet is dropped into the hole, sand rammed into the mold, and the pattern withdrawn. The stem of the radiator chaplet is left protruding in the mold cavity a distance equal to the thickness of metal and ready to support or hold down the core in its proper position.

When the core is set, it rests against the flat end of the wire stem. In many cases this does not provide a sufficient bearing surface when the casting is poured. Additional bearing surfaces can be obtained by putting a round or square core plate on the core, against which the radiator chaplet will press.

The most commonly used radiator chaplet has a shoulder and break-off nicks. This drops into the hole in the pattern as far as the shoulder.

ram-away A defect caused by molding with a sand that has poor flowability and ramming at the wrong angle (Fig. R-2). A section of the mold is forced away from the pattern by ramming sand after it has conformed to the pattern contour.

FIGURE R.1

Radiator chaplets.

FIGURE R.2

Ram-away.

ram off A defect resulting from a section of the mold being forced away from the pattern by ramming sand after it has conformed to the pattern contour. This is caused by careless ramming, when the mold is rammed vertically and then on an angle, causing the vertically rammed sand to slide sideways and leave a gap between the pattern and the sand. It results in a deformed casting. Another cause is using a sand with poor or low flowability.

ram-up core A core set against the pattern or in a locator slot in the pattern (Fig. R-3). The mold is rammed and when the pattern is drawn the core remains in the mold.

rapping bar and rapper The rapping bar consists of a piece of brass or steel (cold roll) rod which is machined or ground to a tapered point (Fig. R-4). The rapper is made of steel or brass and is shaped exactly like the frame of a sling shot.

The purpose of these tools is to rap or shake the pattern loose from the sand mold in order to draw it easily from the sand. The pattern is shaken in all directions to drive the sand slightly away from the pattern. The resulting mold cavity will actually be a fuzz larger than the pattern. The pattern should only be rapped enough to free it from the sand. You will be able to see when it is loose all around by the movement of the pattern. Over-rapping will distort the mold cavity which may or may not matter depending on how close you wish the casting to hold a tolerance.

The operation is quite simple: the bar point of the rapping bar is pressed down into a dimple in the parting face of the pattern with the left hand. The rapper is used to strike the bar with the inner faces of the yoke.

FIGURE R.3

Ram-up core.

FIGURE R.4

Rapping bar and rapper.

rat A lump on the surface of a casting caused by a portion of the mold face sticking to the pattern.

rat tail A minor casting defect. A small buckle occurring as a small irregular line or lines on the casting surface.

receiving ladle Usually a ladle (often stationary in front of the cupola) into which the metal is tapped and where any innoculation needed is done. The pouring ladles are fed from the receiving ladle. In this arrangement the receiving ladle becomes in fact a tilting forehearth.

red brass Red brass is defined as a brass alloy containing 2 to 8 percent zinc with the tin content less than the zinc. The lead content is less than .5 percent. This alloy is not often used in the production of castings. The leaded red brasses and semi-red are called red brasses. A leaded red brass is a brass with 2 to 8 percent zinc with a tin content less than 6 percent (usually less than the zinc content) and lead over .5 percent. 85 percent copper, 5 percent tin, 5 percent zinc, and 5 percent lead is called red brass but is actually a leaded red brass.

red shortness The brittleness of some ferrous and nonferrous metals when at a red heat. Referred to as *hot shortness.*

reducing atmosphere An atmosphere which is short or lean of oxygen.

refractoriness The ability of sand to withstand high temperatures without fusing or breaking down.

regenerative chamber   A system where the air for combustion is preheated by regenerative chambers—heated brick mazes through which the blast air passes and is heated. They are constructed in pairs; while one is giving up its heat to the blast air, the other is being heated (usually by the exhaust gasses from the melting unit). When the chamber through which the blast air is being heated falls below a certain temperature, a series of valves swap the direction of the air and exhaust over to the other chamber to regenerate the cooled one.

reservoir   A basin on top of a mold designed to hold sufficient metal to pour the mold. It is opened to the sprue by a plug, similar to a bottom pour ladle (Fig. R-5).

return scrap   Home generated scrap consisting of gates, risers, chips, and borings from the castings produced. In some cases as with steel, the return scrap from a given casting can be greater or equal to the weight of the casting itself.

reverse chill   Also called *inverse chill* (Fig. R-6). The condition in a casting section where the interior is mottled or white iron with a gray iron exterior. It is usually found in thin castings. The usual cause is the presence of nonferrous metals in the iron such as antimony, lead, tellurium, etc., or the casting was poured with a too-high carbon equivalent for the section thickness being poured.

FIGURE R.5

Reservoir.

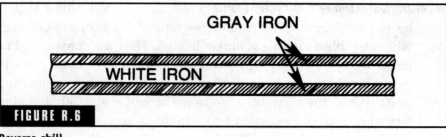

Reverse chill.

ribs Stiffening members on a casting designed to increase its strength and/or utility.

riddle, hand A round riddle or sieve used by a hand molder to riddle sand or facing onto a pattern prior to ramming the mold. Riddles are purchased with various meshes of wire. The most common hand riddle used is a #4—four openings per inch.

risers A reservoir or reservoirs of excess molten metal designed to supply metal in compensation for the shrinkage that cannot be properly fed from the gate (Fig. R-7).

roll-off hinges These hinges allow the flask to be opened like a book (Fig. R-8). The pattern is removed and the mold closed—all without lifting the cope.

FIGURE R.7

Riser.

Roll-of hinge.

rollover machine   A molding machine designed in so that the flask is rolled over before the pattern is drawn from the mold, as opposed to lifting the mold from the pattern (pin-lift machine).

Roman joint   A joint commonly used in the assembly of the component pieces of a large statuary bronze casting (Fig. R-9). The joint is made so that when properly done it cannot be seen. Knife edge ridges at the mating junction are hammered down flat (cold forged) with a peen hammer and then finished with a file and scraper.

rosin oil   An oil made from gum or wood rosins by the destructive distillation and then the fractionating of the distillate into an oil or

Roman joint.

spirit. Rosin oils are used as core binders alone and in combination with other materials.

rough surface This defect can run from mild penetration to spotty rough spots or a completely rough casting. Many factors or combinations are at fault—sand too coarse for the weight and pouring temperature of the casting, improperly applied or insufficient mold coating or core coating, faulty finishing, excessive use of parting compound (dust), hand cut gates not firm or cleaned out, dirty pattern, sand not riddled when necessary, excessive or too-coarse sea coal in the sand, permeability too high for class of work, or the core or mold wash faulty (poor composition).

rubber cement Latex rubber treated with a preservative and used as a core binder. The sand is mixed with latex and water and the core is formed and dried at room temperature. The latex cores have a quick collapsibility and shake out easily. An excellent binder for cores used in thin walled aluminum castings.

runner box A device for distributing molten metal around a mold by dividing it into several streams (Fig. R-10).

runner riser A runner horizontal or vertical in the cope which acts also as a riser to feed the castings (Fig. R-11).

run out Caused by the metal in the mold running out between the joint of the flask. It drains the liquid metal partially or com-

FIGURE R.10

Runner box.

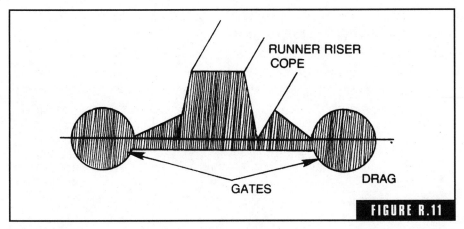

FIGURE R.11

Runner riser.

pletely from any portion of the casting above the parting line. A run out can come through or between the drag and the bottom board from a cracked drag mold. Also, it can come from between a loose or improperly fitting core and the core print. It is caused by insufficient room between the flask and the cavity, insufficient weight on the cope (cope raises during pouring), or improperly clamped molds. Excessive hydrostatic pressure (sprue too tall for the job), no dough roll used between cope and drag (large jobs), or a combination of all of the above.

An attempt to save a run out by placing your foot on top of the cope and applying pressure above the point where the liquid metal is running out is foolhardy and dangerous. Also trying to stop off the run out flow with sand or clay is foolish.

sag   A decrease in metal section due to a core or the cope sagging. The cause is insufficient cope bars, too small a flask for the job, insufficient cope depth. This defect will also cause misruns.

sand slinger   A mechanical device which throws molding sand with sufficient force and impact so that the sand is literally rammed into the mold (Fig. S-1).

The principle is rather simple. The conditioned molding sand is fed via a belt into the hub of a high speed impeller consisting of flat blades. The blades throw or sling the sand downward through the discharge mouth. Both the amount of sand fed to the impeller and the impeller speed is controlled to give the desired impact and flow. The two basic types are stationary and traveling slinger. The primary use is in ramming up large molds, copes, and drags. They are widely used in foundries engaged in *street castings*, sewer rings, sewer covers, catch basins, etc.

The common name in the foundry is *elephant snout*. On large slingers the operator rides the business end of the slinger.

saxophone gate   A gate designed to provide the same conditions as a step gate only delivering metal to the casting at different levels as the mold is filled (Fig. S-2).

scab   Rough thin scabs of metal attached to the casting by a thin vein separated from the casting by a thin layer of sand. Usually found on a flat surface. They are caused by hard ramming, low permeability, and insufficient hot strength. Sand does not have enough cushion material, wood flour, etc., to allow it to expand when heated. Unable to expand, it will buckle and cause scabs along with, but not always, rat tails. Grooves under the scabs are called *pull downs*. It is the pull downs that bring about the scab.

FIGURE S.1

Sand slinger.

FIGURE S.2

Saxophone gate.

scarfing Removing pads, gates, and risers from steel castings with a hydrogen or oxyacetylene torch prior to grinding.

scrap metal Metal purchased from a scrap metal dealer or junk yard. Also celled *foreign scrap*. Scrap that is generated in the shop from the operations is called *return scrap* or *domestic scrap*. Great care should be exercised in buying foreign scrap as to its exact pedigree. It should be properly cleaned and classified. With nonferrous materials this can be quite a trick and requires a great degree of experience.

screen core box vents Round screen vents used in a core box which is blown (Fig. S-3). The vents exhaust the air in the box from the blow. When slotted instead of screened, they are called *slot vents*.

sea coal A finely ground soft coal used as a dry shake-bag facing. Mostly used as an additive to both facing and system sand in amounts up to 5 percent. The most common practice is to keep it in the neighborhood of 3 to 4 percent. Excessive sea coal in any molding sand, whether natural or synthetic, will cause the sand to become brittle, low in resilience, and difficult to mold. Care should be exercised in adding sea coal to any sand; however, properly used it is very beneficial and will produce excellent castings with good peel and a smooth surface. In the proper amounts it will increase the green strength, dry strength, temper, moisture required, mold hardness, and deformation while it decreases the flowability and permeability.

The most common use in molding sand is in cast iron sands. It can be purchased in five grades:

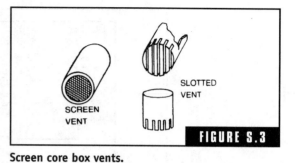

Screen core box vents.

- A—12 mesh for large heavy machine castings

- B—18 mesh for medium weight castings

- C—24 mesh for light and medium weight castings

- D—40 mesh for radiator castings and lightweight castings

- E—100 mesh for ornamental iron, piano plate, stove plate, and hollowware

The average analysis of a good grade of sea coal is volatile matter, 38.49 percent; fixed carbon, 53.84 percent; ash, 4.81 percent; and moisture, 2.70 percent. Contrary to popular belief that sea coal has no use in brass and bronze casting sands, the author has done extensive work with sea coal in every weight range from 1 pound and less to in excess of 500 pounds in brass and bronze with most gratifying results. One half to 2 percent of silk-bolted or air-float sea coal in any brass sand works very well.

Petro Bond sands are improved with the addition of sea coal or graphite. The flowability and moldability is increased by 100 percent.

semi-centrifugal When a casting is symmetrical about its own axis, such as a wheel or gear blank casting and poured through its hub or center, the process is called semi-centrifugal (Fig. S-4).

semi-killed, steel Incompletely deoxidized steel. Permits the sufficient evolution of carbon monoxide to offset solidification shrinkage.

semi-steel A misnomer when referring to gray iron when the cupola charge consists of a high percent of steel scrap.

set gate pattern If a pattern is made for a gate but not attached to a pattern and only placed against it while making the mold, this pattern is called a set gate pattern.

set sprue A wooden *sprue stick* set in a sand mold during the ramming of the mold. Usually a simple, round, and slightly tapered

FIGURE S.4

Semi-centrifugal casting.

wooden stick (Fig. S-5). Some are bell shaped at the top to form a pouring basin.

set-up core A core print made of a dry sand core to provide a stronger bearing surface for a heavy core should a green sand print prove inadequate (Fig. S-6). A common practice in large green sand work.

shake bag A porous cloth bag used to shake dry parting or blacking materials on a pattern or mold surface.

shellac pot A glass or metal pot with a domed lid so that the brush can be left in the shellac. The cover forms a seal when closed (Fig. S-7).

shell process A process where a resin-coated sharp sand is dumped on a hot metal pattern and allowed a long enough time to produce a heat-cured shell of the desired thickness to form a shell mold (Fig. S-8). The remaining uncured sand is dumped back into the dump box and the cured shell is stripped from the pattern. The cured shells (two halves cope and drag) are assembled by bolting, gluing, or clamping. They are backed with shot or sand and poured.

BELL SPRUE

FIGURE S.5

Set sprue.

Cores are also made by the sand shell process with hot metal core boxes, which make excellent lightweight hollow cores. They are used not only in shell molds, but in sand and permanent molds as well.

Set-up core.

When the sand shell system was first introduced into the foundry industry, it was looked upon by some as a panacea. Before it found its true place in the industry, it took a heavy toll not only in botched-up castings but in money.

It is a good system when properly used and its limits are understood. The same problem exists with any system. Investment casting, particularly by art bronze casters, is another with definite limitations. I have seen some costly messes made by investment casters who try to cast a life-size casting all in one piece in investment when the casting could have been done in French sand with not only a finer finish but at half the time and cost. Use the right medium for the job at hand.

shift block   Dry sand, wood, or cast iron blocks that fit prints on cope and drag pattern boards (Fig. S-9). The blocks are placed in the drag prints and the mold coped. The corresponding prints in the cope mold lower over the shift blocks to prevent a shift in the mold. The use of shift blocks is resorted to only if the only flask available for the job is in no shape to trust. Shift blocks are also used to register cope and drag core molds which are not made in a flask. They are double-faced truncated pyramids or cones.

shifts   There are two classifications of shifts: *mold shift* and *core shift*.

A mold shift occurs when the parting lines are not matched when the mold is closed. The result is a casting offset or one that is mismatched at the parting. The causes are excessive rapping of a loose pattern, reversing the cope on the drag, too loose a fit on the pattern pins and dowels, faulty mis-

Shellac pot.

FIGURE S.8

Shell process.

matched flasks, too much play between pins and guides, faulty clamping, improper fitting (racked) jackets, and improper placing of jackets.

A core shift is caused by not aligning the halves of glued cores true and proper when assembling them.

shrink cavity and shrink depression These defects are caused by lack of feed metal, causing a depression on the concave surface of the casting. The shrink cavity is a cavity below the surface. It is not connected to the surface with a dendrite crystal structure.

shrink rules Steel rules purchased from pattern supply houses that have the desired shrinkage for the particular use worked out over its length. Thus, if you purchase a ³⁄₁₆ shrink rule (for brass), the rule will be divided into 12 inches but will actually be 12³⁄₁₆ inches long or ³⁄₁₆ inch longer than a standard 12-inch rule. The shrink rule is used to dimension the pattern and automatically

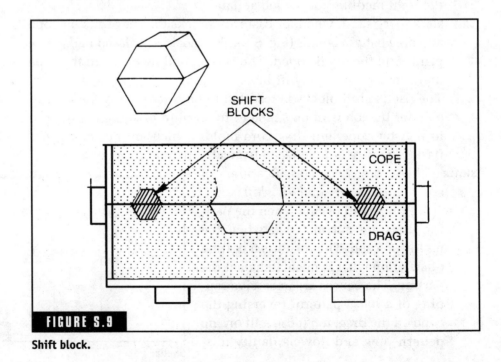

FIGURE S.9

Shift block.

compensate for the shrinkage chosen. Shrink rules can be purchased with any desired shrink or combinations needed, including a double shrink.

silica flour The most widely used inorganic additive. It is used in steel sands to control and increase the hot, dry, and green strengths. With the advent of the use of finer base sands for steel, silica flour is used much less now than in the past.

silicious clay A clay which contains a high percent of silica.

sillimanite A sand $A1_2 O_3 SiO_2$ used as a core sand for precision work. A very fine grained core can be made with sillimanite; it will hold a dimension.

silicon brass and silicon bronze An alloy containing over .5 percent silicon, 4 percent zinc maximum, and 98 percent copper, maximum.

Regular silicon bronze consists of 92 percent copper, 4 percent zinc, and 4 percent silicon. It holds .302 pounds per cubic inch. A patternmaker's shrinkage is ³⁄₁₆ inch per foot.

The pouring temperature for light castings is 2050 to 2250 F. For heavy castings, the temperature is 1900 to 2050 F.

No flux or deoxidizer is needed. It is contaminated easily with lead.

sill sand The fine dust collected from the tops of sills and beams in the foundry. Used as a dry parting material in a shake bag or old sock.

sintering point The temperature at which molding material begins to adhere to the casting; or in the sintering test where the sand adheres to a platinum ribbon under controlled conditions.

skeleton pattern A framework of wooden bars which represents the interior and exterior form as well as the metal thickness of the required casting. This type of pattern is only used for huge castings.

skin The thin surface layer on a casting which is different from the main mass in composition and structure.

skin drying Drying the surface of a mold by the direct application of heat from a torch or coke basket.

skull The film of metal or dross remaining in a ladle after it has been emptied.

slab core A flat plain core used in a mold to form a flat surface or as a cover core.

slag hole The opening in the back of the cupola through which the slag is drawn from the molten metal. Also called the *slag notch*.

FIGURE S.10

Slick and oval spoon.

slag inclusion Slag on the face of the casting and usually down the sides of the sprue. The cause is not skimming the ladle properly, not choking the sprue (keeping it brimming full from start to finish), sprue too big (cannot be kept choked), and gating system improperly choked.

slick and oval spoon This tool is a must for all molders (Fig. S-10). The size needed is determined by the work involved. Most molders have at least four sizes from the little tiny one that is ¼ inch wide to the big one 2 inches wide. This tool is called a *doubler ender* in the trade. One end is a slick similar to a heart trowel blade but more oval shaped. The opposite end is spoon shaped. The outside or working surface is convex like the back of a spoon. Its inner face is concave. This face is never used and therefore is usually not finished smooth. When new it is painted black. Both faces of the slick blade are highly polished.

The double ender is a general use molding tool used for slicking flat or concave surfaces, to open up sprues, etc.

slicking Smoothing a section of a mold with the hands or a molder's slicker. Over-slicking can result in blows and scabs.

slip jacket A metal or wood frame to place around a snap or slip flask mold after the flask has been removed during pouring (Fig. S-11).

slot sprue A rectangular-shaped sprue widely used in aluminum and magnesium casting (Fig. S-12).

slush casting A casting made from a low melting alloy which freezes over a wide range of temperatures. The molds are metal, usually brass or bronze, and mounted on trunnions. They are filled with metal with a hand ladle and rocked back and forth until an inner shell of metal is formed. The center, which is still liquid, is poured out leaving a hollow casting. Slip casting of metal is similar to slip casting a hollow wax form or clay form.

snagging Rough grinding the gates, flash, etc., from a casting.

SAND MOLD   JACKET

BOTTOM BOARD

FIGURE S.11

Slip jacket.

snap bands Metal bands dropped into the cope and drag prior to the ramming of straight-sided snaps; they reinforce the mold at the parting line (cope and drag) to help prevent run outs (Fig. S-13). Also called *bands*.

snap flask A flask, usually made of cherrywood. After the mold is made the flask can be removed by opening the flask and lifting it off the mold, leaving the mold as a block of sand on the bottom board (Fig. S-14).

Both cope and drag have a hinge in corner *A*, and in corner *B*, a cam locking device. In operation the cope and the drag locks are closed tight and the mold made in the usual manner. When finished, the locks are opened and the flask is opened and removed from the mold.

The big advantage of the snap flask is that you need only one flask to make as many molds a day as you wish. With rigid flasks you need as many flasks as the number of molds you wish to put up at a time. I have seen small shops that had only three or four sizes of snaps and a variety of wooden floor flasks.

FIGURE S.12

Slot sprue.

FIGURE S.13

Snap bands.

FIGURE S.14

Snap flask. A. Hinges and B. cam locking devices.

Solders.

soda ash Sodium carbonate used as a flux.

soldiers Square wooden sticks dipped in a clay wash. They are used to reinforce and support the sand in the cope (Fig. S-15). Deep pockets of sand hang from the cope. They are placed in position during the ramming of the cope.

solid contraction The shrinkage a metal takes from its solidification point to room temperature.

solidification shrinkage The shrinkage taken by a molten metal when going from a liquid to a solid state.

sorbite When medium carbon steel is water-quenched it results in a hard close-grained metal. If the quench is not as severe or slower, the steel will be softer. It is then called *sorbite* or *troostite*.

split pattern A pattern made in two halves split along the parking line (Fig. S-16). The two halves are held in register by pins called *pattern dowels*. The pattern is split to facilitate molding.

   The dowels hold the two halves of the pattern together in close accurate register, but at the same time are free enough that the two halves can be separated easily for molding, similar to the pins and guides of the flask.

   The dowels are usually installed off center in such a manner that the pattern can only be put together correctly.

sprue In investment casting, a rod that supports the model while the mold is being made. Sprues provide a passageway for melted wax to leave the mold and also provide the entrance through which molten metal is poured into the mold.

Split pattern.

sprue pick   A molder's tool used to draw a wooden set sprue from the cope (Fig. S-17). It consists of a double-ended tool having a sharp metal point on one end, similar to a dart. The opposite end is pear shaped to give the tool the necessary driving weight. The point is driven into the top of the sprue with a flicking movement like throwing a dart. The sprue is simply lifted out. The tool provides the handle to do this. The sprue pick is also used to draw small wooden patterns from a mold.

stack core mold   A series of mold sections made in dry sand cores poured through a central sprue. Often rotated during pouring or centrifuging.

stainless steel   A wide range of iron alloys having a high content of chromium. They are highly resistant to oxidation and corrosion even at elevated temperatures. The original stainless produced in the U.S. in 1914 was 13.5 percent chromium and .35 carbon.

steadite   The eutectic of iron, iron phosphide, and cementite.

steam gas porosity   This defect usually shows up as round holes similar to holes in Swiss cheese, just under the cope surface of the casting. It comes to light during machining. The cause

Sprue stick.

is a wet ladle, where the ladle lining was not properly and thoroughly dried.

In extreme cases the metal will kick and boil in the ladle. The practice of pigging the metal in a wet ladle and refilling it with the hopes that the pigged metal will finish drying the ladle is sheer folly.

step gate A gate with (Fig. S-18) one or more steps, used to prevent a long metal fall into the mold, which could cause mold erosion; and to produce a more elastic gating system to prevent hot tearing at its junction with the casting.

FIGURE S.18

Step gate.

sticker   A lump or rat (bump) on the surface of the casting caused by a portion of the mold face sticking to the pattern and being removed with the pattern. This problem is caused by poor cleaning, poor shellacking, polished pattern, rough pattern, cheap shellac, tacky shellac, sticky liquid parting, cold pattern against hot sand, or an insufficient draft.

stock cores   Round cores of various diameters and lengths kept in the core room for those odds-and-ends type jobs with a missing round core box or kept to core holes through open sand castings (lifter plates, etc.). Stock cores are made from stock boxes or a coremaking machine resembling in looks and operation a sausage machine.

   These machines have tubes of various diameters which fit on the end (Fig. S-19). The sand is extruded through the tube by an auger turned by hand or motorized. A vent wire produces a vent through the core on its passage through the tube. The core is extruded onto corrugated driers for baking.

strike-off bar   Each time a mold is rammed up the sand must be struck off level with the flask cope and drag (Fig. S-20). The bar simply consists of a metal or hardwood straightedge of sufficient length.

stripping plate   A metal plate through which a pattern projects, and which conforms to the pattern very closely. It is used to mold straight-cast tooth gears with no draft. The mold is rammed in the usual manner and the pattern stripped by pulling it down through the plate with a rack and pinion gear. The plate supports the sand between the teeth, allowing you to draw a pattern with zero draft from the mold without damage to the mold.

FIGURE S.19

Stock cores.

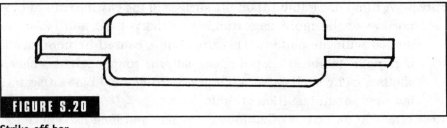

FIGURE S.20

Strike-off bar.

sub-zero metal   Metals that maintain their physical properties at sub-zero temperatures. Manganese bronze and aluminum bronze are among the sub-zero metals. They are not adversely affected at temperatures as low as minus 300 F.

sucker   The sucker is not a purchased tool but one made by the molder. It consists of two pieces of tubing and a tee of copper or iron (Fig. S-21).

Its use is to clean out deep pockets in molds where the bellows and lifter fail, if the pocket or slot is just too dirty to spend the time a lifter would take, or where it would be hard to see what you are doing with a lifter. The operation is very simple.

FIGURE S.21

A sucker is made by the molder.

You simply blow through the elbow with an air hose. This creates a vacuum in the long length which gives you in effect a vacuum cleaner with a long skinny snout. Now stick the long end
down to where the problem is and blow through the elbow.
These jobs will lift out small steel shot, a match stick, or material
which cannot be wetted such as parting powder or silica sand.

sulphur dome An inverted dome placed over a pot or crucible of
molten magnesium containing a high concentration of sulphur
dioxide.

swab A sponge, rag, or hemp material used to dampen the sand
around a pattern before drawing it.

sweep pattern A sweep pattern consists of a board with a profile of the
desired mold. When revolved around a suitable spindle or guide,
it produces that mold. Two are usually required, one to sweep the
cope profile and the other the drag profile.

swell A casting deformed due to the pressure of the metal moving or
displacing the sand. It is usually caused by a soft spot or a too
soft mold.

swing frame grinder A large grinder suspended from a crane or chain
so that it can be maneuvered easily with a swinging action (Fig.

FIGURE S.22

Swing frame grinder.

S-22). Used to grind castings which are too bulky or large to grind any other way.

synthetic molding sand   A molding sand compounded from selected individual materials which, when mixed together, produce the desired properties.

talc Also called *soapstone*. A hydrous magnesium silicate used as a mold and core wash when combined with a suitable binder. The most widely used homebrew mold and core wash is composed of 1 part molasses to 10 parts water with sufficient graphite added to produce the desired consistency.

tally mark A mark or combination of marks to indicate the location of a loose piece of a pattern or core box. Sometimes called a *keeper mark*.

tamastone A high strength gypsum used to make patterns, matchplates, core boxes, etc.

tap hole The hole in the breast of a cupola or furnace through which the molten metal is tapped.

target boss A boss on a casting from which all dimensions are taken or related.

teapot spout ladle A ladle designed like a teapot; the metal poured from the ladle comes from the bottom to ensure clean, slag-free metal to the mold (Fig. T-1).

tellurium An elementary metal, Te, obtained as a steel gray powder of 99 percent purity by the reduction of tellurium oxide or tellurite. Its chief use is as an alloy with lead to harden and toughen the lead.

tellurium bronze Composed of 1 percent tellurium, 1.5 percent tin, and the balance copper. It has an annealed strength of 40,000 PSI.

Also used as a chill core wash. When a section of a core is washed with a tellurium wash, the area washed will act as a chill. A great tool to promote directional solidification on complex cored casting.

temper (verb) To mix water or other liquid with sand.

temper (noun) The moisture content of a tempered sand.

FIGURE T.1

Teapot spout ladle.

temper carbon   The free graphite (graphitic carbon) that precipitates from solution during the graphitizing of white cast iron.

templet   A thin piece of material with the edge contour made in the reverse of the surface to be formed or checked.

temporary pattern   A cheaply built pattern used to produce one or two castings.

tensile strength   The force that holds the sand up in the cope. And, as molding sands are many times stronger in compression than tensile strength, we must take the tensile strength into account. Mold failure is more apt to occur under tensile forces.

Where compression strength is measured in pounds per square inch, the tensile strength of molding sands is measured in ounces per square inch.

Tensile strength is determined very easily.

ternary alloy   An alloy that contains three principal elements. Gun metal of 88, 10, and 2 is a ternary alloy.

test bar   A standard specimen designed to permit determination of mechanical properties of a metal. Also called a *coupon*. It is poured from the same ladle of metal as the casting or is cast as an attachment to the casting and shipped with the casting.

Texas ramming   Term given to the method of ramming a flask cope and drag with the peen end of a molder's shovel and the back of the blade (Fig. T-2). The sand is *riddled* into the cope, filled and *peened*, and then filled to overflowing and rammed by swatting with the back side of the shovel. Keep adding and swatting until firm, then strike off and finish in the usual manner. For shallow copes and drags with small, comparatively flat patterns, it can be quite fast. If executed correctly it produces good fast work, but it takes a lot of steam to keep it up for any length of time.

threaded inserts   Threaded inserts are used where an accurate thread is necessary. They differ from screw shells in that they are machined from black bar stock and can be furnished in many different diameters and thread sizes (Fig. T-3). They produce a much better thread than screw shells and can be designed to meet varying metal thicknesses surrounding the insert. Threaded inserts are used in chilled castings where drilling and tapping are impossible. Either an open-end or closed-end insert can be used.

Threaded inserts are used in a manner similar to that of screw shells. A hole is provided in the pattern large enough to allow the insert to draw freely and the insert is dropped into the hole before molding. If an open-end insert is used, the insert fills with green sand when the mold is rammed and a nail can be pushed

FIGURE T.2

Texas ramming.

FIGURE T.3

Threaded inserts.

into the sand to reinforce it. Open-end inserts can also be used by attaching them to cores.

The closed-end insert is rammed up in the same manner as the open-end type, but it is not necessary to fill it. A wooden plug pressed into the open end maintains the insert in its proper location in the mold. When the casting is poured, the insert becomes part of it.

The outside surface of the insert is knurled to ensure good fusion with the molten metal.

tilting furnace Any furnace that can be tilted to pour out the molten metal.

tin A silvery white metal with a bluish tinge, melting point of 232 C., and specific gravity of 7.298. It is widely used as a hot dip coating on steel (tin plate) or it is electroplated. A widely used metal as an alloy in a wide variety of casting metals and solders.

tin brass A brass with over 6 percent tin and a zinc content even greater. An alloy seldom used in the foundry.

tin bronze A bronze with 2 to 20 percent tin with zinc less than the tin. The most commonly used foundry tin bronze is called straight bronze, 88-10-2 and gun metal. It is 88 percent copper, 10 percent tin, and 2 percent zinc. Its weight per cubic inch is .315 pounds. Patternmaker's shrinkage is 3/16 inch per foot. Pouring temperatures for light castings are 2100 to 2300 F. For heavy castings, 1920 to 2100 F.

tin tubes Tin tubes find many diversified uses in foundry operations, but their principal use is for coring holes through heavy metal sections and reinforcing as well as ventilating intricate cores. They are also used as chills to initiate setting of heavier metal sections at the same rate as thin sections, thereby preventing shrinks and porosity.

These tubes, made of tin plate, have a free fit inside for the diameter listed. Tubes can also be furnished filled with core sand or made from perforated metal. Holes cored with plain tin tubes have a smooth surface after the sand is knocked out.

tramp iron Iron shot, gates, sprues, nails, etc., in the molding sand due to improper conditioning of the sand and not using a magnetic separator to clean it. Tramp iron or brass can be the cause of blowing and chilling defects when they get rammed up in the sand next to the pattern when molding. They always seem to be located just where you want to cut a gate or punch a sprue hole.

transfer ladle A ladle that may be supported on a crane bridge or monorail and used to transfer metal from the melting furnace to the pouring floors or a holding furnace.

triplexing Making steel where the iron is melted in the cupola then transferred to the converter and blown. The blown heat is then transferred to the arc furnace for finishing and alloying.

trunnion A boss-like projection (in pairs) on a flask, ladle, furnace, etc., used to lift and or rotate the object on an axis (Fig. T-4). Flask trunnions are used to lift the flask with a beam bail and to roll it over. Large slip and pop flasks are fitted with half trunnions or split trunnions—half on the cope and half on the drag. When the mold is closed it can be rolled on the trunnions.

FIGURE T.4

Trunnion.

FIGURE T.5

Tubular sprue cutter.

tubular sprue cutters   A tapered steel or brass tube used to cut a sprue hole in the cope half of a sand mold (Fig. T-5). It is sold in sizes from ⅞ to 1¼ inches in diameter. All are 6 inches long.

tucking   Pressing sand with the fingers under flask bars, around gaggers, and other places where the peen or rammer does not give the desired density. An important operation with hand ramming as well as some machine molded work.

tuyere   An opening in the cupola or blast furnace through which the blast air is forced.

upset   Any frame metal or wood used to increase the depth of the cope or drag (Fig. U-1). On a snap pop-off or slip flask it is usually screwed to the flask. In the case of rigid wood or metal flasks, they usually have tabs which extend down inside the flask being upset in place during molding and pouring. A square or round frame used to increase a sprue or riser height is also referred to as an upset.

U.S. sieve series   A series of nesting sieves used to determine the average grain fineness and distribution of dry sands. The sieves are stacked

FIGURE U.1

An upset increases the depth of the cope or drag.

in order from the most coarse on top to the finest on the bottom and a pan on the bottom. The sample to be checked is weighed and placed on the top sieve. The sieves are shaken or vibrated. The sieves are dissassembled and the retained sand on each screen weighed. The percents are then plotted against the beginning known weight. A complete set consists of the following meshes: 4, 6, 8, 12, 16, 20, 30, 40, 50, 70, 100, 140, 200, 270, and the pan.

vanadium   An elementary metal V. A pale gray metal with a silvery luster with a specific gravity of 6.02 and a melting point of 3236 F. It will not oxidize in the air. In the percentages of .15 to 0.25 with a small quantity of chromium, it is widely used to alloy steel (*vanadium steel*).

ventilated flasks   A metal flask with round or oblong holes through its sides and ends. The holes allow steam and gasses from pouring the casting to vent more freely than if the flask were not perforated. It is believed by some that the resistance of a solid flask wall to the escape of mold gasses builds up the pressure in the molds, leading to casting defects such as pin holes.

vent plate   A plate containing a series of vents (screen or slotted) used under an open-ended core box for blowing the cores (Fig. V-1).

vent plugs   A vent made in a permanent mold by drilling a hole in the mold and plugging it with a square plug (Fig. V-2). Vent screens and slotted vents installed in metal core blowing boxes are also called vent plugs.

vent wire   A slender pointed wire with a loop at its top. It is used to punch vent holes in the cope and drag a sand mold to provide easy access of steam and gasses to the outside during the pouring of the casting. The venting is done prior to the pattern removal. The vent wire is pushed down into the sand to within close proximity of the pattern. The first and second finger straddles the wire each time it is withdrawn as a guide.

FIGURE V.1

A vent plate.

FIGURE V.2

A vent plug.

vitrification point The temperature upon heating at which clays reach the condition of maximum density and shrinkage (vitrified).

volumetric shrinkage The volumetri shrinkage of a molten metal from its liquid state to its solidification temperature.

wash   Any number of refractory compounds used to coat molds, cores, ladles, cupola spouts, etc. Increases the refractiveness of the surface to which it is applied.

washburn core   A washburn core consists of a riser necking core which conforms to the shape of the casting at the point of riser attachment (Fig. W-1). Its purpose is to keep the riser open so that it can feed the casting and at the same time reduce the size of the riser attachment, resulting in a great saving in riser removal and grinding. The core can be made of various kinds of refractory material (fired ceramic shape) or a rodded oil sand core. There is a straight-line relationship between the thickness of the core and the neck diameter.

washing and erosion   The sand is eroded and washed around in the mold. Some of it finds its way to the cope surface of the casting as dirt sand inclusions. It can come from the gating system or in the mold cavity. The causes include a too-low hot strength, a too-dry molding sand, poor gating design, a deep drop into the mold, washing at the point of impact, metal washing over a sharp edge at the gate, metal hitting against a core, or a vertical wall during the pouring.

water soluble wax   A wax primarily used in investment casting wax, such as spacers between the blades of high speed impeller blades. The pattern is assembled with regular wax and water soluble wax spacers. When complete, the water soluble spacers are dissolved leaving precise spacing between the blades.

web   A plate or member lying between heavier sections (Fig. W-2).

weep hole   A hole placed in a casting to allow drainage of moisture.

well board   A board fitted with pins or guides to match a flask (Fig. W-3). The board has a well into which a pattern board fits flush. The use of well boards allows a quick pattern change and standardizes the pattern mounts.

Washburn core.

Web.

whirl gate A gate or sprue arranged to introduce the metal tangentially, thereby imparting a swirling motion (Fig. W-4).

whistler A small (¼-inch) opening through the cope of a mold at the highest point on the casting; used to tell when the mold is full when pouring (Fig. W-5).

white iron A cast iron in which all the carbon is in the combined state and none is thrown out during solidification as free graphite, as opposed to gray iron. Most of the carbon is in the form of graphite, mechanically mixed with the iron. White iron is used to cast parts where high wearing qualities are desired. It is extremely brittle and cannot be machined by normal methods.

COPE PATTERN

MALE PINS

COPE
WELL BOARD

PATTERN

DRAG PATTERN

WELL

DRAG
WELL BOARD

FEMALE
GUIDES

FIGURE W.3

A well board allows quick pattern changes.

wind box   The chamber surrounding a cupola through which the blast
air is conducted to the tuyeres. The wind box has a pressure
equalizing effect, therefore each tuyere will receive approximately the same volume and pressure.

wood flour   All wood flours are not the same. Foundry wood flours
should have the largest portion of resinous material removed.
They should possess a low ash content. The normal percentages
used in natural and synthetic sand mixes usually run up to 1½
percent. In core mixes use ¼ to ½ percent cereal and ½ percent

FIGURE W.4

Whirl gate.

WHISTLER

COPE

DRAG

FIGURE W.5

A whistler is a small opening through the cope of a mold.

wood flour. Wood flour additions will reduce volume changes, hot strength permeability, and dry strength while increasing green compression strength, mold hardness, moisture, deformation, and density.

wood's metal 25 percent lead, 12.5 percent tin, 50 percent bismuth, and 12.5 percent cadmium. This alloy has a melting temperature of 154.4 F.

Z

zinc   A bluish white crystalline metal which melts at 419 C. and boils at 907 C. Zinc is a widely used metal for alloying. Also used in various chemical reactions, plating, etc.

zinc tracks   This defect is found on the cope surface of high-zinc alloy castings. The defects are caused by the zinc distilling out of the metal during pouring. This zinc oxide floats up to the cope and forms worm track lines on the casting when the metal sets against the cope. The problem is caused by pouring too hot (metal flaring) in ladle or crucible or pouring the mold too slowly with insufficient gates. The mold must be filled quickly before the damage can be done.

zircon sand   Zirconium silicate comes chiefly from beach sands. It is used for mold facings, cores, and when flour is used as mold and core washes.

zirconium   A silvery white metal which melts at approximately 1850 C. and has the specific gravity of 6.5. It is difficult to reduce to a metal form as it combines easily with oxygen, nitrogen, carbon, and silicon. It is produced by reacting *zircon sand* with carbon. Used as an alloy with ferrous and nonferrous metals and widely used as powerful metal deoxidizer.

INDEX

Note: **Boldface** numbers indicate illustrations.

C. W. Ammen is a lifetime metalcaster, a consulting chemist and metallurgist with clients around the world, and one of McGraw-Hill's most popular technical writers. He is the author of *The Metalcaster's Bible*, a bestseller since its 1980 publication and the basis for this book. He is a member of the American Institute of Chemists, the American Chemical Society, and Pyrotechnics Guild International, Inc.